# THE GERMAN HISTORIANS

**BLACK ROSE BOOKS**

C.P. 1258
Succ. Place du Parc
Montréal, Canada
H2X 4A7

*Please take a moment to fill in this brief questionnaire, and to return it, by mail. Your answers will enable us to offer you the best possible service, while making available the most interesting books. Thank you.*

I found this card inside the book entitled:

I was made aware of this book:
- ☐ by a friend
- ☐ by looking through your catalogue
- ☐ in a bookstore (name & city)

- ☐ in a library (name & city)

- ☐ by reading an article or review

This book was of interest because of:
- ☐ the subject-matter
- ☐ the author
- ☐ the title
- ☐ the cover and/or the text on cover
- ☐ the table of contents

Name: _____

Address: _____

City: _____

Postal/Zip Code: _____

Country: _____

Tel/email: _____

*View our entire catalogue at: http://www.web.net/blackrosebooks*

# THE GERMAN HISTORIANS

## Hitler's Willing Executioners and Daniel Goldhagen

### Fred Kautz

*translated by the author from the German*

Montréal/New York/London

Copyright © 2003 BLACK ROSE BOOKS

No part of this book may be reproduced or transmitted in any form, by any means electronic or mechanical including photocopying and recording, or by any information storage or retrieval system—without written permission from the publisher, or, in the case of photocopying or other reprographic copying, a license from the Canadian Reprography Collective, with the exception of brief passages quoted by a reviewer in a newspaper or magazine.

Black Rose Books No. FF316

National Library of Canada Cataloguing in Publication Data

Kautz, Fred

The German historians : Hitler's willing executioners and Daniel Goldhagen

Includes bibliographical references and index.
Hardcover ISBN: 1-55164-213-1 (bound)  Paperback ISBN: 1-55164-212-3 (pbk.)

1. Goldhagen, Daniel Jonah. Hitler's willing executioners. 2. Holocaust, Jewish (1939-1945)--Historiography. I. Title.

D804.3G648K38 2002    940.53'18'072043    C2002-903115-X

This edition is an expanded version of the German edition, entitled *Die Holocaust-Forschung im Sperrfeuer der Flakhelfer: Vom befangenen Blick Deutscher Historiker aus der Kriegsgeneration*, (Verlag Edition AV:Frankfurt a M., 2000). We wish to thank Wolfgang Schneider/Redaktion Konkret for use of the photo of Hans Mommsen.

Cover design: Associés libres

| C.P. 1258 | 2250 Military Road | 99 Wallis Road |
| Succ. Place du Parc | Tonawanda, NY | London, E9 5LN |
| Montréal, H2X 4A7 | 14150 | England |
| Canada | USA | UK |

To order books:

In Canada: (phone) 1-800-565-9523 (fax) 1-800-221-9985
email: utpbooks@utpress.utoronto.ca

In United States: (phone) 1-800-283-3572 (fax) 1-651-917-6406

In the UK & Europe: (phone) London 44 (0)20 8986-4854
(fax) 44 (0)20 8533-5821 email: order@centralbooks.com

Our Web Site address: http://www.web.net/blackrosebooks

A publication of the Institute of Policy Alternatives of Montréal (IPAM)

Printed in Canada

# CONTENTS

Foreword by Helmut Dahmer
vii

Preface
xi

Gold-Hagen and "Siegfried"
1

The Nightmares of Ruth Bettina Birn
115

Kater and Mouse
125

Instead of a Postscript
145

The German Historians
162

Bibliography
164

Index
185

*For my children Jacob and Rania*
*who went through the hardship that was entailed in writing this book*

*and for*

*the historian Julie Freeman*
*of Niagara Falls, Canada,*
*a Cassandra*
*who warned the community of scholars on the other side of the Atlantic:*
*"The Germans are not just like us!"*
*a warning that was so unwelcome to our most distinguished scholars*
*that they closed their ears*
*and sacrificed the skeleton at the feast*
*of routine business*
*in the name of German-American academic cooperation*
*and to an academic Holocaust scholarship,*
*which had degenerated in the context of this shallow harmony*
*of intellectual gymnastics*

# FOREWORD

German historians of the post-45 era—as well as their colleagues from the neighbouring social sciences—have carefully avoided writing their own history, the history of their entanglement in war and genocide. The biographies of the Conzes and Schieders were intimately linked to the history of the Third Reich and World War II. If they would have done research on the "*Volksgemeinschaft*," on the co-ordination (*Gleichschaltung*) of the universities, on the persecution and destruction of human beings, they would always have come into contact with their own deeds. Just like the Germanist Schwerte-Schneider who was able to succeed under any regime or like Max Frisch's literary copy of such a figure, the change artist "Stiller," they quickly slipped in 1945 into another costume, from the field-grey and black Wehrmacht and SS uniforms into academic robes (only to be defrocked by the 68ers).

Twelve or more years were retrospectively "erased" from biographies; with this deletion twelve or more years disappeared from contemporary history as (possible) research topics. Writing the history of the Holocaust and the genocidal war of the Wehrmacht in the East was therefore left to others—to Reitlinger, Hilberg, Browning—but from the specific generational problem they had, the German historians distilled a "methodological" virtue. The generation of the planners, combat veterans, Hitler Youth and auxiliary anti-aircraft gunners (*Flakhelfer*), as well (as their students) were, in the final analysis, able to write (just about) every topic in contemporary history, but not about the protagonists. Just like Waldheim and Barbie-Altmann or their collegial collaborator Papon pretended never to have been there, where helpless human beings had been hunted, deported, tortured, and massacred, so the post-war historians of the war generation devised an "objectivistic" method, which enabled them to reconstruct in obsessive detail events and institutional structures, which constituted the frame thereof, without ever having to deal with the "actors." In their reconstruction of the war and persecution there are missing those who committed atrocious acts and those who had to suffer them. History, as these "structuralists" reconstructed it, was a history that made itself. The history of the "Third Reich" resembled in a stunning way the "history" of a tidal flood or a cyclone. In their obsession to make themselves disappear from history, they also deleted from the recent past the agents of the historical processes. Hence, there was nothing to be learned from their history books, nothing, in any case, that would have provided the reader with answers as to how he or she ought to deal with the problems of today. The interest for orientation (the only thing that motivates the "layperson" to preoccupy him or herself with the past) was neglected. That is the real reason why German historians are no longer read in Germany.

Before this background Goldhagen posed a "new" question to the history of Behemoth, World War II, and the Holocaust. He violated the code of conduct of the German post-war historians, according to which historiography only deserves the predicate "scholarly," if it desubjectivises the history it narrates, i.e., if it brackets out the individuals who are not only in cultural and political conflict with others, but also with themselves, if it squeezes the history of experience out of the history of events. German historians were not psychologically able to raise Goldhagen's question. His question seemed to them to be an illegitimate, compromising, extra- and unscholarly question: in brief, a "moral" question. Since Goldhagen's book is a moral book, it was in their eyes "just a bad book." It was bad—bad for the established academic historiography, for it highlights what this historiography has neglected to write about to this day.

Goldhagen asked anew the 68ers question about the moral make-up of the subjects of the Third Reich, as well as the question about the "Zero hour" in contemporary German history. The campaign, which is launched against him, has as its target the type of historiography he tries to reintroduce, historiography with a moral purpose.[1] The heated polemics against him are explained by the fact that the historians who defend themselves against the audacity of his book,[2] are afraid that they themselves might become the subject of study of a complimentary kind of history—as biased individuals who would have liked not to get involved. The readers of Goldhagen and his critics will eventually have to decide (as they had to decide in the case of Hannah Arendt), whether Goldhagen's historiography will, in future, be regarded as non-scholarly or whether it will bring about a "paradigm change": a change towards the reintegration of the "subject" and of "morality" into historical scholarship. If Goldhagen's "turn to the subject" would be adopted by historiography, it would once again become relevant for "lay people." History itself would become once again one of the subjects: in future it would be narrated as a story that could have been prevented under certain conditions. Yes, history could be narrated once again. And this would be good, for only in narration can the history of events be translated back into the history of experience.

Fred Kautz, a historian himself, reads the reactions to Godhagen's book, which (West) German historians and journalists have published in 1996 and 1997 as a chapter of the intellectual history of his discipline. His diagnosis:

> After 1945 too many German historians wrote contemporary history as structural history. Deep inside of the glass palace of the structuralists there is a forbidden 13th room. Locked up inside it is the personnel that has been banned from the history of institutions: the desk-bound murderers and the execution squads, the tight-lipped fathers and grand fathers of the German post-war German families who had returned as surviving veterans of Hitler's Wehrmacht, those who had gone into hiding with their camouflaged identities, the mutated zombies, once more in office and highly honoured, as well as the silenced victims.

Where there is a forbidden room, there's also a forbidden question, in this case the question concerning the inner disposition of the perpetrators and victims, whose enjoyment on the one hand, and pain on the other, had found no place in the academic portrait of Fascism. Even the psychological state of the victims and their children became only decades after 1945 a subject of human interest and scholarly research. Throwing some light upon the psychological make-up of the Millions of "ordinary Germans" in Hitler's formidable force, was, however, studiously avoided by German historians of Fascism. When eventually an "outsider" came and posed to their profession the question of all questions and even found an answer to it, they flipped out.

Now the history of the Holocaust has to be written anew, has to be told in a different way. For only if the fate of the generations before us is understood as man-made, can we sabotage our fate.

*Helmut Dahmer*
*former Professor of Sociology*
*Darmstadt University*
*Frankfurt, 4.4.1998*

## NOTES

1. In an article about the reception of Hannah Arendt's Eichmann book one reads: "Soon the scandal took on fantastic dimensions. A nation-wide campaign was launched in the United States, which aimed at bringing Hannah Arendt into discredit within the Jewish and academic communities. A whole troop of experts, some especially flown in from Israel, toured the country, denigrating Hannah Arendt as a 'Jewess, consumed by self-hatred,' as the 'Rosa Luemburg of nihilism'...Four big organizations put experts to work, having them scrutinize her text line by line, in order to tear it apart. Of course, these people found mistakes, mostly smaller ones, such as wrong dates and misspelled names." Amos Elon, "Die Exkommunikation. Das Wesen des Bösen in der Politik oder Hanah Arendt und der heftige Streit um ihr Eichmann-Buch," *Frankfurter Allgemeine*, 4.20.1997 ("Bilder und Zeiten").

2. Daniel Jonah Goldhagen, *Hitlers willige Vollstrecker. Ganz gewöhnliche Deutsche und der Holocaust.* [*Hitler's Willing Executioners*] (Berlin: Siedler, 1996).

# PREFACE

This book first appeared in 1998 towards the end of the Goldhagen debate in Germany under the title *Gold-Hagen und die "hürnen Sewfriedte": Die Holocaust-Forschung im Sperrfeuer der Flakhelfer*. An explanatory word for those unfamiliar with the German language and German mythology and the play on words in this title: Siegfried, the Germanic hero of the *Nibelungenlied* was invulnerable, except for a spot between his shoulder blades. Hagen, his adversary, knew about this and waited for the right moment to plunge his spear into it. In a similar way Gold-Hagen found the vulnerable spot of German mainstream historiography, which tries to explain the Holocaust in terms of abstract sounding phrases, such as "implementing the Final Solution" or "the process of destruction," and administered a fatal blow to it by reminding readers that what was actually involved was the cold-blooded slaughter at point-blank range of helpless people.

There was good reason for Hans-Ulrich Wehler, the leader of German structural history, to perceive the Harvard Junior Professor's bestseller *Hitler's Willing Executioners* as a "thorn in the flesh."[1] Daniel Goldhagen's book sticks like a harpoon in the body of German academic history and "Siegfried" cannot shake it off. Unable to deal with the book, the deans of German historiography go so far as to deny that there has been a Goldhagen controversy in Germany.[2] May they continue "the sleep of the unjust," the uncomfortable feeling that Goldhagen comes very close to the truth is spreading, namely that Germany was a nation of "eliminatory anti-Semites" that were in agreement with the "Führer." Eichmann and his staff in the Reichs Sicherheits Hauptamt (RSHA), were not simple policemen who disposed of Jews behind the front lines, like cogs in a wheel who just did their job without giving much thought to what they were doing (as Hans Mommsen and his colleagues would like us to believe). The opposite happens to be the case: They were highly motivated perpetrators who acted in accordance with their anti-Semitic views, fully aware of the consequences of their deeds.[3]

As problematic as it may be to speak of "the German historians," it is nonetheless true that they closed ranks against Goldhagen and rejected his book collectively. The manner in which they rejected it, made it all too clear that they did not respond to the book as trained historians, but as Germans, whose biographies are intertwined in various ways with the Nazi past. By pointing this out in my book, I hit the nail on the head.[4] The smugness and unwillingness of German academics (not only historians) to step down from their pedestal, in order to discuss openly, confirms my thesis. I had to wait for four years before the first, and up till now the only, professional historian, namely my German-Canadian compatriot Michael Kater to take the time to comment on my book. After much begging and flattery on the part of the *Australian Journal of Jewish Studies* he wrote a review. In doing so, he confined himself to a desperate defense of his German colleagues. Solidarity with these colleagues seems to take absolute priority over dealing with the serious problems raised in the book, problems he refuses to address.[5]

The reason for the anger with which Kater attacks my book became all too clear to me when I read the foreword of his book *Das "Ahenerbe" der SS* and learned that he finds himself much in the same dilemma as do his German colleagues Mommsen, Jäckel and Wehler, whom he defends. Kater, too, wrote his dissertation under the guidance of a Doktor-Vater who once had been a strapping Nazi, namely under the guidance of Werner Conze from the University of Heidelberg[6] who made a name for himself in the Third Reich as a *volkish* and anti-Semitic propagandist. I take it that that is news to Michael Kater, even though he could have gotten to know Conze in his published writings as a former disciple of Adolf Hitler, a disciple for whom Jews were traitors, parasites, and devious enemies of the *Volk* who had to be removed. But I assume that Kater didn't want to know this, as—according to some new findings—he didn't want to know anything about the criminal past of the former SS-Obergruppenführer Wolf-Dietrich Wolff from the "Ahnenerbe" Foundation of the SS. According to court records Wolff was an accomplice to the murder of at least 87 Jews in Natzweiler Concentration Camp. Kater wrote on behalf of this Nazi criminal an expert opinion on York University stationary, in which he tried to convince the court "that Wolff just performed...routine administrative tasks within the 'Ahnenerbe' Foundation and hence could not have made any decisions on his own."[7]

The bad news about the Nazi past hasn't reached the generation of Mommsen, Wehler and Jäckel and also the generation of Kater any earlier than now, because they partook in the conspiracy of silence, not because the archives were sealed. Here in Germany a diplomatic silence still is observed; as in a secret agreement nobody mentions to any one else "those critical years." I should, in fact, be ashamed of myself for breaking this unspoken rule in this book. When it appeared for the first time in 1998, I asked a philosopher from the Technical University of Darmstadt, with whose daughter my children had attended Kindergarten and primary school, and with whom I frequently had stimulating conversations after PTA meetings, whether I could count on him for a review. The next day there was a note from him in my mailbox, informing me: "Unfortunately I am unable to review your book, because I know too little about this whole business" (my translation). Truly astonishing, the "well known representative of Darmstadt cultural life" who is an ardent advocate of a "close-to-life philosophy" and who is "concerned about the pressing contemporary problems,"[8] knew too little "about this whole business." The former pupil of an Adolf Hitler Boarding School, whom I mention in my book as the Darmstadt historian who against his better judgment accepted Rainer Zitelmann's apologetic Hitler biography as a dissertation, doesn't seem to be quite as ignorant, but he is dazzled when he sees me. Whenever our ways cross, he looks at me, as if I were a ghost. And the late President of the Technical University of Darmstadt and former Fritz Fischer student, who also gets "honorable mention" in my book, pretends he doesn't see me when he walks by me. The editor of the historical journal *Aschkenas* who is also the Director of the local State Archives, wrote me that he couldn't have my book reviewed in his journal, because he can only spare room for important books, and *Neue Politische Literatur*, the journal of the Darmstadt University's Department of

History, shrouded itself in silence, when I offered my book to the editors to have it reviewed. They didn't even respond to my letter.

However, the book deepened friendships with people who really mean something to me and it even smoothed the way to new friendships. My old friend Claude Owen who had to flee with his parents from Frankfurt in 1938, because of "racial" reasons, and who, after an interim stay in Bolivia, came to Canada, where he taught me German literature, felt that such a book was long overdue. He wrote me: "Your opus appears to me to be of the very highest caliber and of fundamental veracity and necessity." The Australian philosopher and political scientist Harry Redner, with whom I struck up immediate friendship when we met during a public lecture held in a meeting hall of the Jewish congregation in Frankfurt, said to me: "Fred, I think that everything you say in the book is true." The book also paved the road to friendship with Sol Littman, the former Director of the Simon Wiesenthal Center in Toronto, where I met him before his retirement. In view of the difficulties I had and still have with the book, he stood by me over the years and strengthened my resolve with encouraging words such as these: "As the Jewish refusnicks...used to say to each other 'Be strong'." Under no circumstances should I forget to mention Helmut Dahmer, the "obstetrician" who helped me to give birth to the book. If he wouldn't have been there, to whom else could I have spoken unabashedly about Germany and the Germans? Others also need to be mentioned: Julia Frankel, Frances Hanna, Hans-Georg Enger, Torsten Schäfer, Michael Will, Frank Haindl, Wolfgang Günther, Andreas W. Hohmann, Dieter Johannes, Walter Wilkes—and last but not least, my sister Leni Coleman. I am indebted to all of them more than I can express in words. Since my book has reached them, I can take a breather, for I have accomplished something.

What has enabled my accomplishment, and what was it that drove me to write this book? My rootlessness! My roots had been severed in 1955 when I emigrated at the age of thirteen with my parents to Canada. However, the memories remained with me. I identify with Canada's awakening to full independence during the First and Second World War. But if the memory of French-Canadians goes back to Normandy and Brittany and that of Canadians of Anglo-Saxon descent back to England, Ireland, Scotland and Wales, then my memory reaches back into the Third Reich and into the immediate post-war years in a small village in Lower Saxony. As an uprooted German I was virtually predestined to adopt the perspective of the "roaming observer" when I returned to Germany in 1982. I seemed to roam around aimlessly, while looking for something, which I was unable to identify. At a staff meeting in the Hessische Staatsarchiv Darmstadt one archivist is supposed to have wondered: "This Herr Kautz is looking for something; could it be that he is Jewish?" No, Herr Kautz isn't Jewish, but whoever is familiar with the Clifford Geertz book *Thick Description*, can easily guess what was going on. An important essay in this book is entitled "Deep Play." It describes how something unexpected happened to the "roaming observer": While the ethnologist Clifford Geertz runs from the police along with the natives, he all of a sudden discovers the point of intensity, in which everything in the society, he is observing, comes to a point.[9] My *"objet trouvé"* was a former Wehrmacht Lieutenant, whom the Technical University of Darmstadt designated as my faculty advisor. Something happened during an encounter of a peculiar kind with him during his office hours, when, before I knew it, I got into a heated argument with him. The subject of the quarrel was a small town Lutheran minister, whose biography I tried to piece together with the help of documents. In this heated argument everything that was wrong with German academic history came to a point.

The minister in question had been a Nazi and a leading activist of the "German Christian" Movement in Friedberg County. With missionary zeal he had indoctrinated church goers to rally them under the banner of Adolf Hitler and his crony, the Reichsbischoph Müller. In an attempt to understand what went on in the head of this upright Lutheran clergyman, I had thoroughly studied his monthly devotional column, published in a small regional church newspaper, of which all issues from 1927 to 1941 were at my disposal. In it I had found the longing for a "Führer," the gospel about the *Volk* being a part of the order of creation, which had to be guarded against the Jews as enemies of the Christian way of life, anti-communism, anti-pacifism, anti-modernism, philistine sexual morality and a hodgepodge of other things one usually associates with Nazism. I had also obtained from the Berlin Document Center a copy of the minister's Nazi Party membership registration card. In Wiesbaden I had looked at his Denazification trial record, and in the Central Archives of the Evangelical Church in Hesse and Nassau I had studied his personal dossier.

I was even more surprised when the normally friendly advisor, who treated me, as a rule, in a kind of benevolent fatherly way, started to brow-beat me even before I had a chance to sit down and organize myself. "Nein Herr Kautz, that is not how one writes history!" he lashed out at me, accused me of character assassination, and asked me, what this insignificant minister had done to me that gave me cause to write in such a derogatory way about him. He would have preferred seeing a "more merciful approach"; my basic source was, according to the advisor, rather weak.

About "Luther's clear German eyes" we quarreled. To the advisor and ex-Wehrmacht Lieutenant the phrase referred to the "clairvoyance of the religious leader." I had read Walter Kempowski who had collected testimonials from "Old Fighters" and from hysterical women who had just melted away when their "Führer" had subdued them with his commanding glance; and they all swore that their idol had light blue eyes, although Hitler's eyes were brown. I saw my minister prone to a similar delusion when he was captivated by "Luther's clear German eyes," which looked at him in a "compelling" way. Seeing that Lucas Cranach had painted a swarthy, dark-eyed Martin Luther, to the ex-Wehrmacht Lieutenant and active duty academic law enforcement officer, this was of course gibberish, mere "psycho-talk." All in all, what I had written was below all standards, a mishmash of undigested readings, by no means the yield of scholarly research, much rather a "pamphlet." In short, the brow-beating awaiting Goldhagen, I had already received more than a decade earlier and couldn't help but see what was happening, when from the lofty height of his tenured position Eberhard Jäckel rejected Goldhagen's study as "just a bad book," Hans Mommsen whimpered about the "biting sharpness" of the Junior Professor's assertions, and Jost Nolte ridiculed the Junior Professor as a "pamphleteer."

Unbelievable how some Germans are bored by this prehistory. Among the numerous laudatory reviews my book received in non-professional journals, there is one that touches upon crucial events that had led up to its publication, namely the article in the *ötv magazin*, which was not meant as a critical article at all, but rather as a pat on the back from my labor union, the ÖTV, for a rank and file union man who had published something.[10] The substance of the 270 word article is about my odyssey from Germany to Canada and my return to my native land as a GI, a report on my university studies in Canada and the U.S. and my subsequent research trip to Germany, where the academic welcoming committees were already awaiting me full of suspicion. "Ohne Emotion" ("Without Emotion") is the title, which heads the article in fat print, and I do not quite understand, whether the author Dietmar Rothwange refers with this title to himself or to the German historians, whom, according to him, I accuse of writing history, not from the perspective of human beings capable of experiencing joy and sorrow, but from the vantage point of genuine Wissenschaft—as if experiencing joy and sorrow, on the one hand, and Wissenschaft, on the other, were mutually exclusive. In any case, the labor union journalist Rothwange seems to subscribe to this dichotomy. One need not look for value judgments in the article, there just aren't any. "Now Fred Kautz has problems with his native land," the article states in passing and leaves it at that. "Tough luck, buster," the subtext reads. *Das Päckchen*, the high gloss propaganda sheet for the wage slaves at UPS, where I once worked as an unskilled laborer in order to survive, could not have mentioned these problems in a more non-committal way. It took a young Canadian, the reporter Kalvin Reid from the St. Catharines *Standard*, the newspaper of the Niagara Peninsula, to give some thought to the connection between my biography and the book I wrote.[11] His knowledge about what happened "back in the Old Country" during World War II, was not at par with the latest research (so that he let Field Marshal Montgomery's 8th Army advance as far as West Prussia), but the story interested him and this motivated him to do an admirable piece of investigative journalism. He even tracked down some of my opponents, in order to ask them what they thought of the book *Gold-Hagen und die "hürnen Sewfriedte.*" "Two contacts in the history department at the university in Darmstadt refused to comment on Kautz and his work," Reid notes. The German press could benefit from taking tutoring lessons from this enthusiastic Canadian reporter.

And it was left to my Canadian compatriot Sol Littman, the son of a Jewish-Canadian seamstress who helped to unionize Canadian workers in the clothing manufacturing industry, to point out what it means to have come from a working class family and to have acquired a university education. "Kautz is the product of a German working-class family that emigrated to Canada while he was a fourteen year old adolescent" he writes. "He went to school in the small, provincial Canadian city of St. Catharines, attended the local university (Brock) and went on to graduate studies in German history at the State University of New York at Buffalo, and at Darmstadt University. The first in his family to receive a university education, his academic life has not been easy."[12] My father was a farmer in Bessarabia before the war. After the war he had to work as a farm hand in Lower Saxony; thereafter, he cut peat in the bog and jobbed in a road construction crew. In Canada he found work as an unskilled laborer in the construction industry. He worked like a cart horse till his old TB returned. He had originally been struck while fleeing in the winter of 1945 from West Prussia, or perhaps got it in our damp refugee dwelling "back in the Old Country." After he had been cured, he stayed on in the Schaefer Hospital for Respiratory Diseases and worked there as a janitor. To write something was more difficult for him than lifting heavy bricks on a construction site, for he had received at the most three years of schooling in Bessarabia. When he had to sign his Old Age Pension check, he virtually flexed his muscles, because he was not used to holding a writing utensil in his hand.

Hence, I belong—without having had much choice in the matter—to the first generation of those intellectuals who have risen out of the working class and for whom we have no real name yet. That, too, means rootlessness or being homeless. In the words of the German writer Gerhard Zwerenz:

> Return to the inarticulate protectiveness of the proletarian, motherly embrace is no longer possible for those who have gotten used to thinking, who have acquired a passion for the search of truth with all its uncertainties.[13]

PREFACE / xix

I could sing a song about all this as, when I drove from Buffalo across the Canadian-American border to visit my parents in their small house on Lake Street in St. Catharines (just a 45 minute drive).

I abhorred returning to the "inarticulate protectiveness of the proletarian, motherly embrace." I wanted to liberate myself from this stifling embrace. Perhaps, in the past, I wanted to defect to the idols who sit in upper floor executive offices or who hold chairs in university departments. I am no longer driven by this desire. I no longer want to make common cause with them, especially if they still wear the Nazi uniforms of yonder days under their lab coats of "value free" science. The thought of becoming like them repels me.

I feel I owe this confession to the reader. In the words of the Italian historian Carlo Ginzburg:

> Why should we bar the reader from entering the work-shop of the researcher? To present research findings, while blending out the way we got them, distorts things enormously.[14]

May the reader look into the workshops of the historians, especially at those belonging to the generation of the Adolf Hitler Boarding School, the Hitler Youth, and the auxiliary anti-aircraft gunners. Kurt Vonnegut, that master of black humour, might say this to arriving guests: I promised to give you an explanation of why it was necessary to bring out a second augmented edition of this book, which was originally entitled *Gold-Hagen und die "hürnen Sewfriedte,"* but something went wrong in the kitchen. What I wrote here instead of a foreword also turns out to be a report of my last two decades "back in the Old Country," which were by no means a piece of cake.

*Fred Kautz*
*September 2002*

## NOTES

1. Hans-Ulrich Wehler, "Wie ein Stachel im Fleisch," *Die Zeit*, May 24, 1996, p. 40.

2. Wolfgang Wippermann, "Goldhagen und die deutschen Historiker: Strukturalistische Verkürzungen, böswillige Verdrehungen und antisemitischen Untertöne," in *"Die Fratze der eigenen Geschichte"—Von der Goldhagen-Debatte zum Jugoslavien-Krieg*, ed. Jürgen Elsässer und Andrei S. Markovits, Antifa Edition (Berlin: Elefanten Press, 1999), p. 21.

3. Cf. Among others Yaacov Lozowick, *Hitlers Bürokraten—Eichmann, seine willigen Vollstrecker und die Banalität des Bösen*, transl. Christoph Münz (Zurich: Pendo Verlag, 2000); and Ian Kershaw, "Trauma der Deutschen," *Spiegel spezial*, No. 1 (2001), p. 6-13.

4. I no longer stand alone with this analysis of the German Goldhagen debate. The Swiss author Raphael Gross notes that in comparison to Israel, the U.S. and Poland, Holocaust Studies deserving the name have hitherto hardly been conducted in Germany, where they just seem to be getting under way now. In view of this tardiness he poses the question "whether the history of the Holocaust...could have been written any earlier by German scholars." He doubts it, "for it is evident that historians who were enmeshed in the Nazi past couldn't produce studies on the Holocaust, matching the quality of Hilberg's, Reitlinger's, Browning's and Goldhagen's studies. They shied away from doing empirical studies on the destruction of the Jews. And like me, Gross notes:

   > This, however, does not mean that German historians did not exert their influence on the [discourse on the Holocaust]. This influence may be noted in other fields, namely in the "politics of memory," where the remembrance of the Holocaust becomes more and more abstract. In similar evasive words, with which German historians shied away after the war from empirical Holocaust research, they now dabble in the "politics of memory" by producing a highly abstract consensus, ritualistically stressing the "uniqueness" of the Holocaust, insisting that it cannot be compared to any other genocide and that it constitutes everlasting shame etc.

   Even the Holocaust research conducted in Germany today give Gross much cause for concern. He perceives in it "a strange emotional distance to the horrendous event under investigation...and the absence of value judgments." Gross, "Die verspätete Holocaustforschung," *Buchzeichen*, Supplement to the *Tages-Anzeiger*, Oct. 8, 2001, p. 11.

5. Michael H. Kater, Rev., of *Gold-Hagen und die "hürnen Sewfriedte": Die Holocaust-Foschung im Sperrfeuer der Flakhelfer* by Fred Kautz (Berlin, and, Hamburg. Argument Verlag, 1998), as well as my rebuttal, *Australian Journal of Jewish Studies*, 15 (2001), p. 129-148. [Both are to be found in this book in the last chapter, entitled "Kater and Mouse."]

6. Michael Kater: "I am especially indebted for continuing support to my Doktor-Vater, Herr Werner Conze, Heidelberg,." Toronto, May 1973, "Foreword" to his book *Das*

"Ahnenerbe" der SS 1935-1945—ein Beitrag zur Kulturpolitik des Dritten Reiches, Studien zur Zeitgeschichte, ed. Institut für Zeitgeschichte (Stuttgart: Deutsche Verlags-Anstalt, 1974), p. 8-9.

7. Cf. Ernst Klee, "Ein Medizinhistoriker als 'Dienr' eines Nazitäters," in Klee, Deutsche Medizin im Dritten Reich—Karrieren vor und nach 1945 (Frankfurt am Main: Fischer, 2001), p. 293-298 and 306-307; Michael Emmerich, "Die Fehler eines Studenten: Der Sozialhistoriker Michael Kater habe sich zum ' Diener' der SS gemacht, meint Ernst Klee -Vorwurf und Antwort," Frankfurter Rundschau, Oct. 30, 2001, p. 20.

8. Cf. Reinhard Olschanski, "Lebensnahe Philosophie," Darmstädter Echo, May 25, 2002, p. 22.

9. Clifford Geertz, " 'Deep Play': Bemerkungen zum balinesischen hahnenkampf," in his Dichte Beschreibung: Beiträge zum Verstehen kultureller Systeme, transl. Brigitte Luchesi and Rolf Bindemann, suhrkamp taschenbuch wissenschaft 696 (1983; Frankfurt am Main: Suhrkamp, 1987), p. 202-260.

10. [Dietmar Rothwange], "Ohne Emotion: Kollege kritisiert etablierte Historiker," das ötv magazin, No. 10/11, (Oct./Nov., 1999), p. 36.

11. Kalvin Reid, "Writer opens Pandora's box of German history—Ex-St. Catharines man object of academic scorn for his views on German involvement in Holocaust," The Standard, Sept. 18, 1999, p. 1-2.

12. Solomon Israel Littman, "Der zermürbende Kampf von Fredric Kautz gegen den akademischen Betrieb," Graswurzelrevolution, May 2002, p. 14.

13. Gerhard Zwerenz, Der Widerspruch: Autobiographischer Bericht (1974; Berlin: Aufbau Taschenbuch Verlag, 1991), p. 197.

14. Carlo Ginzburg, "Geschichte und geschichten: Über Archive, Marlene Dietrich und die Lust an der Geschichte," [Carlo Ginzburg in an interview with Adriano Sofri], in Ginzburg, Spuirensicherung: Über verborgene Geschichte, Kunst und soziales Gedächtnis (1983; Munich: Deutscher Taschenbuch Verlag, 1988), p. 12.

...and then he says, Is that a new quilt you are working on, Grace?

And I say, Yes it is, Sir, it is a Pandora's Box for Miss Lydia...

And he says, And do you know who Pandora was, Grace?

And I say, Yes, she was a Greek person from days of old, who looked into a box she had been told not to, and a lot of diseases came out, and war, and other human ills...

He is surprised to find I know that, and says, But do you know what was at the bottom of the box?

Yes, Sir, I say, it was hope.

*Margaret Atwood*
*Alias Grace*

# GOLDHAGEN AND "SIEGFRIED"

Newspaper editors have asked me about a dozen times, what I think about Daniel Goldhagen's book. I'll be quite blunt: it is not up to the current standard of research, it doesn't even meet mediocre standards; its just a bad book.

—Eberhard Jäckel

This kind of treatment of an unusually thoroughly investigated area of research should have alarmed the dissertation advisors, the interpretive premise about the embodiment of evil by a genocidal people should have been emphatically rejected by them.

—Hans-Ulrich Wehler

Hans Mommsen (Bochum) felt compelled to state in public that he would "never have conferred the Ph.D." on Goldhagen.

—*Frankfurter Rundschau*, 23.9.1996

"Every writer must transgress illegally some border or other: he will become aware of this early enough when he is being 'shot' at,"[1] wrote Heinrich Böll, who knew best, because without fail he had gotten into the line of fire with the very novels which appealed to the German conscience. Since the appearance of his book about "the ordinary Germans" and the Holocaust,[2] Daniel Jonah Goldhagen, a young political scientist from Harvard has been under fire. The academic law enforcement officers of the German historical establishment react to him as if they had to prevent at all cost his breaking the historiographical "Siegfried Line" of their Holocaust research. Already before the appearance of the German edition of his controversial book they brought their "big Berthas" into action in order to pound it into smithereens with nit-picking and untrue, malicious assertions.

At the 41st Congress of the German Historical Association, the President of this illustrious professional body, Lothar Gall (Frankfurt), leaned back on the softly cushioned chair of academia and tried to dismiss the public debate over the book as mere sensationalism.[3] And at the very same gathering Hans Mommsen raised his hands in consternation, warning his audience against going too deeply into the motives of the perpetrators:

> Things were even worse than Goldhagen had described them—but whosoever opens Pandora's box to poke around in the atavistic dimensions of history would lend forbearance to cultural disintegration.[4]

In other words, Goldhagen's descent into the inner circle of the Holocaust, his "thick description" of mass murder, as well as his passionate, frequently angry style of writing disturbs German academic historians too much in their cool-headed, tedious and pedantic research and interpretation of history.

The book is exceedingly dangerous says Hans Mommsen:

> Goldhagen's narration of cruel and sadistic acts of violence caters to voyeurism. Serious historians of the Holocaust have deliberately refrained from crass descriptions. At best such descriptions appeal only to the emotions and contribute next to nothing to our understanding. We may assume that Goldhagen was not aware that his appeal to the base instincts is the real cause for the phenomenal sale of his book.[5]

Where is the originality and profundity in this argumentation? The great Hans Mommsen, who claims a monopoly for himself in Holocaust research, seems to have plagiarized this criticism of Goldhagen's supposed violation of the rules of propriety from Ulrich Raulff, who in turn seems to have copied it from the Canadian sociologist Y. Michael Bodemann[6] who chastises Goldhagen for having instrumentalized a "pornography of horror" in *Hitler's Willing Executioners*. Tipped off by Bodemann, Raulff pushes Goldhagen's book away in disgust, saying:

> To clear up any misunderstanding, I am concerned about the representation, not about the brutality of the facts themselves. Historiography in our time has [as a rule] refrained from resorting to a crass style; even when dealing with the most brutal wars and with blood-curdling mas-

sacres, historians have maintained a dispassionate distance. Especially in the description of Nazi horrors, they have been careful not to go beyond the dictates of decent language. It was as if Hilberg, Mommsen and whoever else dealt with the Holocaust, had instinctively observed an unspoken law, forbidding the showing of pictures...One can appreciate this tactfulness or criticize it as an expression of a deep-seated aversion to really deal with the subject. Be this as it may, Goldhagen's disregard for analytical scholarly prose and his resorting to highly emotional images violates a boundary, which up till now serious historiography hadn't dared to transgress.[7]

So the matter is all settled: the book has no redeeming value, it is dangerous, and should be forbidden! Should we accept the judgment of these historians in good faith rather than read the book? Should we dutifully obey the call of the German deans of academic history and get spiritually into step with them? I have reservations. The same arguments occur again and again. To me this monotony seems to throw light upon a particular kind of sensitivity among German historians, rather than upon the weaknesses in Goldhagen's book. It raises questions and reveals something about the self-image of German historians; questions and information about what German historians consider to be permissible in the historiographical treatment of the Holocaust; questions and no real answers as to why German historians preoccupy themselves with the mass murder of six million Jews; and in conjunction therewith, the question about what readers they have in mind when they write about the Holocaust or whether they even bother thinking about what problems people outside of the 'ivory tower' might have with the Holocaust. In other words, all the negative pronouncements on Goldhagen's book, coming out of the mouths of the leading German historians, create the impression that those who occupy chairs in history departments of German universities are not even interested in entering into dialogue with the public at large and would rather be left alone, being quite content, chatting with each other to no end about "functionalism" and "intentionalism" and having these scholastic exercises paid for by the Friedrich Ebert—and Volkswagen—Foundations.

Precisely the hullabaloo over Goldhagen's supposed disregard for propriety seems to be the most appropriate place to start, if one wishes to find out more about the psychological state of the German historians. The reason being that the problem at hand is one of aesthetics, a problem having to do with the ways and means of dealing with the historical imagination. It cannot be suppressed, it will not tolerate being chained down and calls for permeation with rationality. The controversy over Goldhagen's book gives reason to believe that the Harvard scholar's German opponents wish to castrate our thinking by calling for a ban on imagination. The debate shows beyond this that the underdeveloped understanding of historiography as a part of literature is one of the major weaknesses with which the anti-Goldhagen coalition is stuck, seeing that the prominent historians within this group are representatives of socio-political history, a stream of historiography which encourages historians in their indifference to questions of aesthetics, rather than problematizing this indifference. These historians are not at all in an enviable position when they parade around as self-proclaimed judges in matters having to do with good taste.

The problem, as they present it, raises the question of whether the representation of the mass murder of the 1700 Jews of Lomazy on August 19, 1942, that killing orgy in a deep pit in which the butchers stood knee deep in bloodied mud and ground water, with dead bodies and dying men, women and children floating around them, would have pleased the German connoisseurs of dignified writing more had Goldhagen imitated the prose of the Goethe Prize winner Ernst Jünger, that frosty stylistic perfectionist who could write so beautifully about death by firing squad, leisurely, somewhere in between the detached chattiness of Theodor Fontane and the modest lyricism of Eduard Mörike ("Doch in der Mitte liegt holdes Bescheiden"), in a refined classical tone, avoiding all excitement and expressiveness, lest an outburst of emotion spoil the elegance of his prose. And in contrast to Mr. Raulff, one would not just have to speculate in passing, but ask persistently whether one can really talk about a deliberate ban on images in the historiography of the Holocaust. One would have to analyze very thoroughly whether tactfulness or repression is involved in all the excitement about "propriety of language."

When it comes to Raul Hilberg, Raulff is most definitely leading his readers astray when he ascribes to him a self-imposed ban on images. Hilberg above all others was concerned with finding out who the perpetrators were and what they looked like. Only in retrospect did it occur to Hilberg that in doing so he was swimming against the current of Judaic tradition. In his autobiographical book *The Politics of Memory* he confesses how much his magnum opus *The Destruction of the European Jews* violated his ethnic-religious tradition. For in it he writes:

> Jews of today are aware just as much as their forefathers of antiquity about giving the perpetrators a face and personality, and letting them think, or admitting that they could experience doubt or feel remorse—in short, to admit that they were human. And what had I done? Again and again I stepped on forbidden territory, describing Amalek in every detail as a mass of German officials.[8]

If these officials appear nonetheless only as blurry silhouettes in Hilberg's standard monograph, then this has little to do with concern about the propriety of diction or with deep seated defense mechanisms, but rather with the structural approach, which Hilberg borrowed from his teacher Franz Neumann, and with the fact that the documents produced by Nazi bureaucracy fail to give sufficient information about the individuality of the perpetrators. And before Raulff makes any pronouncements on unspoken, but binding rules of diction in the representation of the Holocaust, he also should know that on Raul Hilberg's initiative a whole wall of photographs depicting well known and not so well known perpetrators from government bureaucracy, from the military, from industry, and from the Nazi party was put up in the United States Holocaust Museum in Washington.

But even this wall, which the planers call respectfully the "Hilberg Wall," does not satisfy the man who dedicated his life to not letting the memory of the Holocaust fade. One cannot help but note Hilberg's disappointment when reading his comment on this wall. He says, "A few perpetrators are shown, but only in the prisoner dock, awaiting sentence."[9] He probably would have preferred it, if "Amalek" had been depicted in each and every detail as a "common civil servant with uncommon tasks,"[10] as loving husband and father, who was legitimized in his capacity as a scholar to make profound pronouncements on certain topics, and who (in order to show off before his colleagues and to demonstrate that he was in step with the new age) stated in 1938 that the Aryan Paragraph alone was not enough to get rid of Jewish influence, thereby evoking thundering applause (as, for example, Dr. Günther Franz on June 6, 1938), or the way Goldhagen represents him, as a sadistic thug who, while escorting his designated victim to the place of execution, had a direct personal relationship to this Jewish child, "a little girl, eight or ten years old."

Not until I came to Germany did I encounter a mortal fear of pictures or of puzzle pieces, such as names, from which one could put together the picture. When I arrived in 1982 from Canada to commence my research in the Hessisches Staatsarchiv (Darmstadt) and asked for Nazi court records, I was referred to a high ranking archivist who asked for my understanding concerning the restrictive access to such documents. Mr. Hochhuth, the playwright, had found out through such records that Mr. Filbinger (then Premier of Baden-Württemberg) had been a navy judge in those days and had blown this up into a scandal, which did a lot of damage. He had to be careful, lest a misfortune like that would happen again. And even though this high level archivist was a very busy man, he insisted on xeroxing many of the documents I asked for himself. First he would make a preliminary copy, then, instead of blacking out names with a felt-tip pen, in a tedious procedure he would use scissors to cut these names out. He would put this paper spaghetti on the copying machine once more and make a second copy which he would give to me.

And there is no doubt in my mind that Wehler's brand of anti-individualistic and abstract *Historische Sozialwissenschaft* established as the predominant school of historiography in Germany, had something to do with an aversion to graphic description. Rarely, if at all, does this school of historical writing depict real people. This leads Golo Mann, the master of historical prose, to say:

> The basic fault of this new, modern type of history is that it doesn't concern itself enough with people of flesh and blood; in other words, that it plays "Hamlet" without the Prince of Denmark.[11]

Mann attributes this to a lack of sympathy for human beings.

How right he is! For isn't it an indicator of hard-heartedness when Hans Mommsen, one of the leading representatives of this modern, academicized historiography, pontificates about the "process of elimination,"[12] especially so, since he is constantly using unemotional and neutralizing phrases like the "implementation of genocide," the "implementation of the Holocaust," the "implementation of the 'Final Solution'?"[13] He might as well have stuck to the diction of the Wanasee Protocol, which uses phrases free of value, such as "natural diminution," "practical implementation of the final solution," or such and such Jews were to be "processed in accordance with the final solution."

"Language will bring it to the light of day,"[14] says Victor Klemperer in his book *LTI*. Here it brings to light the nature of the German "functionalist" school of Holocaust research, thus showing how diligent its leading proponents are in applying their historiographical skills in order to avoid being confronted with the graphic picture of the exact nature of the crime. Mommsen's article "Die dünne Patina der Zivilisation" bears witness to the fact that this dean of German history is so afraid of pictures that he leaves nothing undone to discredit Daniel Jonah Goldhagen, who spreads them out before him. Mommsen in his own words:

> He [Goldhagen] likes to see himself as one of the first researchers to use photographs as a source—in the files of the Hamburg State Attorney's Office there were contemporary snapshots—but little is he aware of how difficult it is to date and determine the relevance of photos, which in isolated instances have been handed down to us. Characteristically the book does not mention where these photographs came from, an unforgivable sin of omission.[15]

Why this nit-picking? This book, which was brought out in the U.S. by Alfred Knopf Publishers and in Germany by Siedler, is not a dissertation, but a condensed version thereof, in which Goldhagen's work is made available to a wider reading public. If a dissertation is published as a bestseller, something which occurs only very rarely, the publisher edits the text and the bibliography in order to make the book marketable by reducing the cost. The general reader is, in any case, not too concerned about where which document is deposited, because he has neither time nor money to verify the authenticity of sources. It may just be that Goldhagen's text has been edited when it was transformed from a dissertation to a best seller. If Mommsen wishes to come forth with well founded criticism and not just hair splitting, he should order the dissertation via inter-library loan from Harvard.

Beyond this, doesn't Mommsen "shoot himself in the foot," when he says, wedged into a sentence and just in passing, that the pictures Goldhagen uses are all to be found in the files of the Hamburg State Attorney's Office, which in the sixties and seventies conducted investigations of the members of Police Battalion 101 (as if he wanted to say that he is not impressed by Goldhagen's archival research, because the material he presents is not new: Christopher Browning had used it ). Is research in primary sources only legitimate if after much tedious work such research brings to light hitherto totally unknown documents out of some obscure archive? Interpretation would then only be of secondary importance and could be totally void of originality; indeed, the less originality the better, because lack of imagination is the best protection against subjectivity, which is frowned upon.

According to this notion, nothing original could be said anymore about Goethe's *Faust*, because it has already been discovered and interpreted by literary historians. No new Hitler biography could be written anymore, because Hitler's book *Mein Kampf*, his table talks, his medical and dental records, and what have you, have been read line for line by historians. Yet, Hitler biographies keep appearing one after the other and I dare say that good Hitler biographies, which will revise and modify what has already been said, will also be written in the future.

How sincere and productive is Mommsen's excessive skepticism concerning the authenticity and relevance of the photographs Goldhagen used? Many of them are, as mentioned, deposited in the files of the Hamburg State Attorney's Office. Isn't it legitimate to assume that in the course of the investigations these photos have been critically scrutinized by forensic experts and criminologists in order to establish their authenticity and relevance? Why is Hans Mommsen so set on depreciating Goldhagen's commendable achievement that he tries to discredit him in two mutually exclusive ways: on the one hand, he pretends to have doubts concerning the authenticity and relevance of Goldhagen's pictorial sources, on the other he nit-picks that Goldhagen made use of materials which had been neatly assembled by a German governmental agency, thereby shirking real archival research, thus disqualifying himself from being recognized as a genuine researcher.

And what is it that Mommsen is trying to prove with impeccably dated and authenticated photographs? His theory that "many...perpetrators didn't know themselves what motivated them?"[16] That will hardly be possible. There is, for example, an 8mm amateur film, documenting the mass shooting of Jewish men, women, and children near Liepaja in Latvia (July 1941). It was later used as incriminating evidence during the *Einsatzgruppen* trial in Ulm, Germany. The amateur movie photographer, a former petty officer of the German navy, by the name of Reinhard Wiener said this about the making of the film:

> I was, in any case, not hindered while making the movie, not even by an SS man who saw me just before I finished the roll of film. He asked me whether I had gotten "good" shots.[17]

It seems to me that this concerned and 'friendly' question of the SS killer and the fact that he turned his face to the camera, proves much of Goldhagen's thesis about the shameless, willing German executioners, than Mommsen's thesis about insignificant, confused sheep who "just obeyed orders" and didn't have the foggiest notion what the action in the killing fields was all about.

Aside from this, my desk copy of *Hitler's Willing Executioners* leaves me with the impression that Goldhagen was quite conscientious about dating and establishing the origin of photographs. The snap shots on page 225, depicting Jews herded together on the athletic field of Lomazy, waiting to being marched off to the execution site, are a case in point. In the accompanying text one reads:

> The reverse side of the third photograph was inscribed by the photographer as reproduced on the next page.

Turning to the next page, one sees a facsimile of the backside of that photo. The exact reproduction of the handwritten note reads:

10 / THE GERMAN HISTORIANS

> Verurteilte Juden
> Lomartzie 18 Aug 42
> 1600

It is followed by Goldhagen's exact translation:

> Condemned Jews
> Lomartzie18 Aug 42
> 1600

Commenting on the scribbled note, Goldhagen says:

> This man wrote down the pertinent information, made sure that years later he would not confuse or forget the accomplishment of the day. By his count, they killed 1,600 Jews.

Or what about the picture on page 407? Goldhagen carefully notes when and where the photograph was taken and even finds clues, as to why it was taken, and writes:

> The following photograph of a German soldier killing a Jewish mother and child was sent home through the mail. On the back of it was penned: "Ukraine 1942, Jewish Action, Ivangorod."[18]

Should Goldhagen also have provided the home address to where the photographs were sent? Unfortunately there are the privacy laws of the Federal Republic of Germany, with which the "ordinary Germans" of today keep the Nazi past at a safe distance. But doesn't it suffice for our purposes just to say: "Ukraine 1942, Jewish Action, Ivangorod?"

What more does one need? If Professor Mommsen can do a better job, who is stopping him? Germany's leading newspaper, *Die Zeit*, illustrated his contribution to the Goldhagen debate with four photographs, which show, how in 1941 in the Ukraine Wehrmacht soldiers tortured and humiliated a Jew by cutting off his beard—pictures of the kind which can also be found in Goldhagen's book. To dispel rumors that had been spread, according to which these photographs were fakes, the German Federal Archives in Koblenz issued a news release, stating: "These pictures were made in July 1941 by the war correspondent, Gehrmann, who belonged to Propaganda Unit 691."[19] The German Federal Archives have a collection of over a million negatives of photographs, taken by propaganda units of the Wehrmacht. What's Professor Mommsen waiting for? *Hic Rhodus, hic salta!*

But the problem is that Mommsen doesn't want to see, Wehler doesn't want to see, Jäckel doesn't want to see! With their craftsmanship, nit-picking, and excessive concern about impeccable scholarship they resemble a man about whom Freud said that he continuously took off his spectacles to clean them, in order not to be able to see. Where is one of these high priests of learning driven by real curiosity, which expresses itself in frustration over the inadequate sharpness of a picture they are looking at, as, for instance, in a sentence like this: "We cannot observe the bureaucrats in their offices; who supported the system with their work?" Where does one of these "great white hunters" express anger over the stifling misuse of German privacy laws when the task at hand calls for making public carefully guarded secrets, anger as expressed in this sentence:

> All photographs of Police Battalion 101 that are described here but not shown cannot be published because of an interpretation that a local official has made of the privacy laws of the Federal Republic of Germany?

Or where does one hear out of their mouths urgent appeals like this one:

> The first task in restoring the perpetrators to the center of our understanding of the Holocaust is to restore to them their individualities, grammatically by using not the passive but the active voice in order to ensure that they, the actors, are not absent from their own deeds (as in "five hundred Jews were killed in city X on date Y).[20]

The first cited sentence is Raul Hilberg's sigh of frustration, vented while working on his book *The Role of the German Railroads in the Destruction of the Jews*. Tell tale evidence had directed his attention to the *Reichsbahn*. In its offices, he got a glimpse of the murderers, who sat at their desks and killed with the stroke of a pen, but their contours were blurry. He couldn't get a sharper picture, because the train schedules of the *Generaldirektion der Ostbahn*, the telegrams of the German railroads, and the bank records of the ghetto administration did not yield a sufficient amount of information.[21] The other two quotations are from Daniel Jonah Goldhagen.[22] His appeal and complaint, as well as Raul Hilberg's sigh of frustration are true indicators of curiosity and hunting fever. German academic history shows no sign of ever having been infected with this fever and its curiosity remains well within the prescribed bounds of propriety. At least the generation of historians to which Hans Mommsen, Hans-Ulrich Wehler, and Eberhard Jäckel belong, seems to be rather smug and immune against hunting fever. Lothar Gall appears to speak for all of them, when like a primary school teacher, he lays down the law: "We historians must counter this bloody plasticity with analytic research."[23]

Strange, very strange! As in Schiller' play *Wallenstein* one could say here: "Vor Tische las man's anders!"[24] "Vor Tische" was the case of Lothar Gall when he wrote his book about the Bassermann dynasty, a well-to-do middle class family. The book was a real work of art, in which millers, innkeepers, merchants, politicians, scholars, and actors were not interchangeable heroes, so that this saga of a German family could in a certain sense be seen as a counterpart to Gerald Green's Holocaust novel about the unfortunate Weiss family. At that time Gall played deliberately on the emotions of the reader. The title of the book was *Bürgertum in Deutschland*. On the dust jacket it was advertised with the following blurb:

> [Gall] does not talk about the middle class in an abstract way, but rather about representatives of this class, about real human beings. In doing so he sticks to Alexander Pope's dictum: "The proper study of mankind is man."[25]

"Vor Tische" was also just before the noisy German historians' controversy of the eighties, when Martin Broszat, the noted historian and Director of the Munich *Institut für Zeitgeschichte*, complained:

> When the Third Reich begins, authors start keeping a safe distance. Empathetic understanding for historical circumstances ceases, as does the pleasure of historical narration. The history of National Socialism is no longer suppressed, but it degenerates into compulsory reading.[26]

What historians were producing were black and white analyses, presented in abstract, academic prose, which were borrowed from political science. And since the historians knew the outcome of the story in advance, the verdict was a foregone conclusion. Guilty! What was missing, was the portrayal of psychologically credible human beings.

Then again I remember, how the same Martin Broszat demonstrated smugness, shielding academic history from the *Spiegel* editor Heinz Höhne. On the occasion of the televising of the American docudrama "Holocaust" the latter wrote:

> German historians, for whom the televising of "Holocaust" became a Black Friday, have good reason to contemplate the meaning and usefulness of their work. It has rarely been certified so dramatically that an entire academic discipline has for years talked past the needs and interests of the general public. It's time for change.[27]

Broszat didn't even understand the accusation. Proud as a peacock, he pointed out that a survey of the curricula of 22 universities had produced a "surprisingly positive" picture: these centers of learning and research had in the past 18 semesters offered 650 courses and seminars, dealing with the Nazi period. He conceded that most standard works, written by academic historians, only ascertained the Nazi crimes instead of exposing their specific and graphic details, which, according to him, had nothing to do with the suppression of truth, but rather with stylistic embarrassment. Broszat verbatim:

> Mass executions and gas chambers present a "stylistic" hurdle to the language of historicism, which is only accustomed to sublime ideas, a hurdle the historian is trying to leave behind as quickly as possible.[28]

However, this sublime language is supposed to be just right for bone-dry topics like the social insurance system of the Third Reich, because topics like these Broszat would like to see represented with historical empathy and psychologically credible human beings.[29]

The dichotomy: here "serious" analytical research, there "trivial," close to life, vivid description constitutes evasive reasoning. Vivid description and historical analysis are not mutually exclusive; by and large they are dependent on each other. To narrate history without analysis is trivial, but to only analyze history without narrating is banal. In the debate over narrative versus analytical history the same historians are at one time all for vivid narration, at other times against it—namely when the topic to be discussed has to do with Nazi crimes. It already dawned on Karl Dietrich Bracher that something was not right here. Hence, he objected to a radical academization of history, chiding the overeager adherents of this trend, because while turning to a modern, supposedly more realistic analysis of National Socialism, they were trying to push aside the question of guilt and responsibility.[30]

But in all seriousness: Are there legitimate moral or aesthetic reasons, which speak against the evocation of the Holocaust by means of imaginative, graphic images? When talking about the destruction of the Jews, authors like Peter Weiss, as well as the German historians suppress their imagination, trusting that the documents will speak for themselves. If this ascetic approach would enjoy unconditional, universal validity, Goldhagen could only have avoided being criticized by suppressing all his feelings, letting the documents speak for themselves. This, in any case, seems to be the opinion of Ulrich Raulff, who says:

> The horror of the real Holocaust requires neither aesthetic tricks, nor rhetorical manipulation. Whoever wants to experience it, should just read the record of the Auschwitz trial.[31]

What Goldhagen had produced, was a scandal, a desecration of the real Holocaust, because he had taken the liberty of taking the gruesome incidents, which are mentioned in the documents and arranged them according to the "horror movie aesthetics" of Hollywood.

Let's just play along with Raulff for a while, let us resort to the mimesis of classical theater, where rape murder, and manslaughter take place behind the scene, in contrast to the blood-curdling baroque tragedy, where torture, stabbing and gouging are acted out in front, before the spectators. Let us open up the Auschwitz trial once more and listen to the cross-examination of former SS Master Sergeant Kaduk, without asking any questions of our own:

> *How come you were posted to Auschwitz?*
> KADUK: Well, to Auschwitz I was taken by the SS-9 Regiment. I'm then on the Eastern front. I was, and then I have come to the West and in the East, there, I got Malaria. And then I came to Glaz, fifteen of us,

from there we got to Belau, reserves, there I am told that we are gonna go to a troop training area, and they lied to us. And then we found out that it was a concentration camp.

*When you first entered that camp, what was your impression?*
KADUK: Oh, well, you know, I was a bit shocked. I'd believed...we'd seen all the inmates. I was shocked. But I couldn't do nothing.

*Were people shot there?*
KADUK: Yes, they was shot, in Block 11. There the political branch, was in charge.

*And why were they shot?*
KADUK: Hm, that I can't tell you no longer now, all right. There arrived a list from Berlin for us, and the list went to the Protective Custody Camp commandant, political branch, the political custody camp and I ordered these here people for the next day and I say we don't go out to work. And then they went to Block 11 and there the political division picked them up, shot them. Why that wuz I dunno.[32]

How should he have known? Nobody told him anything! When I read all this and see the stupid face of SS Master Sergeant Kaduk and how he stands at attention before his judges, with his hands at his trouser seams, then I remember that brave "Private Schwejk": "Sir! Reporting as ordered: I am stupid!"

It just can't be true that just a bunch of simple folks, who couldn't afford the luxury of their own opinion "implemented" the Holocaust. There must be more to it than that, there must be more specific details begging for an explicit, graphic description. Raulff's notion about the tasteful mimesis of the Holocaust seems to be just an opinion that is being circulated at academic cocktail parties, nothing more than a sublime kind of rumor (Raulff heard it from Bodemann, Mommsen from Raulff, a work colleague of mine stuck the *tageszeitung* with Bodemann's article in my face, and so on)—a "smoke screen," which fogs up the real problem.

Every historian who has dug in the archives, knows quite well that one doesn't get very far, if one suppresses the imagination and reads the documents just for their literal content. If one takes the records of the Auschwitz trial, as Raulff recommends, then one finds out something about the SD man Boger's preference for certain torture methods, but one cannot see behind him the fee paying honorary SS members, i.e., the gentlemen from industry who flattered Himmler in order to get his permission to set up profitable branch plants on the premises of concentration camps; one learns about the formalities, which SS Oberscharführer Erber had to observe while selecting able bodied men at the camp, while sending the others on to the gas chamber, without quite understanding what this selection process had to do with anti-Semitism, and one learns about the gruesome daily chores of Rapportführer Kaduk, but his underdeveloped, lower class speech and his primitive mode of thinking keep him at a distance, far away from educated decent folks like us.

And if one leafs through volume after volume of the Nuremberg trial records, one cannot find one single document of the *Reichsbahn*, the state owned German Railroads. While gathering incriminating evidence, the victorious allied powers were not looking for railway documents. Hence, not one single page with the *Reichsbahn* letterhead turns up in this comprehensive document collection. In other words, sources never speak for themselves, they only reveal information, if the researcher makes them talk. They only give answers to questions, which one poses to them. If there are no questions, crucial documents may be overlooked. The greater the researcher's historical imagination, the more creative he will be in deciphering the traces of the past, the better he will get into the deeper layers of the text.

Discussions on the complex business of interpretation and understanding Raulff could have found in the theoretical writings of Marc Bloch, Lucien Febevre and all the great French masters, whom he reveres. Seeing that he is one of the most knowledgeable German historians—as far as French historiography is concerned—he would know these better than I do, but he perceives Goldhagen's historical imagination as something obscene, and he is offended by how the pieces of the puzzle fit together in the light of this imagination. Consequently he rejects Goldhagen, saying that the young Harvard scholar's book is a potboiler which has borrowed heavily from the aesthetics of Hollywood horror movies. The real Auschwitz was, of course, much worse, and, above all, very different. It is legitimate to ask whether this refined revulsion of

Auschwitz does not take flight into the criticism of the historiographical representation of Auschwitz.

For whoever tries to disqualify Goldhagen with the help of aesthetics, must have forgotten that the conflict at hand has preoccupied poets and thinkers for more than 200 years. The Classicists and Romantics discussed it under the heading: The Representability of Evil in Literature. The unexamined creed, which haunts the newspapers and journals these days, and which is blindly accepted by Raulff who swings it as a club against Goldhagen. I refer, to that article of faith according to which the extreme case of the Nazi mass murderer cannot be represented in literature, which would have surprised these writers.

"In the entire history of mankind there is no chapter more instructive for heart and mind than the annals of perversion," decrees Friedrich Schiller and explicitly gives preference to the exceptional criminal: his example is, according to this German playwright, particularly suited to challenge and to educate the moral sensibility of the spectator. Schiller's preference for the extreme villain is rooted in the intention to shock "the cruel scorn and the arrogant self-assuredness" with which "untested, upright virtue looks down upon its fallen sister."[33] To cure her of this, the imagined distance between the criminal and the spectator has to be reduced. This reduction calls, by necessity, for the humanization of evil.

It confronts the Holocaust researcher who has to represent the reality of the destruction of the Jews with difficulties, which cannot be limited to a question of good taste. To be precise: if, for example, the men of Police Battalion 101 are criminals of the kind identified with "absolute evil," so that there is no trace of humanity to be found in them, then they can in principle only be documented, but not represented by literary means. If, on the other hand, we assume that the officers and enlisted men of the police battalions belonged to the human species, then Raulff's assertion that their horrendous crimes can only be documented, but not represented by literary means must be ascribed to an act of suppression, whose only advantage lies in having blocked out "the dark awareness of having similar potentials."[34]

Using this argument, I can by no means claim to be original. I simply follow the logic of an essay by Peter Schneider, entitled "Vom richtigen Umgang mit dem Bösen" ("Concerning the Proper Way of Dealing with Evil"). Peter Schneider who has a real talent when it comes to breaching taboos, is skeptical in regard to the value of the unimaginative, documentary way of dealing with Nazi atrocities and counters:

> In spite of all moral objections, the question must be asked, whether the indisputability of a document only corresponds to a passive, obedient perception on the part of the observer. The horrendous cruelty, which stares us in the face when we look at photographic evidence of the Nazi genocide, is so overpowering and incomparable that it smothers natural inquisitiveness. The reaction of the ordinary (German) spectator exhaust itself all too easily in aversion: Terrible! Never again! And more subdued, but decisive: We didn't do it, it lies behind us, and by looking at these pictures, we have done our duty![35]

Communication here, is a one-way street. TV stations charged with a pedagogical task transmit, the viewers sit in front of their TV and consume what is sent as long as they like it or as long as they can stand it, and then they reach for the button and switch it off. The documentary model of historical understanding, which seems to serve as a foundation of mutual recognition among professional historians, works in the same way. It is based on the presumption that research is solely based on "hard" undeniable "facts," which may be sifted out of the sources. The only task that is left to the historical imagination, is to fill the gaps in a plausible way. If a past event is to be seen "in a different light," one does not call for a different perception, but for the discovery of hitherto unknown information. The historian goes to the archives, takes a stack of documents and skims through them to gather "facts," in order to inform himself about certain times and places. He takes and gives nothing. And when he has studied the documents of the Dachau Concentration Camp or the activity reports of the *Einsatzgruppen*, he stands there after a days work just like the aforementioned spectator who has just turned off the tube. At the emotional level his reaction exhausts itself in an instinctive aversion: Terrible! We didn't do it, it lies in the past.[36]

This instinctive aversion articulates itself again and again in the negative reviews of Goldhagen's book. Even when just skimming through Rudolf Augstein's review essay "Der Soziologe als Scharfrichter" ("The Sociologist as Executioner"), one stumbles over a plump and tactless sentence like this one: "The question, whether Auschwitz was an incomparable crime, has been dealt with enough and cannot be subject to debate year after year."[37] Revealing Freudian slips like this one, may even be discovered in the review essays of the most highly respected representatives of the German historical profession. Hans-Ulrich Wehler writes, for instance: "In this country one should be able to react calmly to the perceivable moral indignation, which drives the author [Goldhagen]."[38] Here speaks an aloof onlooker. His perspective is that of a grown-up person who takes note of a childish misbehavior, which will disappear with time. If Wehler has ever indulged in such "misbehavior," he has long since learned how to behave, and as soon as Goldhagen grows up, he will hopefully come to realize that what's past is past, there is no use in "crying over spilled milk."

Hans Mommsen is even less amused when he has to face the emotional involvement of a young scholar. With a sour face he notes:

> The corrosive sharpness, with which Goldhagen ascribes to the Germans the will to give in to a "demonic kind of anti-Semitism"...and the way in which he alleges them to be lustful perpetrators, is certainly not appropriate to neutralize resentment, and of no help at all when it comes to grappling with the encumbered past in a sober way.[39]

Here envy at the subconscious level gives cause for the discovery of resentment on the part of the son of a Holocaust survivor. Subconsciously Hans Mommsen views Goldhagen with envy, because this young scholar can afford to despise what the Germans did when they were the masters of nearly all of Europe. Or as the renowned psychoanalysts Alexander and Margaret Mitscherlich would say:

> In a first reading resentment may be characterized as jealous disappointment, which has become preconscious. It surfaces again in the form of projection. Projection makes us succumb to a change in our

perception. Instead of seeing our own envy and our "evil" desires, we start seeing malicious traits on the other person, for instance his spiteful unwillingness to forget, his being prone to exaggerate or to twist the facts in a deceitful way. Our own envy becomes invisible to us, the more we preoccupy ourselves with the bad habits of the other person.[40]

The "ordinary Germans" of today have become real experts in finding and criticizing Goldhagen's "bad habits:" It is disturbing, how a prominent historian like Hans Mommsen assumes leadership in this "fault-finding mission."

Eberhard Jäckel doesn't want to be left behind in the leadership race of this campaign. For him too the Third Reich and the Holocaust are "water under the bridge." Or how else am I to understand it, when he writes about how irredeemably bad Goldhagen's book is, and then concludes this scathing review by expressing in a gentle, almost intimate tone of voice, how it grieves him, having to write about the "failure" of a young American author, who had, prior to the publication of this worthless book, appeared to him as a "promising young scholar." Jäckel states: "I say this with regret, for I remember the author as a polite and intelligent young man."[41] What gives Jäckel the right to remember Goldhagen just as a nice American young man, who had come to him to be lectured in a pleasant conversation of one or two hour duration?

How can Augstein's, Mommsen's, Jäckel's and Wehler's discourse, which lets the past appear as something that has nothing to do with us as individuals, be made to agree with the responsibility, which the "good" German historians—Mommsen, Jäckel, and Wehler included—assumed during the "historians' debate" of the eighties? In case they have forgotten this self-assumed responsibility, they can refresh their memory by re-reading Jürgen Habermas' essay, entitled "Vom öffentlichen Gebrauch der Historie," ("Concerning the Public use of History"). There one reads:

> Even if others are no longer bound by it, we Germans still have the duty to keep alive, not only in our heads, [but also in our hearts] the unbuffered memory of the suffering of those who have been murdered at the hand of Germans. These dead have a just claim to the imperfect recollective solidarity, which posthumous generations can only experi-

ence by means of ever recurring, despairing, and in any case haunting memories. If we willfully discard this legacy [Vermächtnis], our Jewish fellow citizens, or all sons and daughters and grandchildren of those who have been murdered, could no longer breathe in this country.[42]

How can one subscribe to such a manifesto and fail so miserably, when it counts most? Could it be that this failure has something to do with the fact that documentary understanding fails to make the "unspeakable" into a subject of our imagination? That, I think, is the crux of the matter. For the documentary mode of understanding (cf. p. 14 and 16) does not compel the onlooker to put himself into a personal relationship to past events, because it does not put his moral judgment to the test and leaves him at a safe distance.

There, at the abstract level the German opponents of Goldhagen carry on learned disputes about whether the Führer or the structures should be blamed for the destruction of the Jews. While doing so, they studiously avoid to address Goldhagen's most important question, namely whether his book constitutes a path-breaking contribution to the humanization of evil.

In the United States Robert Browning said, Goldhagen had denied that the perpetrators were also human beings. His own book *Ordinary Men: Reserve Police Battalion 101 and the Final Solution in Poland*, which orients itself on the Stanley Milgram experiment, concludes that socialization and evolution have produced "deeply rooted behavioral patterns"...which cause people to obey the instructions of those who are above them, even if in doing so they have to violate commonly accepted norms."[43] Subscribing to this hypothesis, Browning concludes by asking, whether each one of us might not have acted the same way as the members of Police Battalion 101 did, if we would have been in their shoes. The criticized Harvard scholar, on the other hand, feels that it was just his mode of description and explanation that restored humanity to the perpetrators. For he proceeds from the premise that any attempt to explain the Holocaust falls short of its goal, if it fails to take note of the fact that the perpetrators believed that what they were doing, was right. As he sees it, the behavior of the perpetrators doesn't indicate that they operated in a moral vacuum, determined by imposed obligations, in which they could drown their scruples about killing helpless men, women, and children. The opposite was true, according to him. Circumstances were such that ordinary Germans had the opportunity to give uninhibited expression to their beliefs in words and deeds. In other words, the historian from Harvard relies on the insights of modern anthropology, which discovered that man who hasn't been formed by the customs of a particular locality doesn't exist, never has existed, and never will exist. In contrast to the Harvard scholar Browning, the historian from Tacoma, Washington, adheres to the belief that all men are basically the same, regardless of what costumes they are wearing and where they live.

Who is right, Goldhagen or Browning? The issue at stake is, how the variety of cultures can be brought into agreement with the biological unity of mankind. This begs the question of what is the relationship between the individual and society, which is in all likelihood the most important question in history. Is there a clear answer or can we only ascertain a tension between "culture" and "man," by necessity an extreme tension, which cannot be resolved no matter how hard we try? Whatever the answer might be, Goldhagen redirects our attention away from the structures towards the perpetrators, to the men who murdered Jews, and to the population, which engendered these murderers.

That is a transgression, for it demands from the reader of Goldhagen's book to grapple with the motives of the perpetrators. This constitutes perhaps the most unpleasant and most disturbing question, the Holocaust poses to us. It is conspicuous that Mommsen, Jäckel, and Wehler, that particularly these three historians who belong to the Hitler Youth generation which was most profoundly influenced by National Socialism, fight the hardest against accepting Goldhagen's challenge. Jäckel protests:

> Always the Germans (on every page he writes "the Germans," on some pages eight times). If not all Germans, than "the vast majority." The Holocaust happened, because they wanted it to happen.[44]

Hans Mommsen lectured on the TV program "Talk-im-Turm":

> The book doesn't bring anything new...It is to be regarded as an indictment of the Germans but not as a scholarly work.[45]

And Hans-Ulrich Wehler, who of these three chief historians comments most favorably on the book, rejects Goldhagen's interpretation as an "unconditional intellectual surrender," because here, according to him, the "collective guilt thesis celebrates, camouflaged as history of mentality, its pseudo-scholarly resurrection."[46]

I just ask myself, why these three advocates of Simon-purer scholarship didn't work up a rage back in 1961, when Hilberg's study *The Destruction of the European Jews* appeared, or at the latest in 1982, when the German edition came out? It constitutes a three volume indictment of the Germans. Hilberg was determined to break loose a Germany debate. For this very reason he had tried throughout his work to leave no doubt about what he said explicitly in volume III:

> The German perpetrator was by no means an extraordinary German. What we can say about his moral fiber, applies not only to him, but to Germany in general. How do we know?
>
> We know...that every policeman...could have been called upon to go on the beat in a ghetto or to serve as an armed escort on a railway transport destined for Auschwitz. Every legal expert in the *Reichssicherh- heitshauptamt* (Head Office of the Security Service of the SS) could have taken over the command of an *Einsatzgruppe*; every accountant or finance expert in the *Wirtschafts- und Verwaltungshauptamt* (Economic and Administrative Department of the SS) was a natural candidate for service in an annihilation camp. In other words, all required operations were carried out with whatever personnel was available. Wherever one examines it, the machinery of destruction represents a remarkably representative sample of the German population at large.[47]

He also regrets in his standard work that after all that has happened, Jews could not act as if the "consideration and understanding" of the countries, where they lived now, was unlimited, that, for example, in America they had to see Germany with "American eyes" and that they had to reject decidedly the notion of collective guilt, so that their call for massive revenge never could be articulated. According to Hilberg, this unavoidable repression of a just feeling of animosity towards Germany did untold harm to the individual and collective Jewish self-consciousness.[48]

Strangely enough, neither Mommsen, nor Jäckel, nor Wehler was offended by this "overgeneralization." Only the British historian Hugh Trever-Roper grasped what Hilberg was trying to say in its entire meaning, so that he started to see the "Final Solution" in an entirely new light, as " 'a national act'...in which the Germans, even though they denied this, were 'involved as a people'."[49] Could it be that Germans didn't hear Hilberg's indictment, because the author of *The Destruction of the European Jews* had to admit to himself "that it was impossible to scream over a thousand pages, that [he] had to subdue his voice,"[50] because he had to articulate his indictment in a neutral language, which corresponded to the social science usage of the forties and fifties, and because his study of the machinery of destruction focused above all upon the bureaucrats who were too refined to shout and scream, so that they dressed their anti-Semitism in bureaucratic phrases, consisting of automated correctness?

And could it be that Goldhagen gives so much cause for anger in Germany, because he doesn't impose this restraint upon himself, because he is not satisfied with a "paper-thin description" and depicts painstakingly by means of "thick description" the gouging, stabbing, and shooting, because he leaves no doubt about it that even when looking at the killing fields, the perpetrators constituted a remarkably representative sample of the German population at large, and because he mounts evidence upon evidence, which proves beyond the shadow of a doubt that not just a few of these "ordinary Germans" performed their "job" without any inner inhibitions, but that, quite to the contrary, they drew a perverse kind of pleasure from what they did?

I, for my part, believe that it is just this demand to visualize "ordinary Germans" as eager exterminators of Jews, who believed, what they did, was right, which is so unbearable. This seems to be the real reason, why the three leading German historians from the Hitler Youth generation reject Goldhagen's book so emphatically. For what other reason would they insist that certain taboos should be respected? So for instance, Eberhard Jäckel when he writes:

Goldhagen says repeatedly that one would have to look at the Germans and their anti-Semitism..."with the eyes of an anthropologist" (for instance on p. 45). With this demand he betrays his whole approach. "Anthropology" may mean many things. It is also a sub-branch of biology, which examines inherited, in contrast to acquired traits. Racial doctrine has its roots in this biologistic subject of study. From it emanated racial anti-Semitism. Goldhagen's arguments have a suspicious affinity to biologistic collectivism.[51]

Wehler states in the same vein:

> In essence this signifies—without the author intending or taking note of it—that he emphatically transforms the debate over National Socialism and its genocide policy into an ethnological problem. Bringing the issue to a point, it must be said that structurally the same thinking patterns reemerge, which were peculiar to the Nazi mind set: the "chosen people" who deserve to be destroyed, are replaced by the "damned people," i.e., the Germans, who are the incarnation of all evil.[52]

That is not a scholarly argument but the deliberate tabooization of an approach, which has proven to be very useful. What is Eberhard Jäckel's discreditation strategy? He insinuates that Goldhagen's anthropological approach is very dubious by simply noting that one can understand various things under anthropology, as if anyone who wishes to know, couldn't find out what is meant today by historical anthropology. Books on the subject, as for example Clifford Geertz' interesting volume, entitled *Thick Description* or the Wagenbach paperback *Das Schwein des Häuptlings* (Rebekka Habermas and Nils Minkmar, ed.) with essays by Peter Burke, Carlo Ginzburg, Marshal Salin, and other noted scholars have in the meantime become as available as "Wrigley Spearmint Gum" and "Lucky Strikes" at the corner store. But the point is, Jäckel doesn't want to inform himself, but determines himself, what anthropology means, namely something unsafe that has to do with Nazism. And Wheeler agrees with him.

With this denunciation these two avoid coming to grips with Goldhagen's message, but what they say sounds good, because it corresponds to the German way of dealing with the encumbered past, to their compulsion to turn everything around. To say it in the words of Marc Fisher, the Germany correspondent of the *Washington Post*:

> In so many ways, normal life since World War II in Germany has been defined as whatever Nazi life was not. A country, anxious to prove to itself and outsiders it had discarded the old ways, simply banned them.[53]

Since the Nazis apostrophized the word "Deutschland" and derivatives thereof ("Deutschland, Deutschland, über alles!," "Deutschland erwache!," "Deutsches Volk, wehr Dich! Kauf nicht bei Juden!"), a lot of Germans prefer just saying "Federal Republic," dropping the noun "Germany," even though the FRG and the GDR have been reunited to form one Germany. And here Wehler and Jäckel, and Mommsen in all likelihood too, want to ban an open discussion about the uniqueness of the country. Pondering over the "national character" or about the collective identity of the people in this country is taboo to them, because the Nazis abused notions such as "Volkscharakter" or "the German soul." One has to be malicious or very dense, if one construes from *Hitler's Willing Executioners* that the German national character is genetically determined and therefore unchangeable. Since Jäckel, Wehler and many other German critics insist that Goldhagen is saying just that, he writes in the "Preface to the German Edition" of his book:

> The discussion about the political culture of a country implies as little that the people of this country are a tribe with unchangeable traits, as generalizing remarks about the people of a country do imply that one thinks of them as a "race" or as an "ethnic group." It is quite permissible to say that the Germans are good democrats, as it is permissible to say that in the 1930s most Germans were anti-Semites. Neither of these statements are "racist." The only thing that matters in these generalizations is, whether they can be empirically proven, whether the analysis justifies such generalizations.[54]

The generalization, which is so offensive to German ears, is Goldhagen's extensive claim that the majority of Germans were decided anti-Semites, ready to help the Führer to make Germany "judenrein" (to rid Germany of the Jews), moreover that there was no shortage of willing helpers among these people when they were called upon to assist with their own hands in the physical destruction of the Jews, because they believed that the country's salvation depended upon the successful completion of this "national task." German critics are unable to deal with this generalization. Hence, they close ranks behind Hans Mommsen, Hans-Ulrich Wehler, and Eberhard Jäckel, alleging that Goldhagen is burdening the Germans with an untenable "collective guilt thesis." If this thesis should win general credence, Holocaust research would be reverted back to the level of research of the fifties.

The reader should ask: what problem is the Harvard scholar addressing? The prevailing explanations of the Holocaust do not satisfy him, because they "share a number of dubious common assumptions and features." Either they take it for granted that the perpetrators were coerced, that "they were left, by the threat of punishment, with no choice but to follow orders" or they hold that these perpetrators had been subject "to tremendous social psychological pressure, placed upon each one by his comrades," or that they were merely "cogs in a wheel," so that they couldn't "understand what the real nature of their actions was."[55] But the problem with these conventional explanations is that they *assume* a neutral or condemnatory attitude on the part of the perpetrators towards their actions.

> They therefore premise their interpretations on the assumption that it must be shown how people can be brought to commit acts to which they would not inwardly assent, act which they would not agree are necessary or just. They either ignore, deny, or radically minimize the importance of Nazi and perhaps the perpetrators' ideology, moral values, and conception of the victims, for engendering the perpetrators' willingness to kill...The conventional explanations [also] suffer from two other major conceptual failings. They do not sufficiently recognize the extraordinary nature of the deed: the mass killing of people. They *assume* and imply that inducing people to kill human beings is fundamentally no different from getting them to do any other unwanted or distasteful task.[56]

Goldhagen refuses to swallow such doubtful fundamental assumptions. Instead he intends to set out on a fearful venture, looking with "the critical eye of an anthropologist" to discover what has been hitherto unknown. To what degree he succeeds in this endeavor, is another matter, what counts, is that he approaches the problem as a cultural anthropologist. The word "anthropology" and the phrase "thick description," which frequently crop up in the book, are key concepts. The anthropologist is a diagnostician. When he examines a strange culture, he keeps his eye open for symbolic acts, because he is trying to decipher the social discourse. Goldhagen sees symbolic meaning in the thoroughness, with which the police battalions performed their "job" while evacuating Jewish ghettos, so that not a single Jew would escape them. Even when they were not under the supervision of platoon commanders or squad leaders and could have let Jewish victims escape, the policemen combed through the houses with the utmost care, squeezing through narrow entrances, down into basements and breaking open locked cupboards etc., in order to find hidden Jews. All this seems to indicate that they were not negligent and that they considered, what they were doing to be necessary. Frequently they tortured and humiliated Jews before they shot them, especially men with beards and sideburns. This suggests that they were neither willing nor able to see in their victims human beings like themselves, rather they saw them as despicable creatures, as enemies of the Volk, who had no right to live. And they made souvenir photos of such scenes or of mass executions: in one unit the company clerk accompanied the firing detachments, in order to document the incidents of mass murder with his Leica camera. The snapshots were posted on the bulletin board in the orderly room and anyone could order copies for himself. This does not indicate that the policemen were ashamed of what they were doing. Moreover, there is reason to believe that they did not see anything criminal in their acts. On the contrary, they seem to have seen in these acts a heroic contribution in the effort to save the Volk.

It is highly probable that Goldhagen is right when he infers from all of these observations that these men killed their victims without any inner inhibitions, because they believed that Jews had forfeited the right to live. What is so upsetting, is that these law enforcement officers, who so eagerly killed in the line of duty, were ordinary Germans, many of them with families and children, with professions in civilian life, such as barber, lumber retail merchant, or dock worker. They were indeed a representative sample of the German population, a population, whose members were for the most part anti-Semitic, regardless of whether they belonged to the Nazi party or not. This leads Goldhagen to conclude that many of them would have been quite willing to kill Jews, had they been deployed as soldiers or policemen to perform such a task.

Regardless of what Mommsen, Wehler, and Jäckel are saying, this generalization does not constitute a "collective guilt thesis." For Goldhagen only the murderers are guilty in a judicial sense. Neither does he claim that every German in the Third Reich was a potential killer of Jews, he doesn't even make this claim in regard to every German anti-Semite. Cultural theory, like the theory of history, is dedicated to the task of providing interpretations of existing cultural or historical facts. It cannot prognosticate the results of experimental procedures, nor can it infer future events from deterministic systems.[57] Keeping within these stated limits, one can say, for instance, that "good" old Lutheran anti-Judaism, enriched and up-dated with Nazi racist anti-Semitism played a decisive role in the choice made by the Reverend Ernst Biberstein from Kaltenkirchen on the Danish border, when in the summer of 1942 he took over the command of *Einsatzkommando* (EK) 6 in Kiev, where he ordered the mass murder of two—to three thousand Jewish men, women, and children (with mobile gas chambers or firing squads respectively). Venerated German men of the cloth, like Martin Niemöller and Otto Dibelius, as well as the majority of the German Protestant ministers of the Upper Hesse region who preached during the Weimar Republic and the Third Reich, and whose cases I have studied, were also anti-Semites, among them the Darmstadt theologian Heinrich Steitz, who wrote after 1945 the authoritative history of the Evangelical Church in Hesse and Nassau, and who held a chair for theology at the University of Mainz well into the eighties. In 1940 he published an article in a regional historical journal, the *Friedberger Geschichtsblätter*, entitled "Juden in Petterweil," where he observes with a pronounced sense of satisfaction:

> All native families in Petterweil can document their Aryan descent. From times immemorial, the population demonstrated an aversion towards Jews. Apartheid was second nature. This stance precluded racial intermarriage. There is no record of Jews having been baptized in the village. Hence, the history of the Jews in Petterweil constitutes the development and eventual disintegration of an alien body.

And in conclusion he notes:

> They [the Jews] went wherever the wind blew them: some went to Frankfurt, some to Friedberg, and some to Groß-Karben. Of course, from there they occasionally came back to make unwelcome visits until the Führer eventually got rid of this scourge of the earth.[58]

What I mean to say is this: there was wide-spread anti-Semitism amongst German Protestant ministers during the period of the Weimar Republic and the Third Reich. In sum it produced the phenomenon, which Goldhagen calls "eliminatory anti-Semitism." For if these ministers and the Evangelical Church would have gotten their way, they would have put a quick end to "Jewish influence" in the press; universities would have excluded Jewish applicants by means of entrance restrictions, in order to make it impossible for Jews to get established in the legal, medical, and teaching professions; school boards would no longer have hired Jewish teachers, because it would have been taken for granted that the upbringing of German Protestant children could not be entrusted to them; laws would have been passed against kosher butchering, and so on. But all this provides no evidence as to whether Martin Niemöller would have been willing to command an *Einsatzgruppe*. Chances are that he would have refused such an assignment. His biography shows that he eventually spoke out on behalf of the Jews. But while taking note of this, it must be added that Niemöller's eventual partisanship for the persecuted Jews was very much restricted by his German Lutheran mentality and by his deep-seated anti-Semitism. It is much more probable that the theologian Heinrich Steitz who slandered the Jews and praised the Führer in the *Friedberger Geschichtsblätter* would have dedicated himself conscientiously to the destruction of the Jews, if Hitler would have sent him with an

*Einsatzgruppe* or a Police Battalion to Russia or Poland. But the truth of the matter is that we cannot say for sure, whether he would have killed Jews. History has to do with things that have happened, its course is not absolutely deterministic. Hence, historical knowledge doesn't allow for a prognosis of what an individual might have done in an imagined situation.

We should consequently believe Goldhagen when he claims, "I categorically reject the notion of collective guilt."[59] As he states in his book and underscores in the foreword to the German edition, where he says in reply to his critics that he doesn't see Germans as "mindless cogs in a wheel":

> *Hitler's Willing Executioners* is dealing with the world understanding, the deeds, and the decisions of individuals, with the responsibility, which each and every individual has, for what he does, and with the political culture, from which these individuals drew their convictions.[60]

The culture from which these individuals drew their convictions, had been for centuries an anti-Semitic culture. A pastor of the Confessing Church, whose case I studied, wrote after the war in his autobiography:

> My father came from a family of small farmers in Upper Hesse. These small farmers had had many bad experiences with Jewish traders and merchants...My grandfather was a self-employed tradesman who had to struggle hard to provide for his family with eight children. The capital he didn't have—and which was out of his reach—he saw in the hands of the Jews.
>
> Under the influence of my father who was a strong person, I accepted the anti-Semitic outlook quite early.[61]

He accepted it and served as SS-Oberscharführer in the Hersbrück Concentration Camp in order to help the Führer to get an important job done.

One would do violence to historical truth, if one would leave the motives of this "ordinary German" for his active involvement in National Socialism unexamined and place them under the heading "Banality of Evil." The "demonic anti-Semitism" to which he succumbed, was not just a harmless personal eccentricity, such as many people have, which neither bothered the world, nor problematized his life in this world. On the contrary, it was a deep-seated prejudice, which determined his thoughts and deeds. This religious and racial prejudice and the readiness to act under the mandate of this prejudice are the subject of Goldhagen's book. This he emphasizes in the foreword to the German edition:

> Tens of thousands of ordinary Germans, like Captain Hoffmann [of Police Battalion 101] participated in mass murder with the aim to exterminate a people. It is the intention of this book to understand the motives and attitudes of these killers.[62]

This problematization, which addresses directly an open secret, namely that there was a decisive causal connection between German anti-Semitism and the Holocaust, seems to be unbearable for Mommsen, Jäckel, and Wehler. The way they fly off the handle is in a certain way reminiscent of the verbal battle in Heinrich Heine's narrative poem "Disputation" (*Werke* 3/I, p. 158-172). Only the casting and distribution is different. Confronting each other are not an equal number of monks and rabbis. Instead we have a single Hagen on one side and three "hürnen Sewfriedte"[63] on the other. At their side fight elderly knights, like the *Spiegel* editor Rudolph Augstein, and shield bearers, like the middle aged historian Jürgen Kocka. The Hagen in this disputation is not the sinister Germanic knight with the eye patch, but a Jewish Hagen, namely Gold-Hagen, who is seen at least by many younger Germans as the champion of enlightenment. When the Berlin historian Wofgang Wippermann defended the young Harvard scholar against his adversary Hans Mommsen, by pointing out that the former had focused research anew upon the cardinal question as to why the Holocaust could only have happened in Germany, he exclaimed: "Goldhagen is a credit to the political culture of this country!"[64] The audience responded with roaring applause.

With the concentration on the responsibility of the individual perpetrators, Goldhagen is appealing to the emotions of his German readers. And as Volker Ullrich, the editor of the political book review page in *Die Zeit* notes:

> The readiness to agree with Goldhagen seems to be carried by a deeply lodged feeling that finally someone openly states, what has been taboo

for so long; namely that the differentiation between "Nazi criminals" and "ordinary Germans" has been wrong; that the willingness to commit mass murder, going into the Millions, came out of the midst of German society; that Hitler and Himmler were able to find hundreds and thousands of volunteers to help them in the extermination of the Jews; and that even if the vast majority didn't actively support this horrendous crime, it could only happen, because of the moral indifference of this majority. That someone openly states this plain truth, seems to be perceived by not just a few Germans as a kind of liberation.[65]

This displeases the German "academic law enforcement officers" so much that they feel compelled to smear Goldhagen who had become something of a celebrity. Mommsen ceaselessly raves that the young Harvard scholar's bestseller is not a scholarly work, but an unwarranted indictment of the Germans. Jäckel accuses him of reverting "to primitive stereotypes." And in Wehler's learned opinion he makes every "ordinary German" into a "crazed monster, obsessed by the will to exterminate all Jews." They have inherited the orthodoxy, pedantry, and self-righteousness of the Franciscan monks and rabbis, whom Heinrich Heine ridicules in his poem. Hence, one could also report about their heroic defense of their historiographical "Siegfried Line" in neo-Heineian verse. It would sound somewhat like this:

*Bochum's champion, Dr. Mommsen, Vents his rage in holy fury*
*Over Goldhagen's conclusions. Mommsen—self appointed jury.*

Dr. Mommsen is quoted in Germany's leading newspaper, Die Zeit:

From the Holocaust he [Goldhagen] concludes that German anti-Semitism was "eliminatory"; from the fact that the rank and file members of the police battalions were recruited from all segments of German society he concludes that the attitudes of these policemen were representative for German society at large: "As a professional historian I cannot condone such generalizations."[66]

Well, if a coffin maker sees himself merely as a professional cabinet maker, an embalmer merely as a specialist for the conservation of tissues, or a historian not as a story teller, but merely as a professional historian, they draw psychological advantage from their expertise: it suppresses unpleasant emotions, preventing these from entering consciousness. I strongly suspect that Mommsen is using his self-understanding as a "professional historian" as a shield against Goldhagen (who according to him does not belong to the exclusive club of "professional historians"), in order to protect himself psychologically. A certain defensiveness may be seen in his claim that it is inadmissible to apply generalizations about the police battalions also to the German population at large, although the membership of these battalions was undoubtedly representative for the German population. It is not very likely that it is the overstretching of a generalization that bothers Mommsen.

The bone of contention seems to be Goldhagen's interpretation as such, seeing that Mommsen raises no objection to the even more sweeping generalizations that are presented in Christopher Browning's book *Ordinary Men*, which draws conclusions from just one single unit, from Police Battalion 101, and applies them to all normal males (be they U.S. Marines in the Pacific, GIs in My Lai, or Japanese soldiers on their course of rampage through Manila); Mommsen holds up this latter book as a foil to *Hitler's Willing Executioners*, contrasting its "depth of interpretation" with Goldhagen's "shallowness."

But this juxtaposition is misleading; the two books do not distinguish themselves so much by the different levels of interpretation, but rather through different modes of interpretations. Browning sees the behavior of the members of Police Battalion 101 from a situational perspective: "Every war—especially a war with racist aspects—leads to brutalization, which expresses itself in atrocities."[67] This is a behavioristic approach, which limits the choice of fundamental presumptions so drastically that laws are only applicable to a causal relationship between stimulus and response. Within such a frame of reference nothing can be said about intentional action.[68]

Goldhagen, on the other hand, interprets his data in an actionistic way. He proceeds from the premise that human actions, as confusing and ambivalent as they may be, can be traced back to intentions, that these actions may be understood from statements, which express intent, and vice versa, that a person is only capable of such actions, which do not stand in contradiction to innermost convictions; in other words, human actions must agree in some way with the concept of right and wrong, good and evil, sensible and nonsensical. Aside from this, Goldhagen's explanatory strategy is an individualizing one. His German critics should have understood this when Goldhagen said:

> About Germans one can say: without Germans no Holocaust. This we cannot say about any other national group. Do we really have to argue over whether the Holocaust bears the stamp "Made in Germany?"[69]

This begs the question: What was special about the Germans, about their politics, society, and culture in the first half of the 20th Century that made them do things which Italians did not do?

To ascribe without careful examination their readiness to commit atrocities to universal human dispositions—such as self-interest and bowing to the power of circumstances—makes no sense, because not all people acted in similar situations the way the Germans did. The Italian Army, for example refused to provide assistance in the deportation of Jews, although Mussolini had instructed his troops to support the anti-Semitic measures of the Axis partner.

Goldhagen focuses on what is unique and continues asking those who had been born and raised in a culture that was saturated with eliminatory anti-Semitism, but who were at the same time intentional actors with a conscience, and responsible for their deeds.

It is quite understandable, why Germans, especially older Germans prefer Browning's book. Whoever wants to, can find evidence in it to prove for himself that "we" didn't do it, because what happened can only be blamed on the circumstances. Goldhagen blocks this escape route by confronting us with intentionally acting human beings. With such a perspective one has to deal with this matter in a completely different way than with omnipresent anonymous structures or with unfortunate circumstances. Whoever is prepared to do this, must necessarily also grapple with National Socialism as a problem of inner disposition. It goes without saying that for Germans, especially older ones, such a soul-searching task is a fearful undertaking. The reason for the refusal of Mommsen and other German historians who belong to the Hitler Youth and Flakhelfer generation to really deal with Goldhagen's book is consequently no mystery at all.

Mommsen sees only a need to explain the Holocaust and National Socialism in terms of structural failures, which victimized the perpetrators just as much as they victimized the real victims And he sees the need for the study of these unfortunate developments and structural failures not in the necessity to work through the past at an emotional level, but in the "social engineering" requirements for today and tomorrow. For he teaches:

> It is not the purpose of the study of the Holocaust and National Socialism to arouse mere emotions; such studies must lead to directives, aiming to prevent the recurrence of analogous constellations of escalation, which produced the progressive moral indifference. The mechanisms have to be laid bare, which explain the progressive moral indifference that took hold of the upper classes in the wake of World War I. To this end it will be necessary to explain the complexity of the conditions, under which genocide could not only be thought of, but also be put into practice.[70]

Grappling with the Holocaust is, seen in this way, first and foremost a problem, having to do with political planning, not a problem of inner disposition, which only others, so it seems, ascribe to Germans, although such ascription has no foundation. If one adopts Mommsen's position, the question of individual responsibility and guilt presents itself only to those who nurture the illusion that human beings have an inner disposition, which predisposes them to act in this or in that way. For Mommsen human beings are in essence empty shells or Pavlovian entities, whose behavior is determined exclusively by external circumstances. Depending on the social system in which they live, the same people can act in completely different ways. Their behavior corresponds to specific situations.[71] This is the actual reason why Mommsen and other historians of his generation accept Browning's book about the destruction of the Jews unconditionally, while they vehemently reject Goldhagen's book, which deals with the same topic. The former confirms their dearly cherished notion about behavior being a derivative of specific situations, while the latter talks about guilt and responsibility.

It is most unlikely that scholars of Mommsen's stature are "babes in the woods" as far as the logic of the social sciences is concerned. It is unlikely that they never have heard about the weakness of the behavioristic approach. Hence, it is more than doubtful that they are defending the theory of behavior being a derivative of specific situations, because it is the *summum bonum* in the explanation of the human condition. However, it stands to reason that this vehement defense of a weak theory is the answer of the Hitler Youth and Flakhelfer generation, which constitutes a rupture in their own biographies. For didn't this generation learn from their own experience that the same people can act in a very different way, if they are put in a different system? In Nazi Germany this age group "functioned" quite well as the Hitler Youth. Three months after having joined the *Jungvolk* (the junior division of the HJ) they passed a test (the Pimpfenprüfung), in which they regurgitated a whole lot of brown knowledge, which had been drummed into them: the Führer's biography, the "sword words" of the Hitler Youth, all verses of Baldur von Schirach's "Hitler Youth Hymn"—the flag leads us into eternity, the flag is more than death—they were proud to carry the Hitler Youth dagger, which bore the etched motto "Blood and Honor," and so on. When the social system of Adolf Hitler ceased to exist, the Hitler Youth and Flakhelfer generation ceased to behave like little Nazis. It decontextualized itself. From one day to the next the members stepped out of their previous biographical context in order to accomplish a smooth integration with re-education. Hans Mommsen, Eberhard Jäckel, and Hans-Ulrich Wehler commenced university studies within this new context. And because these young budding historians knew what was good for them, they meticulously copied the techniques and theories of Marc Bloch, Fernand Braudel, Lucien Febevre, and other Western masters of historiography.

They and their entire generation were patted on the head for being so diligent and for "getting with the program." At first by their fathers, including Wilhelm Mommsen, who wrote in the foreword of his monograph *Politische Geschichte von Bismarck bis zur Gegenwart* (Frankfurt am Main: Diesterweg, 1935):

> I dedicate this book to my four boys who represent a fourth generation, which has not consciously experienced the war. This generation is thriving in unbroken strength, because it takes the experience of growing up in the Reich of Adolf Hitler for granted. Some of the members have already contributed in a decisive way to the Führer's vision. (p. 10)

On other occasion by patronizing Re-education Officers and by a well-meaning international community of scholars—by a Professor Georg Iggers from Buffalo, for example. Full of high expectations he noted in the sixties: "The changing of the guard, which will allow those historians who have been trained after 1945, has just started,"[72] but didn't deem it to be too early to praise these "promising young scholars" for doing everything just right. Prof Iggers said:

> The gap between historiography in Germany and other countries has diminished, because the younger generation of German historians has for the most part turned away from the idealist traditions. More and more it views history as an international scholarly enterprise....For in Germany, too, historians have increasingly come to recognize the importance of the social and behavioral sciences in their own work.[73]

So much for the evaluation of Georg Iggers. Aren't Georg Iggers' appraisals from 1968 and Wilhelm Mommsen's appraisal from 1935 two examples, which strikingly demonstrate the validity of the theory that behavior depends upon the situation? Scholars could smugly lean back and stop pondering over human nature, if this were true! Iggers may be right in observing that the Hitler Youth generation narrowed the gap between German and international historiography, as far as the mechanics of writing history goes. However, when it comes to the aesthetic quality of historical representation,[74] there is a world of difference between the historiography of the Hitler Youth of yonder days, on the one hand, and the historiography of the great French, British and American historians, on the other.

That has to do with a certain kind of consistency, traditionally called "beauty." Franz Neumann appreciates this consistency in the works of the great thinkers of Western Civilization, when he notes in *Behemoth*:

When we read Plato, Aristotle, Thomas Aquinus, and Marcilius of Padua, Hobbes and Rousseau, as well as Kant and Hegel, we are struck by the inner beauty of their thought, their consistency and elegance, as well as by how their teaching stands in agreement with socio-political analyses.[75]

This "inner beauty of thought" is what makes the great British, American, and French historians so appealing to me. When I read, for example, the great books of Fritz Stern I learn that "It is difficult to think of Germany dispassionately."[76] I feel reassured, for here speaks a former inmate of Breslau who is unable to chat superficially about Germany. In other words, when reading his books, I am not wasting my time with a "Germany specialist" who doesn't have to experience Germany for a single day, in order to know what he knows. When I pick up a volume of collected theoretical essays by Philipp Ariès or Carlo Ginzburg, it is as if I am encountering old friends who want to share with me their concerns about the meaning and the material of history. And when I read an exemplary book of the "new school of history," for instance Fernand Braudel's *The Mediterranean and the Mediterranean World in the Age of Philipp II* (1949), then I can almost feel the warmth of the Mediterranean sun.

Historiography, which has been written by academics from the Hitler Youth generation lacks this "inner beauty" and leaves me cold. There is no fire in it, it radiates no warmth. Or in the brutal words of the German historian Ernst Nolte: "Heartlessness is the trademark of the academic discourse." And although Mommsen, Jäckel and Wehler are totally at odds with Nolte on the surface of political discourse, they would most definitely agree with him that the passions have no place in historical discourse. Wehler decrees that the past must be dissected with "the scalpel of rational analysis,"[77] with cold steel, so to speak. Mommsen gives specific orders "to leave emotions aside, when working through the past."[78] For him perplexity is always mere perplexity which distracts from scholarly work; for Wehler it has to do with "soul searching and religious revivalism," which has no business in serious history and should be left to TV preachers like Billy Graham and Pat Robertson; and Jäckel concedes that Goldhagen managed in a few passages to convey the horror of the massacre of the Jews, but at the same time he tries to depreciate this accomplishment by pontificating that such vivid depiction falls outside the scope of the serious historian, his proper task being "the explanation of the interconnectedness of things,"[79] as if vivid portrayal and explanation were mutually exclusive.

It is as if these Hitler Youth of yonder days had secretly conspired to skip re-education. When in a seminar on Western historians Michelet was discussed, we should remember that the master historian makes it clear that to grapple with the past, a Prometheus is needed, "so that the fire, he has stolen, can make audible the frozen voices [of the dead], which hover all around us."[80]

The victorious Allies wanted order and tranquillity in their respective zones of occupation. As Raul Hilberg points out, Americans expected from the victims of Nazism, whom fortune had flushed to the shores of the United States, that they should agree to see Germany with "American eyes." From the former Hitler Youth they expected essentially the same thing. Uncle Sam wanted model students, not rebellious teen-age gangs, bent on quenching their thirst for revenge. Model students bear the label "teacher's pet," because they go out of their way to please their instructor. As first graders they put shiny red apples on the teacher's desk, as grownup scholars they tickle the professor's ego by dedicating a *Festschrift* to him, propagating or defending his ideas.[81] Nothing would be wrong with this, if this obsessive need to please wouldn't be coupled with a certain faint-heartedness. In general model students do not have the courage to pick up a "hot potato."

That may be one of the reasons, why the first edition and even the German translation of Raul Hilberg's *The Destruction of the European Jews* failed to elicit any comments from the Hitler Youth generation, which seems especially grotesque, if one bears in mind that now that this book has withstood the test of time, so that it is regarded as one of the great classics in the field of Holocaust studies. The ex-Hitler Youths, Mommsen, Jäckel, and Wehler use it as a club to browbeat a young Holocaust scholar by the name of Goldhagen. Very well then, where are their welcoming words for Raul Hilberg's magnum opus?

For it should be noted that when it first appeared, Hilberg's work gave rise to a heated discussion in the United States and Israel. Hilberg's portrayal of

Jewish behavior within the process of annihilation was seen in some quarters as a scandal of the first order. He had included in his study the Jewish organizational network, depicting it as an extended arm of the German machinery of destruction. A Jewish tradition of trust in God, princes and treaties had, according to Hilberg, predisposed them not to resist, when the only faint hope for salvation lay in resistance. Their calculation that the Germans wouldn't destroy what they could exploit economically, made them comply to the deadly instructions of the perpetrators. In Hilberg's bleak picture it was this compliance, where outright rebellion and sabotage would have been more appropriate, which contributed in no small way to the misfortune of the Jews. Not just a few saw in such an analysis an "impious defamation of the dead."[82]

While in Israel and in the United States a heated debate took place as to whether Hilberg's portrayal and evaluation was valid, the Germans kept a studious silence, giving rise to a very unusual occurrence in the German publishing world. Droemer/Knaur Publishers in Munich, which had already signed the contract for translation rights with Quadrangle Books and made a down-payment, broke the contract and declined to bringing out a German translation of Hilberg's work, because the erupting controversy was too hot for them.[83] Perhaps it would have been tactless for Germans to get involved in an inner Jewish controversy, but as already pointed out, Hilberg's book was also saturated with other controversial stuff, which should have provoked a German reaction. Nonetheless, it remained a non-book in Germany, because Germans didn't want to get burnt. This excessive German fear of getting burnt, caught the Israeli journalist, Tom Segev by surprise when he tried to make a movie in collaboration with the German TV network ZDF. "You can't imagine how careful they are," he said, "not under any circumstances do they want to show anything that does not have the Israeli stamp of approval.[84]

"Hot topics" of this kind, which the historians of Mommsen's Wehler's, and Jäckel's generation wouldn't touch, exist in abundance—as for instance the topic "refugees and expulsion." Tendentially, Mommsen and other left liberal German historians have lumped together German refugees and ethnic Germans who after 1945 were expelled from Poland and Czechoslovakia, with the revengist, reactionary bureaucracy of the *Landsmannschaften* (political and cultural organizations of Germans who lived before 1945 in Silesia, East and West Prussia, and other areas, which had before World War II significant ethnic German populations). Hence, not just a few German Leftists, particularly those who lean over backwards for the sake of political correctness, are of the opinion that ethnic Germans who had to flee or who were expelled from East and West Prussia and from the Sudeten Land have to blame no one but themselves for their misfortune. This camouflaged collective guilt thesis was augmented by the fear that openly stating the truth would pour water on the mill of the anti-Communists.

Historians of the Hitler Youth and Flakhelfer generation have also shied away from giving a historical account of the firestorm bombardments of German cities, which they themselves had experienced as auxiliary gunners in anti-aircraft batteries, as signalers in observation towers, or as junior firemen in the Hitler Youth fire brigades. Darmstadt, a city in Germany to which a German-American academic exchange program has brought me, and whose captive I still am, so that I had plenty of time to look around, had been on the target list of the Royal Air Force. The old inner city with its narrow streets and half-timbered houses offered itself as a prime target for the "moral bombing" strategy, devised by Air Marshal Harris and his staff to break the German civilian population's will to resist. In the night from the 11th to the 12th of September 1944 the 5th Bomber Command of the RAF dropped its load of "Christmas trees," incendiary bombs, and thunder clap bombs on the city of Darmstadt. The old city was flattened out. More than twenty thousand inhabitants were killed in the air raid. But if one were to go through the dissertations of the local university, one would look in vain, if one were searching for a historical analysis of this night of horror.

Not that this night is forgotten. The city remembers when the foundation for a new building has to be dug. Then the bomb disposal experts are called for assistance or at least consulted. Even today, over fifty years after the war, they dig up tons and tons of bombs, which were dropped in 1944, but failed to explode and could go off, if struck by a bulldozer.[85]

It stands to reason that what is still in the ground, also spooks around in the heads of older inhabitants of the city. I notice this when I travel on the city buses and trolleys. There I pick up pieces of conversation, which refers to the firestorm of 1944. How much this catastrophe has traumatized the people, I also find out when I talk with an elderly woman who lives down stairs and with whom I now have been acquainted for years. The firestorm has a central place in her memory. Other things that she remembers, group themselves around this central catastrophe: the memory that her parents couldn't afford to buy her the smart BdM86 jacket and how much this grieved her at the time, that she had been married to a 100% Nazi who had been a Storm Trooper before participating as a Wehrmacht soldier in the invasion of Russia, that just before capitulation he still "bumped off a few Yankees," and that nobody today could imagine how both of them had believed in the Führer.

She experienced the aerial bombardment of Darmstadt as an observer in a flak battery. Shortly before the end of the war she "made herself scarce." I interjected that for less than that, drumhead court-martials of the SS strung up frightened young soldiers and battle-weary home guardsmen who were caught malingering in the ruins of the Third Reich, as was the case in Aachen, which was temporarily recaptured by German troops after it had already been taken by the Americans.

> "Never mind Aachen," she cut me off, "also here in the vicinity of Darmstadt they publicly executed deserters just before the end of the war!" "Did you see that?" I asked.
> "Yes, they were children. 'Mama!' they cried."
> "Whoever has seen and experienced things like that, must be traumatized for the rest of their life," I said.
> "Yes," she agreed. "My generation is traumatized. I can't get these things out of my head anymore."

It is as if one were reading about another, less gruesome war, when one hears the testimony of the Flakhelfer historian Helmut Kohl. He reports:

> Already as a twelve year old boy I belonged to a school fire brigade. We fought the fires, set by the many air attacks, which Ludwigsburg had to suffer. Our equipment was primitive, but we proceeded with youthful courage; inexperienced, but ready to take risks.[87]

One gets the impression that here a German Chancellor is telling his voters, forty years after the event, what they like to hear, namely that one has gone through "all of this" with "youthful courage," not shying away from "risks," and above all that one survived all of it without having suffered any lasting bodily or psychological injuries.

Wishful thinking! Germans like to believe that the depressing, shameful story, in which they are caught up, has come to a "happy end."[88] But only cheap drug store novels have "happy endings." In real life stories have no "ending" at all; they just continue, as do the stories of the Hitler Youth. No one in his right mind would want to claim that ten, twelve, or thirteen year old children can survive the horrors of war without psychological injuries. It is even taken for granted that TV brutality affects the minds of children and juveniles. According to the German weekly news magazine, *Focus*, four out of five Germans are sick of TV violence, and it is said that they have petitioned the legislators in Bonn with 250,000 signatures, urging them to curtail such programs.[89] But these very same Germans would emphatically deny that they themselves have been psychologically scarred by the violence of war, which they themselves had experienced. In other words, one is confronted here with an act of repression that has its roots in a mass psychological factor of mind-boggling dimensions.

It is a matter of concern, if plumbers, electricians, clerks, and unskilled laborers of the reconstruction generation in Germany are bearing lasting psychological scars from the war. How much more concerned should one be, when noting that the historians of this generation bear the same scares, because according to the wise words of the 19th century poet Anette von Droste-Hülshoff, "the frailty of the educated set is rarely without harm, for it contains an added portion of wrongheadedness."[90] In the case of the historians of the Hitler Youth generation this "added portion of wrongheadedness" makes them incapable to visualize things. However, the ability to visualize historical events is indispensable. Real historians, i.e., those, for whom history is not just a job, but a calling, are people who cannot repress images, people who try to get to the bottom of things, because they are haunted by images.

Thucydides was haunted by images and couldn't sleep. Among other things he visualized the spreading epidemic in Athens, about which he writes in the second book of his *History of the Peloponnesian War*: "having caught the disease myself and having seen others suffer, I want to describe the dreadful epidemic" (II, 48). In other words, he was not willing to trivialize his traumatic experience. This enabled him to vividly describe, how "one passed the sickness on to the other, so that people succumbed like sheep." (II, 51)

Philippe Ariès was pursued by the picture of the transference of the remains of his brother from a make-shift war grave near Bibrach in the Black Forest to his final resting place in a quarter, set aside for fallen French soldiers, on the community cemetery of Thias near Paris. In his memoirs he writes:

> Via the detour of the funeral of my brother, the subject of death entered my thinking. This sad event helped me to faintly visualize the great tragedy of death. Now the idea came to me to examine death with the instruments of the historians, the only instruments, which I had at my disposal. Someone else might have turned to philosophy, theology, spiritualism or poetry. For me history was a substitute for all that.[91]

For Raul Hilberg the traumatic event was the Anschluss of Austria. Seeing in 1939 endless convoys with Wehrmacht soldiers roll towards the Czech border, the twelve year old boy was struck by the thought: "Someday I will write about this."[92]

And Daniel Jonah Goldhagen is drawn to the snapshots, which were found in the wallets of dead or captured soldiers of German police battalions, snapshots, which these police soldiers frequently saved together with the pictures of their mothers and girl friends. Such pictures undoubtedly give some kind of clue to the private feelings and mentality of the owners. A case in point is one of these pictures, in which the amateur photographer combines in a grotesque way the posture of submission, imposed on the Jewish victims, with the cliché like composition of the middle class group photo. As heads of the Jewish congregation the two rabbis are made to pose up front, down on their knees, hands raised above the head. Behind them and to either side of them stand the torturers with content, stupid smiles on their faces. What kind of human beings were these German executioners? What happened to the Jewish victims right after they were photographed? Were they put on freight cars and sent to Auschwitz? Were they taken to a tank ditch to be shot? Or were they burned in the barn that can be seen in the background of the photograph? Such questions preoccupy Daniel Jonah Goldhagen.

In contrast one cannot find vivid images in the historiography of Hans Mommsen, Eberhard Jäckel, and Hans-Ulrich Wehler. They systematically block them out and suppress them. This has to do with the fear of fire, which is common to burned children. Members of this generation who viewed themselves after their ill start in the Third Reich as the "skeptical generation," were thankful for every Chesterfield and Pall Mall they received from a patronizing Re-education Officer, but they wouldn't have wanted him to give them his Zippo lighter, much less would they have wanted to steal it from him. Erroneously these burned children associated any kind of fire with torch light parades, Teutonic yule fires, and the twilight of the Gods:

*We are the flame, we are the fire,*
*We kindle on Germany's sacred pyre,*
*And carry the drum through the realm,*
*We are the movement's crier!*

While the stacked logs cave in, in the sparking flames, life comes into the hollow square of Hitler Youths. The boys move in a circle around the pyre, and each in turn jumps through the flames, This time I do not have to ponder very long to decipher the meaning. This celebration, which mingles the future and death so persistently, sending the boys, one after the other, into the flames, is undoubtedly the diabolic evocation of the massacre of the innocent, to which we are marching.[93]

This scene is to be found in Michael Tournier's novel *Der Erlkönig*. It will bring back memories to Mommsen, Jäckel, and Wehler, which they'd rather forget. For what else could be hidden behind the taboo, when Hans Mommsen emphatically warns against opening "Pandora's box." To avoid coming into contact with the "atavistic dimensions of history," what else but the enticing power of this ritual fire, but also fear and shame vis-à-the fires in the crematorium of Auschwitz? Perhaps they knew more about this fire than they are ready to admit to themselves.[94] And the trauma of the firestorm bombardment, which they had experienced and barley survived, weighs heavier upon them than they are prepared to admit.

This excursion about the discourse on situational behavior and the lack of fire in the historiography, written by the Flakhelfer historians may have taxed the patience of the reader, who is concentrating on the reaction of these historians on a book, dealing with the Holocaust. However, the reader who has paid close attention, is now better prepared to critically evaluate Hans Mommsen's counter-explanation of the Holocaust. Mommsen writes:

> Most recent research shows that there was an interaction between local and upper echelon actors, which led to the consensus that all Jews under German control were to be exterminated. The impetus did not only come from ideological considerations, but also from self-made material and psychological factors. For instance, the Soviet Union's connivance with the Nazis to let them resettle hundreds and thousands of ethnic Germans from the Baltic region, from Wolhynia and Bessarabia to the Warthegau and other regions in Eastern Central Europe was the decisive cause for the deportation of the Jews and for the establishment of Ghettos on Polish territory under German rule.[95]

Aside from the academic phrase "most recent research shows," this almost reads like one of Tolstoy's historio-philosophical interjections, but what is missing, are the deep historical insights to be found in the epic novel *War and Peace*: "One 'coincidence' hundreds and thousands of 'coincidences' placed power in his [Napoleon's] hands, and as if by mutual agreement, all people conjoin to consolidate this power; "mass movements from West to East and from East to West."[96] Tolstoy's narration deals with "coincidences" such as unexpected early frost, Napoleon's head cold at Borodino, and a spark that set Moscow ablaze, while in the case of Mommsen we are dealing with "processes of cumulative radicalization," which lead to the "implementation" of the Holocaust. However, in contrast to Tolstoy, Mommsen doesn't present the sum total of human decisions as the result of actions and reactions of protagonists who distinguish themselves from one another through individual character traits, but rather as the sum total of the actions and even more the reactions of people without any individuality, people who just function: soldiers who came to attention and stood at ease and who—if they wasted any time in thinking—thought what business of mine is it what I think?" when they opened fire on designated groups of human beings; mayors, county commissioners, and other civil servants whose job it was to make public administration function smoothly and who, as a matter of routine, signed over 1000 regulations, emergency decrees, and procedural guidelines, directed against Jews; railroad personnel who were responsible for the transportation of Jews to Auschwitz and who applied themselves to this task like robots; etc., etc. They all do not count as individuals, for it is as if Mommsen had internalized the scholastic motto "individuum est ineffabile,"—individuals are not worth mentioning. For Germans this has the benefit that it doesn't rob them of the delusion that human beings are prisoners of obscure processes which are beyond their understanding. All of them were caught up in processes, in which they were puppets, rather than actors, for as such they were pushed and shoved by a malicious deus ex machina by the name of "Eigendynamik" ("self-propulsion") from one inescapable situation into the other, so that in the end they had no other choice but to "implement" the Holocaust.

Sounds familiar! The majority of the German historians maintained, in the fifties and sixties, that Hitler did not fit into the frame of German history, so that National Socialism could be regarded in a way as an unfortunate accident.[97] As much, as it grieved them, under the pressure of a critical international historical science, they had to throw overboard the notion that National Socialism was just an unfortunate, unforeseeable accident in German history. Today they would at least like to be left in the belief that the Holocaust came out of the blue and that no one could have foretold it. The way leading up to it is supposed to have been a winding road ("the twisted road to Auschwitz"). In order to maintain this illusion, and to combat the fear of getting lost in the "atavistic" dimensions of history, they take care not to stray an inch from the narrow road of the history of events, which leads from one decision to the next.[98] The notion that these decisions on the level of the history of events were co-determined by driving forces, emanating from the nether regions of the German collective consciousness, is intolerable for Mommsen. It doesn't matter, how explicit Hitler is in *Mein Kampf* about what he intends to do with the Jews, for Mommsen these threats remain "within the frame of traditional anti-Semitism" and mean nothing. The fact that at the end of the war the Germans under Hitler kept on fighting, when defeat was foreseeable, only to complete the central intention of National Socialism, i.e., the systematic destruction of the European Jews,[99] proves to Mommsen the inner logic of the internal dynamics of uncoordinated processes and of the "process of cumulative radicalization."

In Mommsen's functionalist explanation it is not permissible to concede that German anti-Semitism played a central role in the Holocaust. Hence, German historians concentrate all their efforts on denying that German anti-Semitism was really as pernicious as Goldhagen claims that it was. "Differentiation" is part of the denial strategy. To be precise, one proceeds like Mommsen, who is apparently coming half-way to meet Goldhagen. Driven by the love for truth he already concedes in the title "Anti-Semitism was a necessary, but by no means a sufficient cause for the Holocaust."[100] This leaves sufficient room to argue that all kinds of other factors "had additionally to come into play," in order for the "incomprehensible" to happen. This opens the gate to a pseudo-scientific discourse, consisting of common-place wisdom, cheap truths, and speculative stupidities, presented in a contorted, long-winding lecture. What was needed in addition, was the local and upper echelon protagonists, who tried to outguess the will of the Führer, while competing for his favor; the problem with the ethnic Germans, for whom room had to be found; the impracticality of the various programs of resettling Jews on reservations on the fringe of civilization; and the unforeseeable course of the war. In this ramification of factors, anti-Semitism eventually just appears to be a peripheral factor. And one tops it all off by speculating as to whether the Holocaust could also have been "implemented" without anti-Semitism. This at least is Mommsen's strategy, when at the end of two pages of print in the weekly newspaper *Die Zeit* he stresses that "neither Himmler, nor Heydrich, nor Eichmann and many of those, serving under him," fitted into the category of perpetrators, "possessed by an extreme anti-Semitism."[101] Or one comes right out with it, like Eberhard Jäckel and simply says: "It is in all seriousness highly debatable whether anti-Semitism in the Nazi period was highly virulent," and "even if it was rooted much deeper than previously assumed, this means very little." Hence, Goldhagen's approach is misdirected, "because anti-Semitism had existed before, without it leading to such deadly consequences."[102]

Mommsen says, for instance:

> So Raul Hilberg had to conclude in his study about German railway officials who organized the transports to Auschwitz that they went about their business of sending Jews to death camps, without giving much thought to what they did.[103]

Or Jäckel:

> That Richard S. Levy took note of the decline (downfall) of the anti-Semitic parties between 1908 and 1914, that Donald L. Niewyk (*The Jews in Weimar Germany*, 1980) registered a fading away of anti- Semitism around 1928 [etc.], is not mentioned by Goldhagen.[104]

Must Goldhagen take certain citation syndicates[105] seriously? Experienced historians, who had to deal with Hannah Arendt, as for instance her classmate Golo Mann or her companion in American exile, Raul Hilberg, think very little of her thesis about the "banality of evil." Hilberg, who cannot suppress a certain *Schadenfreude*, when he mentions that the authorities do not consult Hannah Arendt, but him when they conduct investigations on Nazi war criminals, comments with disdain on her Eichmann book:

> She fails to recognize altogether the genius of Eichmann. He had an iron grip on the *Judenräte* in nearly all of Europe; he meticulously organized the confiscation of Jewish property that was left behind in Germany, Austria, and Bohemia and Moravia; he drafted anti-Semitic legislation for the satellite states; and he saw to it that Jews were transported without problems to the shooting pits and death camps. No, Arendt fails to grasp how gigantic his deed was. There was nothing "banal" about this "evil."[106]

Such words from Raul Hilberg do, of course, undermine Hans Mommsen's thesis about "what were, in the final analysis, uncontrollable processes, which resulted in the murder of millions of people."[107] Regardless of this the renowned Bochum historian acts, as if the pieces, he broke out of *The Destruction of the European Jews*, reinforced his diametrically opposed thesis.

In the eyes of Hilberg the tendencies leading up to the Holocaust displayed a fearful straight forward direction. Hence, he notes: "With an unfailing instinct and a surprising pathfinding ingenuity the German bureaucrats found the shortest way to their objective."[108] And as embarrassing as it might be for those who wrap Goldhagen's knuckles for "having decidedly ethnicized the debate on National Socialism,"[109] while citing Hilberg against the young Harvard scholar, it should be noted, Hilberg's basic arguments also proceed from the premise that the Germans have a particular, non-interchangeable national character. He doesn't scream it out at the top of his lungs, but he, too, sees in the differentiation between the "criminal Nazis," on the one hand, and the "ordinary Germans," on the other, a distortion of historical truth. Hence, he talks about the "German Nazis," about "German social structures"—and he never forgets that the administration, charged with the extermination of the Jews, was in the final analysis a German administration. This is for him the key to understanding, leading him to offer explanations like this one:

> The German bureaucracy wouldn't allow itself to be discouraged by problems; the Germans never came up with sham-excuses, the way the Italians did; they never resorted to apparent solutions, as did the Hungarians; and unlike the Bulgarians, they never used delaying tactics. The moving force in the German administration was the will for perfection. Unlike their collaborators, they were not content with the minimum. They always did their very best.[110]

Moreover, if one follows Hilberg's explanation, then the bureaucrats who always did "their very best," were not faceless pencil pushers, separated from the population by mountains of bone-dry records, but typical "ordinary Germans" with expert knowledge: technocrats of the armaments industry, postal clerks of the *Reichspostministerium*, top-notch legal authorities, crack insurance experts,—and when it came to digging up obscure baptismal records for proof of Aryan ancestry—members of the Christian clergy who were deaf and blind to Jewish suffering.

> Hence, there wasn't any real difference between the machinery of destruction and German society in general. Differences that did exist, were only functional. The machinery of destruction was, *to be exact*, nothing but a special function of the established society.[111]

As Goldhagen would say, this society was pregnant with "eliminatory anti-Semitism" or to use Hilberg's words:

> When Hitler talked about the Jews, he was moving on terrain that was familiar to the Germans. When he made derogatory remarks about the victims, he revived medieval patterns of thought. When he poured out his poisonous, anti-Semitic invectives, it was as if he were waking up the Germans in order to lead them on to challenges long forgotten.[112]

It remains a mystery to me, how anyone can summon Raul Hilberg as a crown witness in the trivialization of German anti-Semitism or in the ramblings about "the twisted road to Auschwitz."

Moreover, the holes in the arguments cannot be plugged with the other monographs, which are cited in evidence by the German "experts." Richard S. Levy's book *The Downfall of the Antisemitic Parties in Imperial Germany* (1975) does, of course, show that the demagogues of the anti-Semitic parties failed to succeed in the Reichstag, and it also contains catchy phrases, like "the road traveled by Liebermann and Boeckel led not to the 'Final Solution,' but to a dead end."[113] However, it doesn't answer the question as to what happened to the anti-Semitism that poisoned the atmosphere after it failed to gain victory in institutionalized political discourse.

It should be pointed out, anti-Semitism as such, was by no means rejected categorically. It was an integral part of the German way of seeing things. The educated middle classes didn't read muckraking authors, like Gerhard Hauptmann or Heinrich Mann, but highly successful writers, like Felix Dahn, Gustav Freytag, and Arthur Dinter,[114] who celebrated things German by using the Jews as a foil. Aside from this, the Herr Kommerzienrat and the Lieutenant of the Reserves had an aversion to political anti-Semitic agitators, like Böckel and Ahrwald, whose political diatribes smacked of populism. They were seen as troublemakers, because they raved simultaneously against "Junker und Juden." Chancellor Caprivi went so far, as lumping them together with the Socialists.[115]

For this very reason it might be worth mentioning another author, namely Peter G. J. Pulzer, who looks at the same developments, Levy is examining, but who arrives at a diametrically opposite conclusion:

> The [anti-Semitic] parties and their leaders were without influence. This is to miss the point. Thirty years of incessant propaganda had been more effective than men thought at the time; anti-Semitism was no longer disgraceful inside social and academic circles; the vulgarities of men like Bielohlawek and Ernst Schneider in representative assemblies permanently lowered the tone of public debate...It was merely a question of waiting for the order to fire.[116]

Isn't this perspective worth considering? As might be expected, Mommsen will object here that as a professional historian he cannot condone "circular arguments" of this sort. However, it would be more honest, if Hans Mommsen wouldn't hide behind the shield of professionalism and grapple instead with his great-grandfather, Theodor Mommsen, who appears in Pulzer's book as chronicler of the loss of human orientation. Tired of constantly having to take a stance against anti-Semites like Heinrich von Treitschke, he makes this discouraging remark:

> You are mistaken if you believe that I could achieve anything in this matter. You are mistaken if you believe that anything at all could be achieved by reason. In years past I thought so myself and kept protesting against the monstrous infamy that is anti-Semitism. It is useless, completely useless. Whatever I or anybody else could tell you are in the last analysis reasons, logical and ethical arguments which no anti-Semite will listen to. They listen only to their own envy and hatred, to the meanest instincts. Nothing else counts for them. They are deaf to reason, right, morals. One cannot influence them.[117]

But enough with the "commentaries and treatises, to which one ought to submit." As far as Mommsen's, Jäckel's, and Wehler's references to the canonized literature is concerned, Goethe would say, "man merkt die Absicht und man ist verstimmt" ("one notices the intention and is put off). Literature with the greatest explosive power, as for example the standard work of Raul Hilberg, they defuse, to make it fit their purposes. Monographs with much less hitting power, as for example, Richard S. Levy's book *The Downfall of the Antisemitic Parties*, they use as decoys to simulate "heavy Flak."

The last argument of which "the Flak trio" takes up a defensive position, when all other dams break, is the assertion that most Germans were not real anti-Semites, but that they did not particularly object to the anti-Semitism of the Nazis. Let's have a close look at this argument in Hans Mommsen's *Zeit* article, "Die dünne Patina der Zivilisation." He writes: "Regardless of how regrettable it may be that many Nazi sympathizers were not particularly offended by the anti-Semitism of the Nazi party, the fact remains that anti-Semitism as such played only a minor role in the decision to vote for the NSDAP."[118] At another place in the same article he doubts whether the people in the Third Reich really knew as much about the mass murder of the Jews, as Goldhagen claims they did. At the same time he considers this to be a superfluous question, which to pursue, would be futile. In his mind "it is doubtful, whether wide spread knowledge of the genocide would have evoked a publicly relevant attitude of protest."[119] Here we see, how useful a catchy phrase, like "the banality of evil" can be, if one is not so keen on knowing too much. Just about anything can be put unexamined into this spongy concept, be it careerism, be it the voter's choice for Hitler, without said voter having been a convinced racial anti-Semite, or be it the indifference in the face of news that seeped through about the mass murder of the Jews.

It would be more productive, although more embarrassing for the Germans, if they wouldn't accept with such haste the apparent indifference in the face of the deadly anti-Semitic policies of the Nazi regime as an excuse. For this phenomenon begs the question, whether this indifference was not in itself an indicator of a spiritual poisoning. Or as Jan Philipp Reemtsma puts it:

Whoever proposes to reduce the population to a manageable size by expelling or killing all Jews, must be an anti-Semite, and if such a proposal doesn't get him at once into serious trouble in regard to quality of life and career plans, he must be living in an anti-Semitic environment.[120]

Neither in Imperial Germany, nor in the Weimar Republic did anti-Semites have to fear such consequences. In 1933 one of them was heaved to power. Even "ordinary Germans" who were by no means fanatical anti-Semites, voted for him, for anti-Semitism as such was no longer tainted with the stigma of bigotry, bad taste, and maliciousness. In short, it had become socially acceptable. It cannot be stressed strongly enough that Hans Mommsen's assertion, according to which Hitler came to power, not because of, but in spite of his anti-Semitism, is based on a contrast that has been construed after the fact. Such a contrast can hardly have existed in the heads of those who were fascinated by Hitler. It is highly questionable whether they could differentiate between the wish that Hitler would nurse the defeated nation back to health and that he would punish the nation's enemies, on the one hand, and the prevailing anti-Semitic sentiments of the time, on the other. There should be no doubt about it, for contemporary Germans this sentiment and this wish were virtually one and the same thing.

No less problematic is Mommsen's concession that wide spread knowledge of the genocide of the Jews would not have evoked any protest worth mentioning. Isn't the historian called upon to explain this lethargy? Spreading knowledge of the Nazi "Euthanasia Program" gave rise to protest. Unfortunately, the Nazi rulers did not stop the killing of the mentally impaired altogether in the wake of this protest, but they did respond to the public pressure by becoming more secretive about "mercy killing." And it would be worth investigating, whether this added need for caution did slow down the murder of the mentally retarded and of social misfits. Why was there no equivalent protest against the mass murder of the Jews?

I think, this had to do with "indifference." It was not an "indifference" without content, but an anti-Semitic "indifference." An edition of Gestapo interrogation protocols, edited by the Gießen historian, Jörg-Peter Jatho, directs the spotlight upon this inobservance.[121] The protocols deal with a small intimate circle of people who listened to enemy broadcasts. This circle had been infiltrated by a Gestapo informant. In the wake of the tip-off, this woman informer gave to her superiors, the small group was arrested on February 6, 1942.

In order to listen in secret to the BBC and to Radio Beromünster, this group, the so-called "Freitagskränzchen" ("Friday Circle"), had met in the apartment of the Gießen pastor and orientalist, Dr. Alfred Kaufmann, who between 1896 and 1906 had been the minister of the Lutheran congregation of the German Lutheran church and the German school in Alexandria, Egypt, and who, during this time had had Rudolph Hess as one of his pupils. Another one of the regular listeners was the painter Heinrich Will who would have liked so very much to be a Nazi, but couldn't, because his wife was Jewish. She accompanied him regularly to these conspirative meetings.

Significant, are the confessions of the Gestapo prisoners for the interpretation of the "indifference" vis-à-vis the racial anti-Semitism, which had been given by the Nazis the status of state doctrine. These clearly reveal that rumors of the "mercy killings" had reached the conspiratorial listeners, which only shows how much one could know if one really wanted to. They even knew that the victims of the "euthanasia" program were put to death by means of poisonous gas. But as far as can be inferred from the Gestapo interrogations, the grizzly topic of the persecution and destruction of the Jews wasn't addressed even once in the conspiratorial circle. The statement of the Gestapo informer, who was brought to trial after 1945, gives reason to believe that the topic was carefully avoided in these meetings. The records of the Regional Court of Kassel, where this woman informer was tried, mentions a telling incident concerning this avoidance:

> One day the accused asked the witness Z., a female friend of Will, explicitly, whether Frau Will had a certificate of "Aryan" descent. The witness Z. gave an evasive answer and left the question open.[122]

Why did she leave the question open? One was among friends, more than that, among friends who were critical of the Nazi regime. No one knew that the woman who posed the question was a spy. More than likely, because all, with the exception of Frau Will the Jewish wife of the painter Heinrich Will, were anti-Semites. For them anything that had to do with Jewishness was tainted.

The "Friday Circle" was for Frau Will as a Jewess in certain ways off limits. To the listeners of the enemy broadcasts it was, of course, known that Elisabeth Will was not Aryan. However, excluding her from the intimate round would have been too unpleasant for all those involved. Hence, there must have been an unspoken agreement, "not to wake sleeping dogs."

According to the unspoken rules of this make-believe acceptance, it was expected of Frau Will that she behave "like a lady." She wasn't allowed to test the borders of her sham-acceptance. It would have been considered in bad taste on her part if she would have mentioned her Jewish background. Even more unacceptable would have been if she would have complained about the repressive measures which she drew upon herself by her Jewishness. For the "Aryan friends" the maintenance of this tactful distance brought with it the advantage that they never had to become aware of their own tactlessness and the limits of their tolerance. In this respect, even the Nazi laws made it easy for these "Aryan do-gooders." As a "Jewess in a privileged mixed marriage" Frau Will didn't have to wear the yellow star.

Dr. Kaufmann's claim that prior to having been told (presumably by the Gestapo), he had been unaware that the wife of his friend Heinrich Will was Jewish, a lie he told to protect himself. How could it have remained a secret to him, what had put such a sudden end to the career of his friend? He didn't want to know anything about the problems of the Will couple, didn't want to hear about it, because as a German Lutheran minister, and as a child who had been raised in a German Lutheran parsonage, he was a "dye in the wool" anti-Semite.

One only has to read his article "Bethlehem, die Weihnachtsstadt" in the *Orient-Rundschau,* a kind of newsletter for veterans who had fought in World War I in Palestine under the command of Liman von Zandern. In this article Kaufmann describes the city of the birth of Jesus Christ, which he had visited frequently while serving from 1892 to 1894 as minister and teacher at the Syrian Orphanage in Jerusalem. On the surface the text radiates dazzling light.

Bethlehem is mentioned as "a small town" way up in the Judean Mountains "that is engulfed in uniquely radiant light." This "abundance of light" is praised throughout the article as the characteristic beauty of the oriental landscape. While painting this scenery, Kaufmann contemplates "the clarity of our Lord." At the same time this article casts in relation to the Jews a dark shadow into the future. If one avoids getting blinded by all the "light," one becomes aware of this ominous darkness, as for instance in Kaufmann's sociological classification of the Bethlehemites along confessional lines:

> The city has approximately 12 000 inhabitants, most of them Arab Christians belonging to either the Greek Orthodox or Catholic Church, and only a few hundred Moslems: like Nazareth, Bethlehem has maintained, in spite of four hundred years of Islamic and Turkish rule, a predominantly Christian Character. Jews are not tolerated.[123]

The matter-of-factness, in which Kaufmann notes "Jews are not tolerated," indicates that he is in total agreement with this politico-demographic peculiarity. For the German Lutheran minister no special explanation is required for Jews not being allowed to live in the city of the birth of our Savior Jesus Christ. Along with this self-explicitness went Kaufmann's aversion to recognizing that Elisabeth Will, the wife of his "friend," was persecuted on racial grounds.

In short, spongy notions, like "indifference," "lack of concern," and "inattention" cover up all kinds of bigotry one would rather not know about. These modes of behavior must themselves become a subject of study in German history instead of accepting them as explanations for the conduct of the German population during the period of the Third Reich. Goldhagen has made a major contribution to historiography and deserves credit for having refused to accept indifference as an explanatory factor for the unchecked "cumulative radicalization" of the persecution of the Jews. He categorically demands:

> Before the concept of "indifference" should be used, at least two issues must be addressed. The first is its meaning. How could Germans have been "indifferent"—in the sense of having no views or predilections on the matter, in the sense of feeling no emotions, of being utterly neutral,

morally and in every other way—to the mass slaughter of thousands of people, including children, which the people themselves or their countrymen were helping to perpetuate in their name?...The public vitriol against Jews was so ubiquitous in Germany during its Nazi period that it was as impossible for Germans to have had no views about Jews or about the elimination of Jews from German society as it was for Whites in the American South during the heyday of the civil rights movement to have had no views about Blacks or the desirability of de-segregation. "Indifference" was a virtual psychological impossibility.

If, however, somehow "indifference" existed, if somehow many Germans had no views about Jews and no views about the justice of what their countrymen were doing to the Jews, then this cognitive state still must be elucidated.[124]

However, concentration on the perception and will of "ordinary Germans" seems to be in the eyes of the historians of the Flakhelfer generation an unacceptable breech of propriety. In this matter Mommsen is expending more energy into putting Goldhagen into the wrong, than into contributing something constructive in an exchange of views, which could elucidate what went on in the heads of said "ordinary Germans." For instead of addressing the posed question, he vents his displeasure about Goldhagen not having been able to soar up to the lofty heights of "functionalist" abstractions, up to the question of how National Socialist policy on how to deal with the Jews, had produced very difficult problems, which in the end one thought, could only be solved by "implementing" the "Final Solution." Goldhagen loses sight of this crucial question in *Hitler's Willing Executioners*, Mommsen points out. Disgruntled he continues: "In doing so, it is his [Goldhagen's] prime concern to underscore the insurmountable cruelty of the German perpetrators, which for him is rooted in their specific anti-Semitic attitudes." This cannot be condoned, for such deviation from the time-honored scholarly approach fails to deal with the uniqueness of the Holocaust, which, as the experts agree, was "a planned, bureaucratically well thought through process" with no room for emotionality.[125]

This is indeed a strange attitude on the part of a researcher since it tries to uphold the pure doctrine about the uniqueness of the Holocaust by trivializing research findings, such as the cruelty of the perpetrators, which are, page after page, meticulously documented in Goldhagen's book. This is all the more strange if one considers that the surest way of finding acceptance in the community of scholars is generally achieved by bringing attention to a hitherto "unjustly neglected fact." But what is at stake here, is not *Wissenschaft* and research, but rather a creed. As a successful graduate of re-education, one is not required to grapple with the Nazi past in an existential way, but one is forbidden to say anything, which might blur the contours of the Holocaust as a uniquely industrialized mass murder. Whoever is careless enough to do that, exposes himself in the eyes of these former Hitler Youths and "born again" democrats as too simple minded to participate in the deliberations with the experts.

Time to say it openly: What these people are up to is discreditation and discrimination pure and simple. It is deplorable that German historical scholarship resorts to such underhanded methods, especially so, since Mommsen professes that German academic history has addressed itself ceaselessly to the task of "uncovering the mechanisms," which explain "the progressively increasing moral indifference"[126] and since Wehler loudly protests that German historians "have tortured themselves" for over half a century, addressing the main questions that have been raised by research on the Nazi past and the Holocaust."[127] Hidden in the German refutations is the thinly disguised wish to finish off Goldhagen who poses painful questions. Paraphrasing this daring American scholar, the former Hitler Youths try to inflict "academic death" upon him. No argument is devious enough to prohibit using it in discrediting an unwelcome intruder in the historical discourse. And what could be in worse taste and more effective than hiding behind the broad back of a prominent Israeli Historian, whom one harnesses to the German defensive mechanisms. Wehler is not ashamed to polemicize: " 'What has happened at Harvard,' Yehuda Bauer, one of the grand old man [sic.] of Israeli Holocaust research, asks." One shouldn't have let it come to the point where Goldhagen "dresses down, with an arrogance that can't be matched, all historians of National Socialism and the Holocaust." Someone should have told him that things just don't go that way. Aren't there mentors, second readers, and outside readers? It's the job of these "small academic work groups...to keep up the state of the art, to continue the discussion on the reached level of knowledge, and to advance it with rationally controllable arguments." But in America, Herr Professor Wehler notes, this doesn't seem to be the case. There renowned universities, particularly the Ivy League colleges, are notorious for not living up to their duties as academic law enforcement agencies. They have even been known to pass absolutely botched up work. To top it all off, they have praised it, so in the case of the dissertation of David Abraham. Critical scholars can consider themselves fortunate to have won after a bitter controversy, for the unworthy Ph.D. candidate had the backing of Chicago and Princeton. In 1992 there was the scandal with Liah Greenfield's comparative study on nationalism, "which was praised and accepted by illustrious figures of the Harvard 'community of scholars'." Such forbearance was unwarranted, because this study presented the road to Auschwitz as a one-way street with no exits. The litany on American academic sins closes with the remark: "And now new depths have been reached in the case of Goldhagen. It is not funny at all to see once more how a sub-standard piece of work slipped through the academic filter." What is at stake here, according to Wehler, is "the question concerning the observance of elementary academic control mechanisms." One should be able to rely upon them.[128]

This attempt to discredit the American higher education on the part of a German professor can backfire. As the saying goes: "People in glass houses shouldn't throw stones." The "small academic work groups," into which Wehler puts so much trust, are no better and no worse than the society whose bread they eat. Moreover, it is one of the characteristics of academic screening that everything that goes against the grain gets stuck and that these screening processes let through just about anything the examination committees and their sponsors want to let through. This is the natural state of things, for the doctoral degree is not to be acquired as slick as a whistle, obtaining it is an extremely complicated matter. Just think of all that has to be taken into consideration. To start, verification as to whether the candidate has successfully passed all his high school subjects is required; then, one has to check whether all courses and seminars the candidate took can be accepted; that he hasn't passed the age limit, so he can still be considered a "promising young scholar"; that his dissertation proposal meets stringent academic standards; that he has not plagiarized; and countless other things. Otherwise just about anybody could come and say, he wants a Ph.D. And since there are so many factors involved, things may unexpectedly go wrong. I wouldn't know where to start, if I wanted to tell what has slipped through the German academic screening and what got stuck in it, or if I wanted to tell how the German system of controls proved its worth, in spite of human error on the part of the examiners, by letting through what people wanted to let through or by screening out what they might have considered harmful.

Where should I start? Tell me where! Perhaps at *Faust und das Faustische*. I read the book as a student of German literature in Canada at Brock University, one of these dubious North American colleges, which—lacking a sense for the sublime in scholarship—had conferred an honorary doctorate on a hockey player, namely Stan Mekita, the star forward of the Chicago Black Hawks. Paging in the Brock library through the *Faust* study with the awe inspiring title, I wasn't even thinking about how discriminate an examination committee has to be in order not to bestow honors upon an unworthy person. Exactly twenty four years later, on May 8, 1995, I bought a copy of the weekly magazine *Der Spiegel* at the newspaper stand just around the corner. To my consternation I had to read in the issue I'd just picked up, how in the case of the Habilitationsschrift[129] *Faust und das Faustische*, the examination committee seems to have been sleeping on the job.[130] Or this "little academic work group" must at that time have been so overburdened with the verification of citations and footnotes that it didn't get around to checking the personal credentials of the candidate. Said candidate had forgotten his name. Schneider is as common a name in Germany as Smith or Johnes in the English speaking world. This may have been the reason for his forgetfulness. Who can blame him for that. Whatever the case may be, said candidate submitted his manuscript under the name of Hans Schwerte. But that wasn't all. He also had forgotten that he already had a doctoral degree, beyond this that he had done his Habilitation on the theme "Dance and Tree," that he had been promoted to the rank of SS-Hauptsturmführer, because of his high achievements as a Germanist, and that in this capacity he had been assigned to the personal staff of Heinrich Himmler.[131] But *honi soit qui mal y pense*, after the Nazi interlude, German academics were consciously trying to avoid picking up from where they had left off in 1945. Aside from that, what's in a name, especially so, since Ranke urges the historian to efface himself in the name of objectivity.

Or should I tell about how an honorary doctorate for Aziz Nesin was torpedoed by the good folks at the Technical University of Darmstadt? Without having thought of anything evil or malicious, the faculty of Social and Historical Sciences had decided on February 8, 1990 to initiate the procedure, at the end of which the TUD would have paid its respects to the noted Turkish writer Azisz Nesin, by conferring upon him an honorary doctorate. A commission was appointed to evaluate Azis Nesin's literary work. Unfortunately the gentlemen of this commission and of the faculty in question allowed themselves the luxury of thinking that world renown as a writer would suffice for the TUD to bestow the honorary doctorate upon this Turkish dissident. While indulging in such reckless thoughts, they had not taken into consideration that in far away Turkey their enthusiasm might create a bad impression, that way down there one might have suspected that the TUD had instigated this academic honor in order to signal its protest against Turkish interference in academic freedom and against torture in Turkish prisons. Such suspicions would, of course, have been unfounded, for said German institution of higher learning is not known as an exporter of subversive ideas and it avoids, like the plague, getting mixed up in the internal politics of another country. Quite the contrary, the TUD is a serious center of teaching and research where a clear distinction is made between academic matters and politics. In other words, the TUD is only interested in constructive international scholarly cooperation, as is attested by the smoothly functioning partnership between the Technische Universität Darmstadt and the Middle East Technical University (Ankara). This latter institution tows the line of the Turkish government and is not tainted by the odious stigma of subversion. Nonetheless, one cannot stress strongly enough how sensitive these Turks are. Why should one then have given forbearance to a misunderstanding? Fortunately the TUD had a reliable system of controls. Thanks to this system one arrived at the wise decision, not to confer the honorary doctorate upon Aziz Nesin, who had a police record and who had served time in Turkish prisons. But since all of this was so complicated and too hard to grasp for simple folks, the Office of the President of the TUD tried to clear up any possible misunderstandings by issuing a simple worded press release. In this modest statement a public relations official pointed out on behalf of the President of the university, the Fritz Fischer student Helmut Böhme, in a differentiated way:

> The Technical University of Darmstadt goes about in a sparing and responsible way with the conferral of honorary doctorates, because such conferrals constitute the highest honor for academic achievements (and only for such) that the university can bestow...The applicant cannot be spared the risk of defeat, because such an eventuality is part of the democratic process...
>
> Untrue and quite irresponsible is...the accusation that the Senate of the TUD yielded to the pressure of Turkish agencies...
>
> All this has nothing to do with the commendable literary work of Aziz Nesin and with the sincerity of his political activism.[132]

The decision had been reached in a clinically sterile operating room. Once again the academic screening had been doing its job, unbiased scholarship had triumphed.

The same way unbiased scholarship had triumphed in the case of Rainer Zitelmann. In his case the "tactful consideration among colleagues" inserted itself into the system of controls as a self-regulating corrective. Karl Otmar Freiherr von Aretin, the mentor of Zitelmann, who is situated right of center in the political spectrum, who in his extracurricular capacity is the Director of the Institut für Europäische Geschichte, which is substantially subsidized by the German Foreign Ministry, and who went on record as saying: "all the talk about the encumbered German past is pure nonsense," saw in the dissertation of his ward a stroke of genius.

Hans-Christoph Schröder, who belongs to Wehler's citation syndicate and who is recognized in Darmstadt as an authority on the history of German Social Democracy, felt, in contrast, that accepting Zitelmann's dissertation would be an affront to academic history. But the opponents remained sober, didn't let things come to a show down, viewed the matter in a "differentiated" way, and resolved the conflict in an amicable fashion by agreeing that what Zitelmann had submitted was a scholarly contribution of "the highest quality," marred by a few minor errors, none of them so bad as that they couldn't be fixed up with light cosmetic changes.

This way the vast body of Hitler literature, which had already been augmented by contributions from German scholars, such as Rudolf Olden, Werner Maser, Joachim Fest, Helm Stierlin, Eberhard Jäckel, and others, was enriched with another Hitler biography—with Rainer Zitelmann's monograph *Hitler: Selbstverständnis eines Revolutionärs* (Hamburg, 1987) [*Hitler: The Self-Understanding of a Revolutionary*]. This new study presented a decriminalized Hitler, a hitherto unknown Führer, a friend of the little man and a combatant in the vanguard of the proletariat who ought to be positioned on the left of the political spectrum, a wise statesman who only tried to achieve rational economic goals in his war against the Soviet Union. According to Zitelmann, this Hitler didn't even believe himself in his rallying cry against the "judeo-bolshevik sub-humans."

All were content. Even critics of Zitelmann saw in the acceptance of the dissertation the lesser evil. Strife would only have disrupted teaching and research. How, for instance, could Aretin and Schröder have continued to direct jointly the advanced seminar if the latter would have stuck to his principles. Beyond this, could Schröder's favorite students still have been considered for stipends from Aretin's Institut für Europäische Geschichte? However, thanks to the "tactful consideration among colleagues" and thanks to a "differentiated" practical way of looking at the matter, scholarship was spared all these mishaps.

Unfortunately, practical examination procedure, which orients itself on "Realpolitik," cannot please everybody. It leaves casualties. In the examination of Zitelmann, Schröder seems to have suffered some injuries. Some time after Zitelmann's straight upward launch into a model career, after Schröder, with the help of revisionists who grouped themselves around him, had conquered the cultural pages of the conservative press, I met his former secretary. As usual we talked about how unfair life can be. Life was being unfair to her former boss. He no longer dared to submit his manuscripts to the Ullstein Publishing House, because Zitelmann had become there the editor for contemporary history. "He has my sincerest sympathies!" I said and didn't know which way to pull my facial muscles, up into a grin, expressing Schadenfreude, or down to signal consternation and fear.

But enough of this talk about the unreliability of the academic system of controls. Instead I invite the reader to the movies, to be specific, to a kind of Mel Brooks movie. The material for the script would be provided by a nightmare I have. In this nightmare I imagine that Goldhagen had tried to obtain his Ph.D. in Germany—Bochum, Bielefeld, Stuttgart, or Darmstadt—where he would have been completely at the mercy of one of these "small academic work groups." This group would consist of the self-appointed examination committee, namely of Hans Mommsen, Eberhard Jäckel, and Hans-Ulrich Wehler. The work of this imaginary commission would start neither in the library, nor in a quiet scholarly study, but rather it would commence in time-honored tradition on the race track of vanity, the dueling place of power politics, the port of exchange for smuggled rumors, the take-off and landing strip for academic high altitude and devious low flights—in the hall of the History Department. Before my inner eye I see the committee assembled at the meeting place, where today communication and exchange of ideas are cultivated (unlike in yonder days, under the Linden tree on the village square), standing around the Xerox copying machine. It is one of those rare days, on which Mommsen is not away on a lecture tour in America, on which Wehler is not under stress having to prepare for a conference, and on which Jäckel can spare some time because the galley proofs for his newest book have not arrived yet, time enough to take care of one of those irritating tasks which one had set aside time and again: the bothersome task of dealing with the dissertation of a visiting doctoral student from the United States, whom one had, up till now, not deigned important enough to give him the time of day.

After some back and forth: "My dear colleague, please start!" "No, dear colleague, you start, I'll join in!" and so on, Mommsen would rise and appoint himself, in Napoleonic manner, chairman of the committee and open the deliberation among colleagues with the following remark:

> Our young guest from America wants to provoke, but the dissertation he submitted clearly falls behind the current state of research; it is based to a large degree on insufficient sources, and brings no new insights! Wouldn't you agree? (Cf. *Die Zeit*, August 30, 1996, p. 14.)[133]

Wehler, who would play the role of court-appointed counsel, would now say:

> But please my dear colleague, about the internal functioning of work camps for Jews we still know very little. And where are there at least a few scholarly monographs which analyze these 'death marches'? Isn't it understandable that Goldhagen wanted to fill this research gap a little? (Cf. Wehler in Schoeps, ed., 1996, p. 196.)

Mommsen, who'd rather swallow his tongue than utter a word of praise, would respond to this:

> But listen, also the commendable descriptions of 'death marches,' which go beyond the current state of research are cluttered with serious mistakes! (Cf. *Die Zeit*, August 30, 1996, p. 15.)

Wehler, still playing the defense counsel, would object:

> Whoever doesn't have a heart of stone, will be deeply moved when reading Chapters 13 and 14. (Wehler in Schoeps, ed., 1996, p. 196.)

That would be enough for Mommsen who would cut off his learned colleague Hans-Ulrich Wehler at this very spot by bursting out:

> Ah, mere emotionalism, when I hear it, I'd like to throw up; it explains nothing! (Cf. Mommsen in Diner, ed., 1987, p. 85.)

In response to this strong statement Wehler would concede:

> We Germans should be able to be more relaxed about the perceivable moral indignation, which motivates the author. Nonetheless, I do agree with you in principle, emotionalism spoils the sublime research process. (Cf. Wehler in Schoeps, ed., 1996, p. 194.)

Finally Jäckel's turn would come. All the time he had been impatiently waiting to get a word in. Not having learned anything from his premature praise of the forged "Hitler Diaries," he would have verified the inferiority of the doctoral candidate in the forefront by skim-reading parts of the submitted manuscript. That Goldhagen had dealt in this manuscript with him and his two learned colleagues, would have escaped Jäckel's attention in this quick perusal. He would now exclaim: "I have looked at the candidates bibliography. He hasn't even read the pertinent literature. We cannot accept this sub-standard piece of work, no way! I reject the submitted dissertation! Are there any objections?" This would be the end of it. Goldhagen's academic career would have been destroyed and neither Habermas, nor anybody else, would have raised a voice in protest.

This is how "Master Proper," "Mr. Clean," and "Herr Saubermann" would swiftly deal with Daniel Jonah Goldhagen, if they only could. Yet, they wonder and are indignant, because said Daniel Jonah Goldhagen took precautions not to be silenced by them and the likes of them. With much concern Wehler registers the predominantly positive reception of *Hitler's Willing Executioners* in America and sees the cause for this agreement with the author in deep-seated anti-German resentments, which supposedly slumber close beneath the surface over there and can be revived at any time. Hence, he admonishes:

> Such antipathies could not have been unknown to the author. It reveals much about his sense of responsibility, if, as a political scientist, he took advantage of this resentment by instrumentalizing it in the media. Thereby he has inflicted considerable damage on Holocaust studies, not only in the eyes of scholars, but also in the eyes of the general public.[134]

This lament of one of the high priests of German history is picked up by the devoted congregation. By sheer coincidence I met the aforementioned, now retired secretary of the Darmstadt History Department. Still devoted to her former lord and master, the way personal secretaries are, she also stuck up for his dear colleagues, Mommsen, Jäckel, and Wehler. Their deep hurt had touched her motherly heart, so she had to tell me, how "sensitive" these "elderly gentlemen" are and how inconsiderate Goldhagen was for not taking their feelings into consideration. On the day before, she had seen on TV how this young troublemaker had been interviewed just before boarding a plane at the Boston airport. "How that man advertises his book," she observed. "That's not dignified; he should leave that to his publisher."

Dignified or not, heaven help those who have no publicity at all. They end up in the dirty laundry of the Saubermanns.

All that's been said so far leads to the unavoidable conclusion that far more is involved in the Goldhagen controversy than professional bickering over dry facts and figures. What's at stake are two diametrically opposed ways of dealing with the encumbered past. There are two options, either one identifies with or one distances oneself from one's own past. Mommsen, Jäckel, and Wehler, although they would deny it, have opted for the second choice. They fear that getting in touch with their roots would confront them with the guilt of their parents. With the help of "professional standards," abstinence of emotions, and abstract language they blend out this guilt. They speak as "professional historians" and as "experts," thereby taking cover as Germans who experienced "all of that" at a critical age—be it as children who grew up in Nazi families, as Hitler Youth or Flakhelfer. Modern scientific thought, as it has been developed by Galilee, Descartes, and Bacon comes to their aid in doing so, because in its endeavor to find out the truth, it doesn't place too much value on memory.[135]

The bone-dry, impersonal style of the Flakhelfer historians and of the "promising young scholars" who have been taught by them, which is so characteristic of German historical writing, as is the pedantic, school-teacherly tone, can, in the final analysis, be ascribed to this escapism. For the Germans who have to be taught, reminded, brought up, and kept in check, are those others who live out there. In this kind of discourse about the past any kind of intimacy between writer and reader is avoided like the plague. The last thing the writer wants to let his reader know is that they have "eaten bread and salt together," meaning that they have shared the most fundamental nourishment, suffered the same hardships, experienced the same joys, and that together they are inescapably entangled in the encumbered past.

Mommsen, Jäckel, and Wehler are speaking as typical post-war Germans. Their historical writing is a product of the damaged German collective identity, of that inhibited, up-tight feeling, which Friedrich Christian Delius captures so magnificently when he describes how Paul Gompitz, an East German, tries repeatedly in vain on St. Wenceslas Square in Prague to strike up a conversation with West German tourists:

> Gompitz: "Oh, how nice to meet another German here in Prague! I am also German; I come from the GDR, from Rostock." And with the question, "from where do you come?" and "what brings you here?" he is trying to draw out the conversation, until—without seeming too pushy—a bridge is built to an invitation for a cup of coffee. The first attempt fails after three minutes, the second after one, the third after five, the fourth after seven. The people don't want to be talked to, and when you address them as compatriots, they clamp up completely.[136]

Whether West Germans on St. Wenceslas Square or German historians, like Mommsen, Jäckel, and Wehler, busying themselves with the production of knowledge, neither of them is seriously interested in claiming the repugnant Nazi past as their own. The only achievement of the latter consists in having juggled the unresolved pieces of the past, thereby having "transformed them into history." Whether they want to or not, by ordering, explaining or relativizing the unresolved pieces, they are providing the German present with the illusion of some kind of normality. They are creating the false impression that this past is already history and no longer part of the present. They are trying to get rid of their past and deny their origin.[137]

Goldhagen goes the other way, the way of identification, which leads back to his "roots." He is writing as a member of a community with a common experience, in which—had he lived in 1942—he would have been a candidate for the gas chamber. Whatever he discovers, he treats as something that is of immediate concern to him. Identification manifests itself on every page of his book, starting with the dedication "to Erich Goldhagen, my father and teacher," a survivor of the Rumanian-Jewish ghetto in Czernowitz, up to the "thick description" of the massacres, a description which betrays that the author is moved by pity for the victims, that he re-experiences their mortal fear, and that this identification evokes in him a just anger which motivates him to ask what went on inside the killers, what did they feel when they were shooting at point-blank range at helpless women and children.

Be it that the chastisement from a number of renowned scholars has hurt his feelings, so that—cost what it may—he is trying to win their recognition (the correspondent of the prestigious German newspaper *Die Welt* is quoted by the father, Erich Goldhagen, as saying: "This is ein wissenschaftliches Werk.")[138]—or be it that he is neither willing nor able to talk with the critics from the land of the perpetrators at the emotional level, as a historical human being he is keeping a low profile in the debate his book has engendered. He doesn't pay them back in the same currency when they insinuate that he, as a Jew, is too biased to make objective scholarly statements about the Holocaust. He could, for example, have replied to them in the lofty literary language of their captions,[139] which would have sounded somewhat like this:

> And I, from the seed of Abraham, have thawed out with the fire of the burning bush, in which YAHWEH appeared to Moses, the cries of the victims and the hellish laughter of the murderers, which are lying frozen on the shelves of the Central Investigation Agency in Ludwigsburg, so that you may hear them.

Instead he demands:

> Every decent human being should respond to this shameful part of the discussion by demanding that scholars and other reviewers should concern themselves only with "*Wissenschaft*" and not with the origin, identity, and supposed character traits of the author of the work under discussion.[140]

However, by taking cover as an historical individual behind "unadulterated" *Wissenschaft* (science), he merely maneuvers himself into a position which is not unlike the one the Russian historians found themselves in, when, as academics, they tried to explain their country's victory over Napoleon in the time-honored categories of classical military history they had internalized during their studies. About this victory and the explanations of this victory in contemporary Russian school books Tolstoy writes in his epic novel *War and Peace*:

We try to imagine two people who, as good sportsmen, engage each other with daggers according to the rules of fencing. The duel has already lasted for some time. Suddenly one of them notices that he has been wounded. Now he becomes aware of the fact that they are not doing this just for fun, but rather that they are fighting for their very lives. He throws away his dagger and grabs the next best club, which he can get hold of, and starts thrashing around with this rudimentary weapon.

We further try to imagine that this man who was sensible enough to use the best and simplest means to achieve his objective, is also someone who extols the rules of chivalry, so that he wishes to obscure what really happened, by claiming in retrospect that he achieved his victory according to the rules of fencing. It wouldn't be too difficult to imagine what kind of distortion and obfuscation would spread as a result of his nonfactual description.

The fencer who insisted on fighting a duel according to the rules of classical fencing stands for the French. His opponent, the one who threw away his dagger in order to grab a club, stands for the Russians. The people who try to explain what happened according to the rules of fencing, are the historians who wrote about the event.[141]

In the debate that takes place, Goldhagen finds himself, without giving it much thought, in the role of the fencer who notices suddenly that he has been wounded. He argues with hurt feelings and pays no mind to whether he hurts the feelings of his opponents or not. And by insisting now that in the controversy one ought to concern oneself only with *Wissenschaft*, he is providing in retrospect a distorted explanation of his victory, which is in some ways similar to the explanation of Tolstoy's fencer who extolled the rules of chivalry, so that in retrospect he distorted what really happened by claiming in all seriousness to have won in accordance with the rules of fencing.

It may well be that Goldhagen is aware of these complexities, or that they dawn upon him, now that the dust has settled somewhat. On the occasion of being awarded the 1997 Democracy Prize of the prestigious journal *Blätter für deutsche und internationale Politik*, he is supposed to have said he only became aware after the appearance of his book that his study does not merely have to do with the past.[142] Ergo, not everything that has happened is over and done with. For this very reason Goldhagen is doing himself no favor when making common cause with Hans Mommsen and the German community of researchers by insisting upon a sober conversation amongst colleagues.

The identification prerequisite in Goldhagen's discourse becomes even more distorted by the imprecise use of the pronouns "we" and "ourselves." It is quite apparent that "we" and "ourselves" stand in contrast to "the Germans," to be exact, in contrast to those Germans who perpetrated the Holocaust as desk-bound bureaucrats, as Concentration Camp guards, or as mass murderers, as well as to those Germans who, because of their particular disposition, saw no compelling reason for opposing the anti-Semitic measures of the state, and finally to those Germans of the pre-Nazi era whose anti-Semitism prepared the way to the Holocaust. If "we" really want to understand them, "we" must approach them the same way anthropologists approach illiterate aboriginal tribes. In doing so, Goldhagen insists, one can "no longer proceed from the premise that the Germans of that time "were more or less like us or, rather, similar to how we represent ourselves to be."[143]

But whom does he mean by "we" and "ourselves?" At times he creates the impression that the American citizen Daniel J. Goldhagen is referring with "we" to his fellow Americans, for instance, when he mentions an American educator who cautioned in 1941: "Nazi schooling...produced a generation of human beings in Nazi Germany so different from normal American youths that mere academic comparison seems inane."[144] In the most comprehensive sense "we" and "ourselves" refers also to all of those, seeing themselves as "rational, sober children of the Enlightenment, who are not governed by 'magical thinking.' "[145]

This comprehensive "we" includes in the final analysis also the Germans of today, on the one hand, because Goldhagen denies the existence of a "*timeless German character*,"[146] and on the other, because his cursory familiarity with contemporary Germany leads him to say in an interview, "they are like us," meaning, just like Americans. Goldhagen emphatically expresses this naive notion in his conversation with Rudolf Augstein, the German media czar, who publishes *Der Spiegel*. To underscore the point he's made about Germany having undergone fundamental changes, he adds:

Yesterday I sat here in Hamburg in the pedestrian zone and had something to eat. I looked around: young Germans, young couples together, people doing their shopping, or just taking a leisurely stroll. So I thought to myself: What do they have to do with the past, what do they have in common with it? Nothing. If I'd sit in Boston, I could see very similar people. Such young people should not let themselves be tortured by the past.[147]

Well, that's how it may seem on the surface. Life in Germany has become more American. They have McDonald's and Burger King, plus TV and democracy. And in the present social and economic crisis the pop philosophy of Dale Carnegie ("Be happy—don't worry!") has here, in Germany, as many adherents as in America. Here, as well as there, the motto is "think positive, win friends, be successful," so that an American on a short visit to Germany, who has little experience in psychological espionage, will come invariably to the conclusion—while observing the busy to and fro in pedestrian zones of Frankfurt, Munich or Hamburg—Germans are just like us.[148]

But the resistance to accepting the reality of the Holocaust as their own past sweeps all these superficial similarities aside and by necessity focuses the spotlight on the differences. I find it hard to believe that Goldhagen, who said in an interview: "As abhorring as the Holocaust literature may seem, it still isn't drastic enough,"[149] would be willing to identify with Lothar Gall, who—as mentioned before—lectures like a school teacher: "We historians must counter this bloody plasticity with analytic research."[150] No less problematic for Goldhagen would it be if he tried to identify with Hans Mommsen, especially so, since the latter objects to the photographs in *Hitler's Willing Executioners*. Not at all possible would be an identification with the recent Chancellor Helmut Kohl, who during a state visit to Auschwitz could find no time at all to talk with former inmates.[151] And although it transcends the Jewish-German dialogue, which is thematized in this book, it must also be stated that for the U.S. citizen Daniel Jonah Goldhagen, who opens the sports page first to read the baseball scores, identification with his former President Ronald Regan would be very difficult. This former President closed his ears to the appeal of the former Auschwitz and Buchenwald inmate, Elie Wiesel, when he desecrated the memory of Jewish victims by presiding together with his German colleague Chancellor Helmut Kohl over a perverse "reconciliation" ceremony, during which the two heads of state paid visits on the same day first to the military cemetery at Bitburg (where among the buried German soldiers there are also SS perpetrators), then to Bergen-Belsen, where children of Jewish survivors had to be evicted first, so that the hypocritical commemoration ceremony could be conducted smoothly.

By saying this, I want to make clear that Goldhagen does what good historians always have done; he identifies with himself and with his own past. Therefore, he is untrue to himself when he tries to make a deal with his German critics. The horse trade he proposes is: Do not paint the ghost of my past on the wall and I will abstain from bringing up the ghost of your familial past. These ghosts have already been set free and haunt the Goldhagen debate, as they haunt every other attempted Jewish-German dialogue after Auschwitz. For any German, Daniel Jonah Goldhagen himself is the ghost they fear most. By his mere existence he signals to them: "I am the child of a Jewish survivor...and you are my prisoner...you are the prisoner of the dead Jews."[152] How else could one explain why a book, which according to Hans Mommsen "doesn't justify the debate it has evoked," has compelled Mommsen to articulate in a flood of words, spread over several newspaper articles and talk shows, what he thinks of this "insignificant" book? What other answer do we have for this, aside from the explanation that he is trying to flee from the problem Goldhagen poses for him, but as much as he tries, he can't escape. And how else would one explain why this book, which contains no such blanket accusation, triggered a heated debate in Germany over "collective guilt?" How else, aside from the fact that an unadmitted, diffuse feeling of guilt eats at every ordinary German's conscience!

However, as children of the perpetrators the Germans of today could also constitute a difficulty for Goldhagen. It seems somewhat problematic to me, the way he is trying to come to terms with them. He absolves them of their past, saying, they have nothing to do with this past, that they have nothing in common with it. Isn't the objective of this kind of talk the avoidance of "guilt by association." For in dealing directly with any individual, who, in whatever way had to do with National Socialism, one runs into taboos. These send out the signal: Don't touch![153]

The protestation that young Germans have nothing to do with the past simply is not true. Should this pretentious assertion find credence, it will rob these young Germans of their history. That they have nothing at all to do with the past, even Goldhagen must find hard to believe. Why else would he continue with the sentence: "Such young people should not let themselves be tortured by the past." They *are* tortured by the past and Goldhagen seems to sense this, for if these young people really had nothing to do with the past, there would hardly be any reason for wishing them a tranquil life, free of tormenting thoughts about the past.

The absurdity is that the Germans of today in their vast majority are innocent. But the more they demonstrate that the past does not bother them, the more they betray themselves as children and grandchildren of the Nazi generation. One just has to think of Chancellor Helmut Kohl. Of all places in the world, he had to choose Israel to proclaim that he is the first German Chancellor who, thanks to the "Gnade der späten Geburt" ("the mercy of late birth") has been spared any entanglement with National Socialism. The present Chancellor Gerhard Schröder is also a case in point. He would like to see in the capital of the reunited Germany a Holocaust monument erected "to which people would like to go." Who, but a politically correct German who has never grappled with the horrendous past at an emotional level, could think of such a thing—a Holocaust monument, which people would like to visit? And then there is the attitude "wir sind wieder wer!" ("we are no longer nobodies!"), which is so pervasive among the children who were born in the years of the post-war "economic wonder." But if one looks closer, one cannot help but see that only with continued U.S. presence the Germans allow themselves to feel comfortable with their increasing power within the European Economic Community.[154] In other words, the enticing call from deep in the subconscious, "Willst feiner Knabe, du mit mir gehen?"[155] has not yet been silenced, and left to their own devices, the Germans still don't feel strong enough to resist.

As long as the past is not really accepted there is still reason to believe that the guilt of the fathers—as if inherited biologically—is passed on from generation to generation. Only then will there no longer be any cause to say: "The fathers have eaten sour grapes, and the children's teeth are set on edge" (Jeremiah, 31:29). The inadequacies of dealing with evil cannot be solved by playing Rumpelstilzchen. Fallacious reasoning, like: "Ach wie gut, daß niemand weiß, daß ich Rumpelstilzchen heiß!"[156] helps no one.

It is the nature of being to be enmeshed in [hi]stories. In the final analysis stories have to do with name and origin, for which we cannot be blamed, but for which we are responsible nevertheless, because it just isn't true that one is only responsible for things he or she has done. Let's think of a stray dog that comes to us—whether we like it or not—we have to take care of the poor creature, otherwise it will starve to death. Name and origin came to us like stray dogs—whether we like it or not—we have to take care of them.

For Grandma Palmer and Cousin Georgia Anderson in the sleepy town of Henning, Tennessee this went without saying. That's why these great-grandchildren of that black slave (who for the sake of convenience was called "Toby" in America) reminded in turn their children and grandchildren: "Yeah boy, dat African say his name was 'Kin-tay'!...He say de guitar a 'ko,' de river 'Kamby Bolongo,' an' he was choppin' wood to make hisself a drum when they cotched 'im!"[157] Trustee responsibility for name and origin was second nature to these old ladies, as it was for the biblical chronicler who reports to us: "And unto Enoch was born Irad: and Irad begat Mehujael: and Mehujael begat Methusael: and Methusael begat Lamech" (1. Genesis, 4:18).

This trustee responsibility makes a difference when we talk about the Holocaust. In the words of the Cornell historian Dominick LaCapra:

> Whether the historian or analyst is a survivor, a relative of a survivor, a former Nazi, a former collaborator, a relative of a former Nazi or collaborator, a young Jew or German distanced from more immediate contact with survival, participation, or collaboration, or a relative "outsider" to these problems will make a difference even in the meaning of statements that may be formally identical.[158]

To illustrate this observation let us consider two statements. Formally they say one and the same thing, although they differ in their substance like night and day.

Statement 1: "The atrocities of the Holocaust do not prove what Germans, but what man as such is capable of."[159]

Statement 2: "Every war—especially any racial war—leads to brutalization, which expresses itself in atrocities. Like a red thread this characteristic can be traced from Bromberg and Babi Yar over New Guinea and Manila to My Lai."[160]

Statement 1 is taken from German Chancellor Helmut Kohl's opening address of the 1986 Berlin congress on the topic of "Jews in Germany from 1933 to 1939." In the address Kohl aspirated remorseful tunes into the microphone: From his awareness of historical responsibility, as he claimed, he infers Germany's special relationship with Israel. However, his generalizing anthropological explanation of the Nazi crimes stands in direct contrast to the supposedly irrevocable acceptance of German guilt, expressing the wish that the unique burden of Auschwitz be not quite as unique and hence, not quite as heavy, and that his nation with a wall down the center of its soul, be not quite as problematic, as it is. To say it quite bluntly, the perceptive listener hears, in Kohl's protestation about having learned the lesson of history, a pitiful longing for normality.

Statement 2 is taken from the book *Ordinary Men: Reserve Police Battalion 101 and the Final Solution in Poland*. The author, Christopher Browning, is by La Capra's standards or by any other standards a relative outsider for he is an American who has neither German or Jewish parents, nor grandparents. To make the suggestion that he is trying to avoid responsibility, because he is explaining the Holocaust in a behavioristic way, would not only be absurd, but also vulgar, for Browning speaks as an American who consciously experienced how his country lost its innocence at My Lai. His vivid description of the atrocities of a German Police Battalion has at its aim—to speak as the German dramatist Friedrich Schiller—to shake up "den grausamen Hohn und die stolze Sicherheit" ("the cruel mockery and the arrogant self-confidence") "with which, as a rule, untested morality looks down upon fallen virtue." In doing so, he intensifies "the dark premonitions of similar dangers."

Or to cite another example: The conclusion that mass murder in Concentration Camps could only last as long as the German Eastern front held, would have a different ring in Goldhagen's mouth than in mine. No one would doubt that he deeply regrets that the Allies were not able to push back the Nazi forces at greater speed. If I would say the same thing, skepticism would be in order, concerning my wish that the Red Army would have overrun the retreating German army at wind's speed, because if this German front in the East wouldn't have held as long as it did, I might not be among the living today. The Wehrmacht's tenacious retreat battle in the East enabled my parents to flee with their children, including me, from West Prussia in the winter of 1945. I owe my life to those German soldiers whose tenacious delaying tactics ensured the continuation of the smooth functioning of Auschwitz.

One could also say that I am deeply caught up in the historical events under discussion. This being caught up in events that took place over fifty years ago, seems to be the touchiest point in the whole debate. Therefore it isn't considered seemly to talk about it. Goldhagen would like to bracket out the direct personal affectedness of the Germans of today. They have nothing to do with the Nazi past he tries to convince himself, as well as them. His German critics appreciate this, for they like to believe that they themselves have remained untouched by the recent past. At the same time they feel it to be their duty to disqualify Goldhagen, because he is not emotionally detached from what he discusses. Major German newspapers, like *Die Welt*, *taz*, the *Tagesspiegel* and other German publications belabor Daniel Jonah Goldhagen's genealogy, stressing that his father, Erich Goldhagen, is a survivor of the Jewish ghetto of Czernowitz in Rumania, who lost most of his relatives in the Holocaust.

"What's going on here?" asks Andrei S. Markowitz in the *Frankfurter Rundschau*. "Since when has it become a custom to discuss in reviews the familial circumstances of an author?" And to make sure that the point he's trying to make is understood, he continues:

> The subtext is clear: Goldhagen, as the son of a father whose life has been affected by the Holocaust in such a devastating way, cannot possibly write an objective book about the destruction of the Jews. The product of his labors can at best be understood as an act of vengeance, with which the son assaults the perpetrators.[161]

Mommsen, Jäckel, and Wehler, the three prominent German historians, say this not quite as bluntly, but rather in a back-stabbing way. At first glance it seems as if it hadn't even registered with Jäckel who the young man from Harvard was, who had visited him. In his review he talks about a polite young American, who—while doing research in the Central Investigation Agency in nearby Ludwigsburg—made a social call at his residence in Stuttgart. With "much regret" Professor Jäckel states now that the aforementioned nice, young man disappoints him very much, because the "bad" book under discussion makes it all too clear that its author had taken none of his good advice. In reality Jäckel must have known quite well what kind of challenge Goldhagen and his book constitute for him. And to me it seems that the father of the wish that the aforementioned Goldhagen would just disappear, was a deep down knowledge about the identity of the troublemaker, as well as a deep down knowledge about his right to speak and to be heard. For all Jäckel says in essence about Goldhagen, is this: I don't want to hear him; I want him just to go away; I'd like to inflict "academic death" upon him! Ditto Hans Mommsen: the idea of having to think through, what Goldhagen thought, outrages him and no way is he willing to look at the photographs Goldhagen is trying to show him. Especially noteworthy in this context is Wehler's round about disqualification of Goldhagen. He doesn't dare say it openly that he thinks Goldhagen is incapable of writing about the Holocaust because he is a Jew, but means exactly this when he writes:

> Should we leave the historiography of the massacre of millions of Armenians...to a young Armenian historian, [which according to Wehler would lead to] seeing this genocide as the final result of a tradition of "Osman butchery," which can be traced back for centuries—having implications for the Turkish war against the Curds?
>
> Should we leave the even greater massacres, which took place under Lenin and Stalin and which lasted for decades...to a young Ukrainian historian [who undoubtedly would see them as a result of a tradition of "Russian barbarism," which can be traced back for centuries—with implications for the war in Chechnya?]

Should we leave the historiography of the virtual annihilation of the American Indians...to a young Navaho historian [who would see the roots to this in the traditional "Americans love to kill"—with implications for My Lai?][162]

It's flabbergasting what perverse ideas are dreamt up in the studies of German professors, where, according to an ancient legend, one seeks the truth unperturbed, "sine ira et studio" ("with diligence and without anger"): the victims of history should not be allowed to write their own history? Armenians should be prevented from writing Turkish-Armenian history! American Indians from writing American history! Citizens of the former GDR—especially, if they were dissidents—from writing the history of the GDR, and so on. According to this notion, Goldhagen would be least qualified to write about the Holocaust, because it can be taken for granted that he's been brain-washed by a father who's been traumatized by the Holocaust. This supposed assault on the son's brain, has allegedly corroded the aforementioned son's common sense so badly that he's no longer capable of writing an "objective" study of the Holocaust. And by the same strange logic, one would have to draw the morbid conclusion that the history of Holocaust best be left to the Germans, where it would be in particularly good hands, for which German, who grew up after 1945, has been pestered with family anecdotes about the perpetration and connivance of his or her own parents and grand-parents? Anyone taking a quick survey among German friends and acquaintances will at best get geographical snippets of information about relatives during the Nazi period. He might hear for example: My father was in Russia. But what he did there, God only knows![163]

But we live after Freud, so we know that frequently untold stories are handed on from generation to generation in a more harmful way than stories that have been told. Aren't the untold stories haunting the heated emotions with which contemporary Germans either accept or reject Goldhagen's book?

The fact is that good history cannot get along without the "emotionalism," which is frowned upon by the German popes of history. "Black History," of which any American university of some standing has a chair, wouldn't even exist if deeply troubled American Blacks, like the Afro-American writer Alex

Haley would not have directed the spotlight on a deficit in American historiography with *Roots* (1996), the saga of his family, whom had been forcibly uprooted from Africa in order to provide slave labour for the cotton plantations of the New World. The same goes for "Palestinian History"; it wouldn't exist, if deeply troubled Palestinian scholars, like Edward Said, hadn't laid the foundation for it. with marvelous books, like *Orientalism* (1979), *The Question of Palestine* (1979), and *Blaming the Victims: Spurious Scholarship and the Palestinian Question* (1984).

If one looks at the historiography of the Holocaust, one would invariable come to the same conclusion. When in 1945 the dimensions of the destruction of the Jews became public knowledge, there was no German outcry. The loss of Jewish life in Germany could not evoke a process of mourning because the Germans had already demonstrated before that they were incapable of respecting, much less loving the Jews in their midst. Not even German historians were willing to deign German-Jewish history, anti-Semitism, and the persecution of the Jews significant enough to include them in the list of canonized topics worthy to be researched. Even today German historiography shirks away from an adequate analysis of the Holocaust, as can readily be seen, when one becomes aware of the inflationary use of the word "implementation" on the part of German chief historians. The excessive use of this word is a striking demonstration of how gas chambers and mass executions constitute a "stylistic" embarrassment for "professional historians" in Germany, who are used to dealing with "lofty" historical ideas. If it were left up to them, they would still be talking about "the German catastrophe,"[164] without ever becoming aware of the "Jewish catastrophe."[165]

The topic was also swept under the rug by the victors. Jewish survivors, whose odyssey ended in America, were advised there that it would be best for them to forget what lay behind them, the sooner the better. Americans for the most part were mainly obsessed with the Cold War against the Soviet Union. The war crimes trials against less prominent Nazi criminals were conducted in the wake of the Nuremberg Tribunal not so much to settle the score with the Germans, but rather to deal quickly with an obscene unfinished business in order to speed up reconstruction and to make West Germany an "honorable" member of the Western Alliance against the Communist threat. Even American Jews were not looking back to Auschwitz, but forward to Israel. And their fears were focused on the danger the Arabs posed for this new State.

In those days the historian Hans Rosenberg who, as a persecuted Jew had found a safe haven in the United States, remarked in passing during a lecture: "The atrocities committed by the French armies in Spain during the Napoleonic wars are unmatched in modern history." Nobody objected, except for an undergraduate by the name of Raul Hilberg.

> I raised my hand and asked: "What do you think about six million Jews that have been killed?" "Oh," Rosenberg replied, "that's an interesting problem," but that he had no time to go into it during the lecture because of the complexity of the subject. The whole incident lasted barely a minute and I thought that I had been very calm. Many years later a woman who had been in this lecture and who vividly remembered the exchange of words, told me that I had been very excited and that fellow students were quite concerned.[166]

If one would pay due attention to this very personal emotional factor in historiography, one would undoubtedly come to the conclusion that starting with *The History of the Peloponnesian War*, over Michelet's *History of the French Revolution*, down to Goldhagen's *Hitler's Willing Executioners*, deep emotional concern, if not disturbance, has always been the driving force, the innovative impetus. Hence, the frame of reference, the by no means value free polarization of private subjectivity (to be frowned upon), versus dispassionate scholarly objectivity (to be encouraged), within which experts discuss Goldhagen's book, is more of a hindrance than a real help in dealing with the aforementioned book or in dealing with each other. For isn't it Goldhagen's achievement that his book *Hitler's Willing Executioners* probes regions which, until this day, have neither been mastered intellectually, nor emotionally. Hasn't it been the intensity of his emotions which enabled Goldhagen to gather hitherto neglected data and to see these under a new perspective, from which an objective emotionally inhibited researcher would have shirked away?

This book, which allegedly hardly deserves all the attention it gets, poses once more the time honored question about the nature and the place of historiography. While Goldhagen and his German critics address each other merely as scholars, or while they try to dispute the opponent's scholarly credibility, history in its dual nature is speaking to us from the pages of *Hitler's Willing Executioners*. Yes, the historian is concerned with knowledge, and knowledge as such has to do with truth and error. Therefore, history can claim a place within the sciences. Yet, as a story telling component of literature it (along with gossip, fables, legends, fairy tales, travel descriptions, mystery novels and the like), belongs to a narrative genre, which has to do with fortune and misfortune. In this latter capacity the subject of history is not so much the truth, but rather the *modus vivendi* with the truth, which falls within the domain of art. The scientists aim is to infer covering laws from the world as it exists. For the artist, these laws are too constraining. He can only accept as a binding law what he creates each time anew in his work. For him the creative act counts for everything. As the Swiss playwright Friedrich Dürrenmatt says:

> I would like to stress that the art of writing a play doesn't necessarily start with the planning of a particular child, nor has it anything to do with love, as the eunuch imagines love to be, but rather with the act of love, which lies outside the capabilities of the eunuch.[167]

From this perspective there can be seen a relationship between the offended writer Goldhagen who writes in an offending way, and his book, which is comparable to the relationship between the artist and his work. The author of *Hitler's Willing Executioners* is the desperate combatant who, at the moment he is wounded, realizes that he's not engaged in a duel just for the fun of it but that this duel is a matter of life and death so that he throws away his dagger in order to thrash at his opponent with the next best stick. All the talk about the Holocaust, that endless discourse about when and why, which orders were given, and the Pavlovian image of man on which this discourse is based, he perceives as an affront. His book is a declaration of war, hurled at those scholarly dignitaries who are leaning back comfortably, taking all the space within this discourse, Goldhagen exclaims, adding: "I describe...the conventional interpretations and I prove all of them to be wrong."[168] He considers them to be wrong and irrelevant, because they give no, or only inadequate answers, as to why orders to kill Jews were obeyed. They are useless for him, advancing him not a step further. In his interpretation of why these orders were obeyed, he can only rely on his creative imagination, not on the prefabricated answers.

What he sees are bloody massacres in which the use of excessive violence and cruelty make it clear time and again that the established description of the Holocaust as mass murder conducted with dispassion is wrong. The blood curdling spectacle, which presents itself to his view, gives him good reason to say that those who are unwilling to take note of the gruesome details, will never be able to see the central mental factors which constituted the driving force. Within the ghastly details of the event can be seen the dimension of freedom and personal choice—in the case at hand, the personal choice to drop all inhibitions, giving free reign to the urge to torture and kill Jews.

Goldhagen's plausible thesis, which is by no means spectacular, is as follows: human beings are not only capable of choosing, more than that, they have to make a choice, each time they do something. Contrary to what Goldhagen's critics claim, this thesis does not by necessity presuppose a sovereign individual in the Kantian sense. As the legal expert Axel Azzola notes:

> The modest presumption of the possibility of being able to decide, from which penal law proceeds, suffices. According to this presumption an individual can be considered guilty, if he or she makes a decision, without external factors forcing him or her to commit the act, or if there are no compelling influences, which would significantly restrict his or her criminal responsibility.[169]

This is exactly what Goldhagen proves to have been the case of the perpetrators. It cannot be said that the gunmen of the Police Battalions shot defenseless women and children to death because they had to fear for their lives: because of irresistible external pressures, or because of a particular kind of psychic abnormality, as for instance blind belief in the Nazi doctrine, after having been brainwashed by the party and its agencies, or because of slavish obedience. This insight is the creative act in Goldhagen's historiography—creative, because he grapples directly with the sources in Ludwigsburg, without letting himself be unduly influenced by the authorized interpretations posited by a corpus of canonized works.

In other words, he doesn't close his eyes to what he sees. This is a childlike way of seeing, accompanied by fear and trembling, an act of great courage for those who have outgrown infancy, an ability, which established scholars who have to be concerned about their reputation, no longer can afford, as Michael Crichton so aptly shows in his science fiction novel *Jurassic Park*. Per chance the laboratory assistant Alice Levine sees the limb of a lizard, which has been sent in from Costa Rica, along with a child's drawing of the unidentified animal. She cries out spontaneously: "Oh, which child has drawn this dinosaurus?" For Richard Stone, specialist for tropical diseases, who has been assigned to identify the mysterious animal by analyzing the sent limb and the drawing, it is out of the question that the animal might be a dinosaurus, because we are living in the 20th century. According to scholarly opinion, dinosauria have become extinct towards the end of the Cretaceous period. Alice Levine, who doesn't have the vaguest notion of what the text books say, but who has a vivid imagination instead, sticks to her opinion: "To me this looks like a dinosaurus." Stone shakes his head.

> Alice responded: "Do you know Richard...if this really is a dinosaur, this could become a big thing."
> "But it isn't a dinosaur."
> "Has anyone already studied the matter?"
> "No," said Richard Stone.
> "Well, than you should take it to the Natural Museum or some place like that," Alice Levin suggested, "you really should!"
> "I'd be too embarrassed."
> "Should I do it for you?" she asked.
> "No," Richard Stone replied. "I don't want that."
> "So you're going to do nothing?"
> "Nothing at all!" He put the bag back into the refrigerator and slammed the door shut. "That's no dinosaur, it's a normal lizard...That's my last word, Alice. This lizard is going nowhere."[170]

Who doesn't recognize Danny Goldhagen in the person of Alice Levin or the notables of German historical scholarship in the scientist Richard Stone? Kept prisoner by recognized scholarly opinions, they have become hearsay literati, for whom secondary literature is, in the final analysis, of primary importance. Hans Mommsen, for instance: As countless books about the Holocaust maintain, was the destruction of the Jews a dispassionate implementation of genocide. From these books Mommsen knows with absolute certainty, that gassing, and beating, and shooting Jews to death was for the "cops" of the Police Battalions and for the Concentration Camp guards just any old job, which, according to his "common sense," they didn't particularly enjoy, on the contrary, which they inwardly disapprove of, while performing their job, beyond the call of duty. But regardless of what's written in all these books, there is plenty of evidence which documents an untold number of incidents of "excessive" violence and of incomparable acts of bestiality. To really address this issue, is, to the renowned Hans Mommsen, about as appealing as a thorough analysis of what may be the leg of a dinosaur to the highly regarded scientist Richard Stone. Although he has no certain proof, he categorically insists: "That's no dinosaur, it's a normal lizard." And although there's much speaking against it, Hans Mommsen maintains categorically: That was no lustfully conducted mass murder of Jews, but the bureaucratic perfection of the dispassionate "implementation" of the Holocaust. Instances of unspeakable cruelty and sadism, which one mentions to him, he twists and turns, until they fit into the picture—the picture, which is identical with the one conveyed by the canonized German Holocaust literature. They were, according to Mommsen, the result of "a mixture of getting used to brutality and cruelty, as well as of a forward charging mentality of men who had burnt all their bridges behind them."[171]

Not just a few "cops" of the Police Battalion 309 must have gotten used to dealing out cruelty in supersonic speed, or they must have burned all bridges behind them very early. Some members of the battalion, as Goldhagen tells us, had great fun, letting old Jews dance before them, and they set the beards of those on fire who couldn't keep up with the music. It is said that one "cop" opened his fly at the sight of some Jews who were on their knees in front of a German general, begging for mercy, and pissed on them. "Cops" of the first and third company are reported to have driven Jews with sticks and clubs into the main synagogue, which they then bolted shut and set on fire. It is reported that one of these "cops" found this particularly amusing, gleefully exclaiming:

"Let it burn, it's a nice little fire [schönes Feuerlein], it's great fun."[172] All this happened on the sixth day of the invasion of Russia. Bialystock, the place, where this occurred, had surrendered without a fight. It would be very difficult to use the theory about gradual brutalization by war or the "flight forward" mentality to explain this blood bath.[173] Goldhagen is right: the massacre, which in its brutality went far beyond what had been ordered from above, was "implemented" by these German butchers with such gusto because they enjoyed killing and torturing Jews. Noteworthy is that the sadistic treatment was only inflicted on Jews. The wounded Usbekian soldiers in the city hospital didn't interest the German policemen in the least, they were too busy liquidating Jewish patients.

Why was Goldhagen able to recognize this lustful wanton murder instantly for what it was and what enabled him to depict the mentality of the perpetrators? And why are Mommsen, Wehler, and Jäckel so dense? I doubt that this has to do with intelligence—that the Harvard scholar is smarter and that the scholars from Bochum, Bielefeld, and Stuttgart are dumber than he is. Neither can it have anything to do with the fact that they are adherents of "structuralism," "functionalism," or of the "historical social science" school, while the American adversary is a graduate of the "intentionalist" school. For truthful, living history is neither the child of pure intellect, nor the result of completed training in a certain school. For the genesis of a poem which appeals to us, it will not suffice to send just any clever lad into a school for poetry, where hard and fast rules of diction and alliteration and regulations for scanning an ode or a sonnet are funneled into his head. Our managers of culture may think that that's how it works, as did the upright city councillors, guild wardens, and town clerks of some 17th centrury literary society (cf. Philipp Harsdörfer, *Poetischer Trichter, die Teutsche Dicht- und Reimkunst, ohne Behuf der lat. Sprache in 6 Stunden einzuflößen*).

Unfortunately, or should I say fortunately, works of art cannot be pre-programmed in such a way. And no "promising young scholar" will become a historian overnight if, after having memorized the master Wehler's instructional booklet *Historische Sozialwissenschaft*, he strictly applies the rules. More is needed. In the words of the great historian Golo Mann:

> To be precise, one cannot throw oneself into history as an inexperienced person....What's needed is above all a rich casuistry taught by life. That's why a beginner will, as a rule, proceed in history in a more naive, more awkward, and therefore also more doctrinaire way than would an older, more experienced scholar. In mathematics this is different. There life experience is of no relevance at all.[174]

Daniel Jonah Goldhagen's study *Hitler's Willing Executioners* verifies the soundness of this observation in a peculiar way. The young Harvard scholar presents his arguments in a dogmatic way. The critics are not amused, because he doesn't take their feelings into consideration. They point out that he doesn't stick to any of the stock in trade interpretations. Quite to the contrary, he is going out of his way to pick a fight with just about anybody who has acquired a reputation in the study of the Holocaust.

The latter, the maverick historian Julius H. Schoeps notes, is the greatest weakness of the book, but as paradoxical as it may sound, also its strength. This, according to him, compels the reader to grapple with Goldhagen's arguments—who, in any case, is not wrong in claiming that eliminatory anti-Semitism had a long tradition in Christian Europe. Undoubtedly the image of the Jew, cultivated by the Church had a lot to do with the attitudes and politics under which Jews had to suffer. The enemies of the Jews were for the most part good Christians and it wouldn't have occurred to them that their attitude towards the Jews was not quite right. Quite the opposite was true, when attacking the Jews they believed themselves to be in the right.[175]

The paradox is that we have in Goldhagen a young scholar who is doctrinaire, but who wrote nonetheless a far better book than is written by many an older and therefore more experienced scholar. The other side of the coin is that in Mommsen, Wehler, and Jäckel we have elderly experts with many years of experience, who—as Paul K. Feyerabend would say—

> ...have to preserve a reputation, so that in consequence thereof they tend to confuse natural knowledge with spiritual rigor mortis. With mistrust they regard any effort to limber up scholarship or any attempt to show that real science (not to be confused with academic science) is

an intellectual adventure, which cannot be kept under the lid, defying all rules—even the rules of logic.[176]

It may seem as if this contradicts Golo Mann's understanding of the maturing of the historian. In reality it substantiates what he says and raises questions about the socialization within the German academic community. The community constitutes a bureaucratized system within which the tenured members enjoy the status and security of civil servants. This makes them weary of innovative change. The system postpones real independence of teaching and research up till the scholar has reached a ripe middle age. Till then tenured professors have the say. They have the power to define the grand lines of research. Thus they control the discourse and define the meaning of concepts. Someone who works his way up through this prolonged immaturity, cannot gather life experience and apply it. It is discouraged by the system, which keeps junior members under guardianship and rewards subservience, getting in step, and fitting in. It's not surprising that German academic law enforcement officers respond with incomprehension to a self-confident young scholar like Daniel Goldhagen and that they want to make him tow the line, the way they once had to tow it. But an "enfant terrible," like the young Harvard scholar needs plenty of room—room which these "rulers of the roost" claim as their own territory and which hitherto was granted to them without any objection. However, new ways of seeing things cannot be found by following the trodden path of time honored routines, but by fresh thoughts which cannot bear being crowded in. They need serious consideration, even if presented in a doctrinaire way and seem bizarre at first.

One more thing is required for the writing of anything good, be it literature or history: the topic must be the right one. It must strike an inner chord within the poet or historian. The selection is, therefore, not only determined by the consideration that this or that topic may be interesting and well suited for a novel, poem, or work of history, but also—if not above all—by how this topic touches the author. The German poet and novelist Theodor Storm says this in an apt way:

> The artist should not willfully choose his topic, the topic should present itself to him by itself; the topic has to choose the artist. If it is the right

one, the particular form of presentation will match up by itself with content of universal meaning.[177]

Couldn't it be said in the case of the controversial book *Hitler's Willing Executioners* that the topic chose the author? It must have pursued Daniel Jonah Goldhagen, the son of the survivor Erich Goldhagen, from the time he was a child. And I venture to say that he succeeded, because his work on the topic was catalyzed by inner involvement.

German historians are pursued by the topic no less, but when they try to confront it, they wear blinders. Especially an older generation of historians in Germany, which still has not stepped down, is incapable of looking squarely into the face of the parent generation. Hans Mommsen says he has a great deal of respect for younger members of the profession who muster the "toughness" "to write with unbuffered realism about the Nazi crimes." He himself does not feel the urge to do this. That's his business, but what's so disturbing is that he would like to ban this "unbuffered realism" from academic history. He claims it is dangerous, fearing that it will "brutalize" the reading public. He warns against opening "Pandora's box."[178]

The lid would already open a crack if German historians would only realize that the perpetrators, which Goldhagen scrutinizes, didn't consist of schematic performers of functions at the highest, the intermediary, and the local level, conditioned like Pavlov's dogs, drooling before the things that were good for them, too inhibited to take hold of them, yet ready to tear a victim to pieces at the sound of a bell. Yet these were their parents or grandparents or at least human beings close to one or the other of them—people, like the *pater familias* Wilhelm Mommsen. His son Hans sharply rejects Goldhagen's charge that the German middle class was a bastion of anti-Semitism. Turning red in the face, he counters:

> Quite honestly, I come from a family where this is not true. It just isn't true that the German middle class was anti-Semitic through and through.[179]

Be this as it may, father Wilhelm Mommsen was an anti-Semite. With reference to the highly respected anti-Semitic historian Heinrich von Treitschke, he participated already in 1930 in the character assassination of the popular biographer Emil Ludwig, whose original name was Emil Cohn.[180] Karl Marx was for Wilhelm Mommsen "a typical representative of Jewish intellectualism," and he held Richard Wagner in high esteem, because this composer was, as he points out, "one of the first" to see "in the Jewish question not just a confessional problem, but a racial one."[181] True, true, son Hans cannot be blamed for the abominable nonsense, his father wrote, but it is highly embarrassing to see him throw a German middle class family, like his own into the scales against Goldhagen.

No less embarrassing is how German academic history reveres its spiritual fathers—mentors like Gerhard Ritter (1888-1967), Theodor Schieder (1908-1984), and Werner Conze (1910-1986)—who after their academic start in the Third Reich acquired honor and dignity in the Federal Republic. They became the founding fathers of West German modern contemporary and social history. It is impossible to think of historical writing in the Federal Republic of Germany without thinking of them. They provided the basic historical concepts and methods. Martin Broszat, Hans and Wolfgang Mommsen, Hans-Ulrich Wehler, and Eberhard Jäckel, to name a few, were trained by them. Up till now, not one of these students has mustered the courage to look his *Doktorvater* straight in the face. In a eulogy to his mentor Theodor Schieder, Hans-Ulrich Wehler beats around the bush when he has to mention his professor's Nazi writings. He wants to see in them an example of "a tested constitutional stance and the cultural tradition of a civilized European nation," which supposedly differs like night and day from the "Lebensraum expansionism of the brown rulers."[182] And in his tearing down *Hitler's Willing Executioners*, he refers to the "Generalplan Ost"[183] in order to show that Goldhagen doesn't know what he's talking about and that in reality everything was much worse, but when it comes to naming the author of the first draft of this devious plan, Wehler is rather tight-lipped.

This author was none other than Wehler's *Doktorvater* Theodor Schieder. In 1939 he wrote on behalf of the "nordeutsche Forschungsgemeinschaft" the rough draft, cf. Angelika Ebbinghaus and Karl Heinz Roth, "Vorläufer des 'Generalplan Ost': Eine Dokumentation über Theodor Schieders Polenschrift vom 7. Oktober 1939," ("Precursors of the 'Generalplan Ost': A Documentation of Theodor Schieder's Poland Memorandum of October 7, 1939").[184]

Whoever mentions such embarrassing trivialities will not only be ostracized by the "horn-skinned Siegfrieds," but will also have to suffer the wrath of their horse valets and shield-bearers, as for example the wrath of Professor Dipper from Darmstadt. He chastises the impertinent maverick Götz Aly for having broken the unwritten code of silence and lectures him:

> Of course, like any other historical document, Schieder's memorandum needs to be interpreted. But to pick up the fine nuances and to listen to what's behind the camouflage language, is not Aly's strength... He lacks hermeneutic expertise and has not enough background in the sociology of knowledge and history of science to enable him to understand such a difficult text adequately.[185]

This school-teacherlike reprimand, alluding to some kind of camouflage language in the Nazi writings of the closet resistance fighter Theodor Schieder, appears to me to be camouflage language itself. It fails to impress Götz Aly, who responds with cutting humor:

> What kind of hermeneutic talents are needed to interpret...Schieder's memorandum of October 7, 1939, in which he calls "for the extraction of the Jewish elements out of Polish cities?" What kind of sociology of knowledge must the analyst be familiar with, in order to decode the "camouflage" language, which on the surface recommends major ethnic cleansing in the annexed parts of Western Poland? And what kind of hearing aid does one need to pick up the fine nuances in a 1936 travel report, in which Schieder informs the German Foreign Ministry, of how "Jewish emigrants from Germany make an unfavorable impression in Estonian sea resorts?" What history of science does one need to study, in order to interpret *lege artis* the fact that Schieder gave in March 1945 a pep talk to young cadets at the SS cadre school at Sonthofen, encouraging them "to fight to the last bullet? By obeying Schieder many a young man went into certain death. A few months later Professor Schieder, who had been unfit for military service (Civilian Replacement Reserve, Class II) wrote plaintive letters to influential

acquaintances, begging them to provide him with character references for his denazification proceedings. (In German slang these dubious references were called "Persilschein" in analogy to the brand name "Persil" of a popular laundry detergent.)

Summing up the shilly-shallying the German high priests of Clio and their altar boys resort to when they have to deal with their biological and spiritual fathers, is the continuation of an age-old story—the story about Noah's hangover, and about the politically correct way in which members of the Noah Business Enterprise dealt with the bosses embarrassing condition. Noah, drunk as a lord, was lying stark-naked in his own vomit, recuperating from a wild night of carousing, when his son Ham (who, incidentally, never had any luck in the Noah Enterprises) entered the tent. Struck by the undignified scene, he turned on his heels to tell his brothers Shem and Japhet what he had seen.

And Shem and Japhet took a garment, and laid it upon both their shoulders, and went backward and covered the nakedness of their father; and their faces were backward, and they saw not their father's nakedness. (1. Genesis 9:20-23)

What is so disgusting in this story is that biological and spiritual children present this looking away, not only to others, but also to themselves, as the love we owe to our parents thereby counterfeiting the very notion of love, for love for one's father and mother cannot be real love if we close our eyes to their guilt. It's the other way around, real love also calls for the courage to see the faults in one's parents so that one may grapple with these blemishes. Once more in the words of Golo Mann: The obsession of German academic history to play "Hamlet" without the Prince of Denmark, has to do with a lack of love.

No one should be surprised by the cold and distanced impersonal relationships within the German historical profession. How warped must have been the relationship between Mommsen, Jäckel, and Wehler, today the deans of history in Germany, on the one hand, and mentors, like Theodor Schieder and Werner Conze, on the other, or between mentors, like Mommsen, Jäckel, and Wehler on the one side, and disciples, like Dipper on the other, when they concealed their true identity from each other, thus not talking with, but to and past one another!

Why has no one rebelled against this phoniness? I understand quite well that it could have become rather touchy for the parties involved to talk with each other in intimate terms if they would have asked each other about familial involvement in National Socialism. More to the point, such familiarity might have endangered careers. It's one of the facts of life that doctoral students are dependent upon their *Doktorvater*—and they don't make themselves particularly popular if they ask him embarrassing questions. But that's the name of the game! Knowledge has its price, sometimes one has to pay with one's career.

The passion of the hunter who's willing to pay this price, runs like a red thread through the life and work of Ernest Hemingway. In an episode of the movie "The Snows of Kilimanjaro" the popular writer by the name of Harry tries to impress his conversation partner by telling him about his exciting life as a member of the fashionable set in Paris, on the Côte d' Azur, and in Switzerland. This just bores the listener and he responds with a tired smile: "But have you ever hunted?"

Mommsen, Jäckel, and Wehler have never gone hunting. They are no hunters; what they lack is the hunting instinct and hunting fever. The Goldhagen debate has made this so very apparent. An abyss opens up and alliances take shape, which would make no sense if one were to remain fixated on what's politically correct: on the one side of this unbreachable abyss stands the Jewish "Gold-Hagen," on the other the "horn skinned Siegfried." The champions of liberal historiography in the Federal Republic were the ones who initiated the collective howl against the disturbing Jewish "Gold-Hagen." It's not surprising that they allied themselves in this effort with those who always collected apologetic arguments for the fatherland. Jürgen Habermas misinterprets what's happening, misses the point altogether, when in a speech in honor of Goldhagen he acts as if the German controversy over the book *Hitler's Willing Executioners* were just another one of those quarrels between the Left and the Right that happen from time to time, pontificating that the controversial book "gave rise for concern among the conservatives."[186] Not the conservatives, but the three leading liberal historians of Germany spearheaded the charge against Goldhagen. Ernst Nolte, Michael Stürmer, and Rainer Zitelmann, the neo-conservative "gang of three" which have been working for some time now on a more positive picture of the Third Reich have maintained a rather puzzling silence in regard to Goldhagen's book. And the German leftist historian Wolfgang Wippermann who has provided the first book-length study on the Goldhagen controversy, also just beats around the bush when he speculates that the strong rejection of Goldhagen's book in Germany has to do with the fact that it constitutes a frontal attack against structural history.[187] Whoever has taken the time to pluck apart the arguments of the three most renowned German historians of today, as has been done here, cannot help but see that the three have reacted first and foremost to the controversial book as Germans, not as professional historians.

As such they can order their feeling of being German to leave the room, but eventually this feeling will come back in through the window, demanding its right. As the German poet Goethe says:

*Bist alsobald und fort und fort gediehen,*
*Nach dem Gesetz, wonach du angetreten.*
*So mußt du sein, dir kannst du nicht entfliehen...*

("Urworte, Orphisch")[188]

Stories have to do with name and origin. In the story, which has evoked such a heated controversy, Daniel Goldhagen is the son of the Jewish survivor Erich Goldhagen, while Hans Mommsen, Hans-Ulrich Wehler, and Eberhard Jäckel are the biological or spiritual sons of fathers like Wilhelm Mommsen, Theodor Schieder, and Gerhard Ritter. The first of these fathers hailed the "new Reich of Adolf Hitler," the second provided Hitler with a memorandum which served as a rough draft for the Führer's notorious "Generalplan Ost," while the third took such care not to observe the Nazi guidelines, keeping his anti-Nazi views so secret that he shouldn't have been surprised when the Gestapo decided to make good use of him in foreign propaganda.[189] The abyss in-between, which we wish didn't exist, is the most difficult communication gap to bridge in this controversy.

That this abyss exists and that one deals on this side and on that side in different ways with the past, is alluded to cryptically by some German historians. Wolfgang Wippermann, for example, notes: "It's quite clear: no German historian writes so emphatic as Goldhagen does!"[190] But to elaborate at length upon this phenomenon is painstakingly avoided on the German side. Dan Diner from Tel Aviv, in contrast, tries to identify the problem by associating it with different schools and methods, speculating that among Jews there are more "intentionalists" and among the Germans more "structuralists!" And that the former bring up the question of guilt, exerting a lot of energy on tying the singularity of the Holocaust to German history.[191] Whether one can let this stand as it is, is another question. But what is certain is that Israeli historians in particular point to the explanatory deficits of structural history, as it is certain that German historians have sadly neglected to do research on anti-Semitism and anti-Semitic politics between 1933 and 1945. It is noteworthy that knowledge in this area has been advanced for the most part by non-German social scientists.[192]

The real difference separating Goldhagen and the German historians is not a matter of methodology at all. Something deeper, more basic even than methodology puts the German historians at odds with Goldhagen. The "intentionalist" Daniel Jonah Goldhagen has much more in common with the "structuralist" Raul Hilberg than with the "intentionalist" Eberhard Jäckel. The same question that bothers Goldhagen, the question of "why did they obey orders?" also bothered Raul Hilberg when towards the end of World War II he saw action in Germany.

In April 1945 his unit was deployed somewhere in Bavaria. During the night the Germans had tried with inferior forces to capture the American position. They were mowed down by volleys of machine gun fire. "What, I asked myself," Hilberg writes, "motivated these men, at this late stage of the war, to run into almost certain death?" He answers this question for himself with the following contemplation:

> When these men commenced their suicidal attack, with screaming officers driving them on, they demonstrated the sturdiness of the system—but why had they obeyed orders? Why had they not rebelled?[193]

It is quite possible that Hilberg and Goldhagen are not in total agreement on what is the answer to this question. Both do, however, agree that the Holocaust was not a "perfect improvisation" but a national project to which the Germans applied themselves with a sense of mission and with the utmost energy. It is very unlikely that most Jews would seriously disagree with this point of view. The Jewish community here in Germany was outraged that renowned German historians chastised Goldhagen in such a flabergastingly arrogant way.[194] And in Israel, as Moshe Zimmermann notes, Goldhagen's book was nothing special, because the author's interpretation of the Holocaust coincided with the conception which the man on the street in Israel has in regard to this topic.[195]

As far as the German way of dealing with the Nazi past is concerned, Dan Diner may be right when he notes that German historians are leaning more towards "structuralism" and that they "are not so much concerned about guilt, seeking explanations instead."[196] But here, too, membership in a particular school is not of prime importance. What brings them together is a diffuse feeling. That Mommsen, Wehler, and Jäckel cling to each other, has to do with the denial of guilt. Jäckel is not a "structuralist," but a Hitler biographer. He expounds the theory that Hitler alone was driven by the explicit desire to kill all Jews and that in essence only he is guilty. This narrows down the question of guilt to only one evil person and absolves the "ordinary Germans." Mommsen and Wehler, on the other hand, are not interested in the question of guilt: as "professional" historians of the "functionalist" or "structuralist" schools, they just want to "explain." As Bracher noted in the mid seventies, they'd rather "brush aside the question of guilt and responsibility."

Therefore it is not surprising that Mommsen, Jäckel, and Wehler find themselves in the same boat with Arnulf Barring, Ernst Nolte, Rainer Zitelmann, and other apologists. Contrary to what's been said, Goldhagen's book doesn't rehash the collective guilt thesis, but it talks about German guilt, about the personal responsibility of the perpetrators. That touches "existential dimensions" in the history which Mommsen, Jäckel, and Wehler seem to regard as their personal property. Not under any circumstance do they want to address the questions Goldhagen's book addresses. That would only disturb them while explaining that the Holocaust consisted of a series of "perfect improvisations," leading to a "cumulative radicalization."

It is precisely their exaggerated academization of historiography, their denial that Clio, the daughter of Mnemosyne, as well as her sisters, the other muses, are charged with the task of "resolving" joy and sorrow. This is the real reason that when confronted with a book like *Hitler's Willing Executioners*, they find themselves in the company of those who have always searched for arguments to exculpate the fatherland. Their scholarly explanations, void of any personal involvement, give forbearance to the derealization of the past, stripping it of its consequences, making it morally unreal.

It might well be asked whether historiography, which just wants to "explain," still deserves to be called history. For as Hayden White recalls, "narrative history" has to do with the subject areas of law, legality, and legitimacy, in short with authority.[197] Who could deny that the Holocaust violated law, legality, and legitimacy? To explain it as the product of some kind of "cumulative radicalization," without passing moral judgment, throws Holocaust studies back beyond the fifties into the Middle Ages, where diligent scribes registered, with the same dispassion, the raids of the Saracens in the year 725, as they registered the rich harvest of the year 722. In their *Annales Sangallenses Maiores* one finds no indication that the raids of the Saracens constituted a transgression that should not have happened. Since everything that happened was seen by the monks as an event that was in accordance with the will of God, it seemed to suffice for them to just take note of it. In a similar way it suffices for the German "structuralists" to just "explain" that the Holocaust happened in accordance with the processes of "cumulative radicalization."

There's another compelling reason for asking whether it is legitimate, or even possible, for the historian to just analyze the past the same scientific way one would analyze a synthetic fiber to which one has no emotional relationship. For what has happened is not history in and by itself. It becomes history in the light of our interest in letting these past events tell us who we are, so that we still can recognize ourselves in the temporal processes of change within ourselves and within the world to which we are connected through what we do and what we suffer. This is a prerequisite for remaining true to oneself.[198]

If we really do want to ask the past who we are—for what else can we do, if we don't want to let ourselves be made into pale, colorless statistical figures, without any personal qualities who are determined by outside forces—then the Germans, as well as I, the son of German parents, have to realize that we are the children of those willing executioners, or at least the children of a society that has brought forth these executioners, as Daniel Johah Goldhagen has to realize that he is one of the children of those to whom our society categorically denied the right to live. Acting as if the gap between these two groups of different, and yet the same origin can be bridged with ease, or to pretend that this gap no longer existed, we just fool ourselves.

If the preoccupation with history is not only a search for the "pure" truth which leads to nothing, or the gathering of data to bolster whatever political correctness, but rather a dialogue with the past which brings the historian in conflict with himself and with others, then we see that beneath the failed dialogue that has been analyzed here, there looms an abyss. The "professional historian" can suppress his identity and talk across this abyss, moreover by his manner of speaking he can make himself forget that this abyss still exists; it continues to exist nonetheless and won't disappear. If Germans and Jews want to talk sincerely with each other, then they come dangerously close to the edge of this abyss. That on either side the speakers shirk back, is understandable. Yet, Germans and Jews remain chained to each other across the historical gap, so that with any attempt to flee, the chains cut deeper into the flesh. Who can stand this? In the words of the German-Israeli historian Michael Wolfsohn who has to resolve this conflict within himself: "Are there no bridges across this historical abyss? The abyss will remain, but bridges have to be built. How? It's our task to find out."[199]

Becoming aware that the task at hand in the present context is "to transform historiography in such a way that it will explicitly allow the historian to participate in liberating the present from the past"[200] would be a step in the right direction. Feelings, will, and intellect, three dimensions of equal value in historical culture, must compliment each other and mingle with one another in order to make possible historical memory.[201] For it isn't the way academic history tried to make us believe, historical knowledge is not just cognitive knowledge. History resists being reduced to the language of numbers and graphs, because it has to do with the secret life of death. It suffices not, if the historian only sees himself as an unbiased expert, he is also a descendant, and he violates the responsibility he has as a researcher, if—like the German deans of contemporary history—he thinks that it is enough to gather data with diligence and without anger. As Michelet would have said it: We owe respect to the dead, a casual greeting just won't do. It is the duty of the historian to accompany them back to the grave and there to separate them from the living, so that their shadows will make peace with each other, allowing the urns with their ashes to be closed.

Whether the ambivalence in the word "we" can eventually be resolved, will, in the final analysis, depend upon compliance with the historians duty, as outlined above. Only if this possibility exists, can Daniel Jonah Goldhagen, the son of a survivor from the Bukowina, and the author of this book, son of parents from Bessarabia, who had complied with the call "to come home into the fatherland," talk with each other without any inhibitions.

*Prientene Daniel, fiul tatalui din Bucovina, eu te salut ca fiu al parintilor germani din Basarabia—daca asa ar fi dorit norocul—care ca vecin ar fi trebuit sa fiu.*

## NOTES

1. Heinrich Böll, "Brief an einen jungen Nichtkatholiken" (1966), in *Aufsätze, Kritiken, Reden* (Cologne: Kiepenheuer & Witsch, 1967), p. 237.
2. Daniel Jonah Goldhagen, *Hitler's Willing Executioners: Ordinary Germans and the Holocaust* (New York: Alfred A. Knopf, 1996).
3. Cf. Rüdiger Suchsland, "Erkenntnis ohne Interesse? Der 41. Historikertag in München," *Frankfurter Rundschau*, 23 Sept. 1996.
4. Cf. Michael Jeismann, "Gegenverkehr—Anthropologische Wende: Der 41. Historikertag in München," *Frankfurter Allgemeine Zeitung*, 23 Sept. 1996.
5. Hans Mommsen, "Die dünne Patina der Zivilisation," *Die Zeit*, 30 Aug. 1996, p. 15.
6. Y. Michal Bodemann, "Die Bösen und die ganz normalen Guten," *die tageszeitung*, 7 Aug. 1996, p. 18.
7. Ulrich Raulff, "'Herz der Finsternis'—Daniel Jonah Goldhagen's Ästhetik des Grauens," *Frankfurter Allgemeine Zeitung*, 16 Aug. 1996, p. 27.
8. Raul Hilberg, *Unerbetene Erinnerung: Der Weg eines Holocaust-Forschers*, übers. Von Hans Günter Holl (Frankfurt am Main: Fischer, 1994), p. 114.
9. Hilberg, *Erinnerung*, p. 114.
10. Raul Hilberg, *Sonderzüge nach Auschwitz*, trans. Gisela Schleicher (Frankfurt am Main: Ulstein, 1987), p. 56.
11. Golo Mann, "Plädoyer für die historische Erzählung" (1979), in *Wissen und Trauer: Historische Portraits und Skizzen* (Leipzig: Reclam, 1991), p. 241.
12. Cf. Martin Buchholz, "Goldhagen ist an allem Schuld," *Neues Deutschland*, 24 Sept. 1996.
13. Mommsen, "Die dünne Patina," p. 14-15.
14. Victor Klemperer, *LTI: Notizbuch eines Philologen*, 14th ed. (1957; Leipzig: Reclam, 1996), p. 16.
15. Mommsen, "Die dünne Patina," p. 15.
16. Cf. Volker Ullrich, "Goldhagen und die Deutschen," *Die Zeit*, 13 Sept. 1996, p. 2.
17. Michael Kuball, *Familienkino: Geschichte des Amateurfilms in Deutschland* (Reinbek bei Hamburg: Rowohlt Taschenbuch Verlag, 1980), II, 117.
18. Goldhagen, *Hitler's Willing Executioners*, p. 405-407.
19. Friedrich Kahlenberg (President of the German Federal Archives in Koblenz), "Die Bilder sind echt: Das Bundesarchiv in Koblenz widerspricht Zweiflern," *Die Zeit*, 29 Sept. 1996, p. 10.
20. Goldhagen, *Hitler's Willing Executioners*, p. 6.
21. Hilberg, *Sonderzüge*, p. 20.

22. Goldhagen, *Hitler's Willing Executioners*, p. 6 and p. 544, note 100.
23. Lothar Gall, talking about Goldhagen's book, in "Worte der Woche," *Die Zeit*, 27 Sept. 1996, p. 2.
24. Meant is the episode in Act 4, Scene 7: A close-knit group of officers in the army of the Imperial Generalissimo Albrecht von Wallenstein, conspires to overthrow and kill their commander. At a banquet, arranged by them to win over non-committed brother officers, they pass around a rather vaguely worded petition, which anybody could sign. After the guests are roaring drunk, an altered version is passed around for signature. Tiefenbach who is still sober enough, notices the foul play and objects: "Vor Tische las man's anders," meaning, "before diner the wording was different!
25. Lothar Gall, *Bürgertum in Deutschland* (Berlin: Siedler, 1989).
26. Martin Broszat, "Plädoyer für eine Historisierung des Nationalsozialismus," *Merkur*, 435 (May 1985), 373-385.
27. Heinz Höhne, "Schwarzer Freitag für die Historiker—'Holocaust': Fiktion und Wirklichkkeit," *Der Spiegel*, 29 Jan. 1979, p. 23.
28. Martin Broszat, "'Holocaust' und die Geschichtswissenschaft," *Vierteljahreshefte für Zeitgeschichte*, 27 (1979), S. 296.
29. Cf. Martin Broszat and Saul Friedländer, [exchange of letters]: "A Controversy about the Historicization of National Socialism," *Yad Vashem Studies*, 19 (1988), 1-47.
30. Karl Dietrich Bracher, *Zeitgeschichtliche Kontroversen—um Faschismus, Totalitarismus, Demokratie* (Munich: Piper, 1976), p. 672.
31. Raulff, *"Herz der Finsternis,"* p. 27.
32. Ebbo Demant, "'Machen Sie fertig den Galgen für 12 Mann': Interviews mit den früheren KZ-Bewachern Kaduk, Erber und Klehr," *Der Spiegel*, 29 Jan. 1979, p. 29-34; extract from Ebbo Demant, *Auschwitz—"Direkt von der Rampe weg..."* (Reinbek bei Hamburg: Rowohlt Taschenbuch Verlag, 1979).
33. Friedrich Schiller, "Der Verbrecher aus verlorener Ehre—eine wahre Geschichte," in *Schillers Werke: Nationalausgabe* (Weimar: Hermann Böhlau, 1954), XVI, 7-27.
34. Schiller, "Verbrecher," p. 8.
35. Peter Schneider, *Deutsche Ängste: Sechs Essays*, Sammlung Luchterhand 782 (Darmstadt: Luchterhand, 1988), S. 91.
36. The German historian Götz Aly, whose stance towards Goldhagen switched with the public mood from patronizing praise to sarcastic rejection, illustrates the point. He writes: "My research concentrates, like that of Hans Mommsen and Raul Hilberg, on the many-sided structures of power in the Third Reich—Goldhagen has, at best, only a vague notion about these. Seen subjectively my approach creates distance, making it possible, when browsing through stacks of documents, to simply skip over or to read just very selectively all that, which Goldhagen painstakingly describes in his book *Hit-*

ler's *Willing Executioners*. I resort to this distanciating approach not for the sake of academic 'seriousness,' but for reasons, having to do with self-protection." Cf. Götz Aly, rev. of *Hitler's Willing Executioners* by Daniel J. Goldhagen, *Mittelweg 36*, 6 (1996), 46-49.

37. Rudolf Augstein, "Der Soziologe als Scharfrichter," in *Ein Volk von Mördern? Die Dokumentation zur Goldhagen-Kontroverse um die Rolle der Deutschen im Holocaust*, ed. Julius H. Schoeps (Hamburg: Hoffmann und Campe, 1996), p. 194.

38. Hans-Ulrich Wehler, "Wie ein Stachel im Fleisch," in *Ein Volk von Mördern?* ed. J. H. Schoeps, p. 194.

39. Mommsen, "Die dünne Patina," p. 15.

40. Alexander and Margarete Mitscherlich, *Die Unfähigkeit zu trauern: Grundlagen kollektiven Verhaltens*, Serie Piper, 168 (Munich: Piper, 1977), p. 126.

41. Eberhard Jäckel, "Einfach ein schlechtes Buch," in *Ein Volk von Mördern?* ed. J: H. Schoeps, p. 187.

42. Jürgen Habermas, *Eine Art Schadenabwicklung*, edition suhrkamp, 1453 (Frankfurt am Main: Suhrkamp, 1987), p. 141.

43. Christopher R. Browning, *Ganz normale Männer: Das Reserve-Polizeibataillon 101 und die "Endlösung" in Polen*, trans. Peter Krause (Reinbek bei Hamburg: Rowohlt, 1993), p 224.

44. Jäckel, "Ein schlechtes Buch," p. 189.

45. Sat 1 TV Station, 28.4.1996.

46. Wehler, "Stachel im Fleisch," p. 199-200.

47. Raul Hilberg, *Die Vernichtung der europäischen Juden*, trans. Christian Seeger, Harry Maor, Walle Bengs, and Wilfried Szepan (Frankfurt am Main: Fischer Taschenbuch Verlag, 1990), III, 1080.

48. Hilberg, *Die Vernichtung*, III, 1119-1121.

49. Cit. from Hilberg, *Erinnerung*, p. 109.

50. Hilberg, *Erinnerung*, p. 76.

51. Jäckel, "Ein schlechtes Buch," S. 191.

52. Wehler, "Stachel im Fleisch," p. 200.

53. Marc Fisher, *After the Wall: Germany, the Germans and the Burdens of History* (New York: Simon & Schuster; 1995), p 28.

54. Daniel Jonah Goldhagen, "Vorwort zur deutschen Ausgabe," in *Hitlers Vollstrecker*, p. 6-7.

55. Goldhagen, *Hitler's Willing Executioners*, p. 11-12.

56. Goldhagen, *Hitler's Willing Executioners*, p. 13.

57. Cf. Clifford Geertz, *Dichte Beschreibung: Beiträge zum Verstehen kultureller Systeme*, trans. Brigitte Luchesi and Rolf Bindemann, suhrkamp taschenbuch wissenschaft, 696 (Frankfurt am Main: Suhrkamp, 1983), p. 34-41.

58. Heinrich Steitz, "Juden in Petterweil," *Friedberger Geschichtsblätter: Beiträge zur Geschichte und Landeskunde der Wetterau*, 15 (1940), 76-83.

59. Goldhagen, *Hitlers Vollstrecker*, p. 11.

60. Goldhagen, *Hitlers Vollstrecker*, p. 6.

61. Hans-Friedrich Lenz, *"Sagen Sie, Herr Pfarrer, wie kommen Sie zur SS?" Bericht eines Pfarrers der Bekennenden Kirche über seine Erlebnisse im Kirchenkampf und als SS-Oberscharführer im Konzentrationslager Hersbrück* (Giessen: Brunnen Verlag, 1982), p. 15.

62. Goldhagen, *Hitlers Vollstrecker*, p. 16.

63. In the *Nibelungenlied* Siegfried acquired an invulnerable horny skin by bathing in the blood of the dragon. These modern day Siegfrieds have a thick skin which protects them against the memory of the past.

64. Cited according to Volker Ullrich, "Goldhagen und die Deutschen," *Die Zeit*, 13 Sept. 1996, p. 2.

65. Ullrich, "Goldhagen und die Deutschen," p. 2.

66. Ullrich, "Goldhagen und die Deutschen," p. 2. [Mommsen indirectly quoted. The last sentence in quotation marks is a direct Mommsen citation.]

67. Christopher R. Browning, *Ganz normale Männer: Das Reserve-Polizeibataillon 101 und die "Endlösung" in Polen*, trans. Jürgen Peter Krause (Reinbek bei Hamburg: Rowohlt, 1993), p. 209.

68. Cf. Jürgen Habermas, *Zur Logik der Sozialwissenschaften*, suhrkamp taschenbuch wissenschaft, 517 (Frankfurt am Main: Suhrkamp Taschenbuch Verlag, 1982), p. 157-183.

69. Daniel Jonah Goldhagen, "Das Versagen der Kritiker," *Die Zeit*, 2. Aug. 1996, S. 13.

70. Hans Mommsen, "Aufarbeitung und Verdrängung: Das Dritte Reich im westdeutschen Geschichtsbewußtsein," in *Ist der Nationalsozialismus Geschichte? Zu Historisierung und Historikerstreit*, ed. Dan Diner (Frankfurt am Main: Fischer Taschenbuch Verlag, 1987), p. 85.

71. Cf. Heinz Bude, *Deutsche Karrieren: Lebenskonstruktionen sozialer Aufsteiger aus der Flakhelfer-Generation*, edition suhrkamp, NF 448 (Frankfurt am Main: Suhrkamp, 1987), p. 142-178.

72. Georg G. Iggers, *Deutsche Geschichtswissenschaft: Eine Kritik der traditionellen Geschichtsauffassung von Herder bis zur Gegenwart* (1968; Munich: Deutscher Taschnbuchverlag, 1971), p. 364.

73. Iggers, *Deutsche Geschichtswissenschaft*, p. 363-364.

74. According to Jörn Rüsen's concept of "historical culture," the aesthetic dimension in history and a certain kind of aesthetic effort in historical memory must be given a place of equal value beside the cognitive and political dimension in historical writing. Cf. Jörn Rüsen, "Was ist Geschichtskultur? Überlegungen zu einer neuen Art, über Geschichte nachzudenken," in *Historische Orientierung: Über die Arbeit des Geschichtsbewußtseins, sich in der Zeit zurechtzufinden* (Cologne: Böhlau, 1994), p. 221-234. Updated résumé in *Geschichte in Wissenschaft und Unterricht*, 45, H. 7, (1994), p. 455.

75. Franz Neumann, *Behemoth: Strukturen und Praxis des Nationalsozialismus 1933-1944*, transl. Hedda Wagner and Gert Schäfer (1944; Frankfurt am Main: Fischer Taschenbuch Verlag, 1984), p. 65.

76. Fritz Stern, "Germany revisited—Berlin 1954," in *The Failure of Illiberalism: Essays on the Political Culture of Modern Germany* (Chicago: The University of Chicago Press, 1971), p. 213.

77. Hans-Ulrich Wehler, "Geschichte—von unten gesehen. Wie bei der Suche nach dem Authentischen Engagement mit Methode verwechselt wird," *Die Zeit*, 3 May 1985, p. 64.

78. Mommsen, "Die dünne Patina," p. 15.

79. Jäckel, "Ein schlechtes Buch," p. 190.

80. Michelet, Journal, ed. P. Viallaneix (Paris, 1959), cited from Jaques Rancière, *Die Namen der Geschichte: Versuch einer Poetik des Wissens*, trans. Eva Moldenhauer (Frankfurt am Main: Fischer, 194), p. 95.

81. Cf. Wolfgang Weber, *Priester der Klio: Historisch-sozialwissenschaftliche Studien zur Herkunft und Karriere deutscher Historiker und zur Geschichte der Geschichtswissenschaft 1800-1970*, 2nd ed., Europäische Hochschulschriften, Reihe III, Geschichte und ihre Hilfswissenschaften, Vol 216 (Frankfurt am Main: Lang, 1987), pp. 189-199.

82. Hilberg, *Erinnerung*, p. 110.

83. Cf. Hilberg, *Erinnerung*, pp. 139-142. [Substitute with ref. to the American original, *The Politics of Memory*.]

84. Mariam Niroumand, "Mit Kastner war die Diaspora angeklagt—Gespräch mit dem israelischen Journalisten Tom Segev, der die Rolle der zionistischen Staatsgründer neu debattieren will," *die tageszeitung*, 21 Nov. 1994, p. 15. [My translation.]

85. Cf. Jörg Feuck, " 'Wir wollen unsere Arbeit im Stillen machen': Der Kampfmittelräumdienst kümmert sich um das explosive Kriegserbe," *Frankfurter Rundschau*, 29 July 1994, p. 22.

86. BdM stands for Bund Deutscher Mädel, the girls' division of the Hitler Youth.

87. Helmut Kohl, "Katholisch, liberal, patriotiisch," in *Mein Elternhaus: Eein deutsches Familienalbum*, ed. Rudolf Pörtner (Munich: Deutscher Taschenbuch Verlag, 1984), p. 362.

88. Cf. Vera Neumann, *Nicht der Rede wert: die Privatisierung der Kriegsfolgen in der frühen Bundesrepublik, lebensgeschichtliche Erinnerungen* (Münster: Westfälisches Dampfboot, 1999).

89. "Kanal Brutal: Der Widerstand gegen den täglichen Horrortrip auf dem Bildschirm wächst weiter—vier von fünf Deutschen haben die TV-Gewalt satt," *Focus*, 27 June 1994, p. 143-148.

90. Annette von Droste Hülshoff, cited according to Doris Maurer, "Keine Pfauenfeder in Krähenpelz: Zum 200. Geburtstag der Dichterin Annette Freiin von Droste-Hülshoff—ein Leben zwischen anpassung und Trotz, Resignation und Wut," *Die Zeit*, 10 Jan. 1997, p. 56.

91. Philippe Ariès, *Ein Sonntagshistoriker: Philippe Ariès über sich*, transl. by Eva Groepler (Frankfurt am Main: Hain, 1990), p. 151.

92. Hilberg, *Erinnerung*, p. 37.

93. Michael Tournier, *Der Erlkönig*, trans. Hellmut Waller (Frankfurt am Main: Fischer Taschenbuch Verlag, 1984), S. 288.

94. Cf. Saul K. Padover, *Lügendetektor, Vernehmungen im besiegten Deutschland 1944/45* (Frankfurt am Main: Eichborn, 1999); Gerhard Spörel, "Stumpf, weinerlich und hoffnungslos," *Der Spiegel*, 23 Aug. 1999, p. 48-521.

95. Mommsen, "Die dünne Patina," p. 14.

96. Leo N. Tolstoy, *War and Peace*, Epilog, Part I, III [I used W. Bergengrün's German translation in a dtv edition.]

97. The historical journal *Geschichtsdidaktik* pointed out over ten years ago the deficits of the functionalist school of history. Winfried Speitkamp wrote then: "At times functionalists tend to lose...sight of the ideological factor, as Schleunes, for example, when they reconstruct in minute detail 'the twisted road to Auschwitz,' while marginalizing anti-Semitism. Hence, this school of thought tends to create the impression that the destruction of the Jews was the result of the competition between various hierarchies, of pragmatism, and of material necessity. This kind of portrayal can hardly explain why the destruction started in the first place or why the process took the direction that it took." "Die Historikerkontroverse und der Holocaust," *Geschichtsdidaktik: Probleme, Projekte, Perspektiven*, 12, H. 3 (1987), p. 220.

98. Over ten years ago the historical journal *Geschichtsdidaktik* put its finger on this problem. In it Winfried Speitkamp noted: "At times the functionalists loose sight of the ideological factor, as for instance when they...following the procedure of Karl Schleunes, reconstruct, by means of micro-historical analysis, "the twisted road to Auschwitz" in every detail, thereby pushing anti-Semitism to the margin. Thus the

functionalist school creates at times the impression that the destruction of the Jews was the result of the interaction of an anarchy of competencies, a conclusion...which can hardly explain...why this deadly program was started in the first place and why it took the particular direction it took." W. Speitkamp, Die Historikerkontroverse und der Holocaust," *Geschichtsdidaktik, Probleme, Projekte, Perspektiven*, 12, H. 3 (1987), p. 220.

99. Cf. Andreas Hilgruber, *Der 2. Weltkrieg 1939-45: Kriegsziele und Strategien der großen Mächte* (Stuttgart: Kohlhammer, 1982), p. 108.

100. "Der Antisemitismus war eine notwendige, aber keineswegs hinreichende Bedingung für den Holocaust," Mommsen, "Die dünne Patina," p. 15.

101. Mommsen, "Die dünne Patina," p. 14. As an antidote to Mommsen's trivialization of the anti-Semitism of leading perpetrators cf. Yaacov Lozowick, *Hitlers Bürokraten: Eichmann, seine willigen Vollstrecker und die Banalität des Bösen*, transl. from the English by Christoph Münz (Zurichand Munich: Pendo, 2000). This study proves beyond the shadow of a doubt that Eichmann and his men were convinced anti-Semites" (Jehuda Bauer).

102. Jäckel, "Einfach einschlechtes Buch," p. 191-192.

103. Mommsen, "Die dünne Patina," p. 14.

104. Jäckel, "Ein schlechtes Buch," p. 189.

105. Scholarship, as practiced in the academy, is after all a system of citing works and authors. Mommsen, Wehler, and Jäckel, for example, cite each other, while persistently ignoring Freud.

106. Hilberg, *Erinnerung*, p. 130.

107. Christian Jansen, "Der ganz normale Ablasshandel-Zwei Jahre nach dem Goldhagen-Schock: Das Buch, 'Hitlers willige Vollstrecker' entfachte ein Strohfeuer: In der Geschichtsforschung spielt es keine Rolle," *Die Woche*, 30. April 1998, p. 30. Worth noting is that Jansen was, until 1994 Hans Mommsen's assistant.

108. Hilberg, *Die Vernichtung*, I, 15.

109. Wehler, "Stachel im Fleisch," p. 200.

110. Hilberg, *Die Vernichtung*, III, 1072.

111. Hilberg, *Die Vernichtung*, III, 1062.

112. Hilberg, *Die Vernichtung*, I, 21.

113. Richard S. Levy, *The Downfall of the Anti-Semitic Political Parties in Imperial Germany* (New Haven, CT: Yale University Press, 1975), p. 265.

114. Dinter's sickening anti-Semitic novel *Die Sünde wider das Blut* (*The Sin Against the Blood*) appeared in 1917, reached 16 editions in four years, and had by 1934 sold over a quarter of a million copies. Cf. *The Sword, the Pen, and the Swastika*, ed. and transl. from the German by Ludo Abicht and Claude Owen (St. Catharines: Brock University Press, 1981), p. xxv.

115. J. Alden Nichols, *Germany after Bismarck: The Caprivi Era, 1890-1894* (Cambridge, MA: Harvard University Press, 158), p. 239f.

116. Peter G. J. Pulzer, *The Rise of Political Anti-Semitism in Germany and Austria* (New York: Wiley, 1964), p. 300.

117. Pulzer, *Political Anti-Semitism*, p. 299.

118. Mommsen, "Die dünne Patina," p. 15.

119. Mommsen, "Die dünne Patina," p. 14.

120. Jan Philipp Reemtsma, "Terrorratio: Überlegungen zum Zusammenhang von Terror, Rationalität und Vernichtungspolitik," in *"Vernichtungspolitik": Eine Debatte über den Zusammenhang von Sozialpolitik und Genozid im nationalsozialistischen Deutschland*, ed. Wolfgang Schneider, Schriftenreihe des Hamburger Instituts für Sozialforschung (Hamburg: Junius, 1991), p. 138.

121. Jörg-Peter Jatho, *Das Gießener "Freitagskränzchen": Dokumentation zum Mißlingen einer Geschichtslegende—zugleich ein Beispiel für Entsorgung des Nationalsozialismus* (Fulda: Ulenspiegel-Verlag, 1995).

122. Strafsache gegen die Hausfrau Dagmar Imgart vor dem Schwurgericht des Landgerichts in Kassel, 3 Ks 1/53, in *Justiz und NS-Verbrechen: Sammlung Deutscher Strafurteile wegen nationalsozialistischer Tötungsverbrechen 145-1966*, ed. Adelheid L. Rüter Ehlermann, H. H. Fuchs and C. F. Rüter (Amsterdam: University Press Amsterdam, 1974), XII, 756.

123. Bund der Asienkämpfer, Balkankämpfer und Orientfreunde e.V., ed.; *Orient-Rundschau*, 13, No. 12 (December 1, 1931), p. 133-135.

124. Goldhagen, *Hitler's Willing Executioners*, p. 439-440

125. Mommsen, "Die dünne Patina," p. 15.

126. Mommsen, "Aufarbeitung und Verdrängung," p. 85.

127. Wehler, "Stachel im Fleisch," p. 204.

128. Wehler, "Stachel im Fleisch," p. 206-207.

129. The *Habilitationsschrift* is an unknown academic hurdle in North American institutions of higher learning. It is a thesis required of a candidate wishing to qualify for lecturing at a university. The candidate has to write this monograph after he has submitted his or her dissertation. With this superfluous requirement the German academic establishment can keep independent thinkers in step intellectually up into a ripe middle age.

130. Walter Mayr, " 'Ich bin doch immune': Spiegel-Reporter Walter Mayr über das zweite Leben des SS-Mannes Hans Schneider," *Der Spiegel*, May 8, 1995, p. 94-97; Ulrich Greiner, " 'Mein Name sei Schwerte'—Ein deutsches Leben: Der frühere Rektor der Technischen Hochschule Aachen, bekannt als Hans Schwerte, war Hauptsturmführer der SS und hieß Hans Ernst Schneider," *Die Zeit*, May 12, 1995, p. 41.

131. "Schneider was, as SS-Hauptsturmführer, one of the leading men in the academic politics of the SS. He was the editor-in-chief of the journal *Die Weltliteratur*, edited numerous other journals, planed conferences and projects, and in 1942 he was appointed coordinator of the 'deployment of Germanic scholarship' in all of Europe. Life experience suggests that in all of these capacities Schneider must have been exceptionally well known in the German community of scholars. After 1945 he counted quite rightly on the discretion of these, because if they would have outed him as a former SS officer, they would have been required to tell in what capacity they had had to deal with him. The ironic pleasure this gave to Schwerte/Schneider, must have been enormous." Dietrich Schwanitz, *Das Shylock Syndrome oder: Die Dramaturgie der Barbarei* (Frankfurt am Main: Eichbaurn, 1997), p. 271.

132. [Marianne Viefhaus], "Verunsicherung? Misverständnis? Demokratischer Vorgang?" *THD Intern*, October 15, 1992, p. 6; see also: F. Hebel, "Senat lehnt Ehrenpromotion von Azis Nesin ab," and Helmut Essinger and Klaus Liebe-Harkort, "Offener Brief: Wissenschaftler der Gutachter-Kommission melden sich zu Wort," *THD-Intern*, October 15, p. 6.

133. To write this imaginary conversation among colleagues, I slightly paraphrased actual statements made by Mommsen, Jäckel, and Wehler. Hence, the bibliographic references to where statements are to be found.

134. Wehler, "Stachel im Fleisch," pp. 207-208.

135. Cf. Harald Weinrich, "Dante und Faust," in *Vom Nutzen des Vergessens*, ed. Gary Smith and Hinderk M. Emrich (Berlin: Akademie Verlag, 1996), pp. 105-131.

136. Friedrich Christian Delius, *Der Spaziergang von Rostock nach Syrakus* (Reinbeck bei Hamburg: Rowohlt, 1995), S. 38.

137. Cf. Gernot Böhme, "Sinn und Gegensinn—über die Dekonstruktion von Geschichten," *Psychs: Zeitschrift für Psychoanalyse und ihre Anwendung*, 54, H. 7 (July 1990), 577-592.

138. Henryk M. Broder, " 'Ich bin stolz':...Über Goldhagen, Vater und Sohn," *Der Spiegel*, May 20, 1996, p. 58.

139. Captions like "Die dünne Patina der Zivilisation" ["The thin Patina of Civilization], "Wie ein Stachel im Fleisch" ["Like a Thorn in the Flesh"], and "Herz der Finsternis" ["Heart of Darkness"], which do not go well together at all with their bone-dry positivistic historiography.

140. Daniel Jonah Goldhagen, "Das Versagen der Kritiker," *Die Zeit*, Aug. 2, 1996, p. 14.

141. Leo N. Tolstoy, *Krieg und Frieden*, Vol. 2, Part VI, I.

142. Cf. Markus Franz, "Preis für den Beobachter der willigen Vollstrecker," *die tageszeitung*, March 11, 1997, p. 4.

143. Goldhagen, *Hitler's Willing Executioners*, p. 27.

144. Gregor Athalwin Ziemer, *Education for Death: The Making of the Nazi* (London: Oxford University Press, 1941), pp. 193-194, cited in Goldhagen, *Hitler's Willing Executioners*, p. 27.

145. Goldhagen, *Hitler's Willing Executioners*, p. 27.

146. Goldhagen, *Hitler's Willing Executioners*, p 582, note 38.

147. Rudolf Augstein, "Was dachten die Mörder?" [*Spiegel* Interview with Daniel Jonah Goldhagen], *Der Spiegel*, Aug. 12, 1996, p. 55.

148. "Like Germans who resist the notion of national differences until they've lived abroad, many Americans arrive in Germany believing that Germans are 'just like us.' They soon find themselves cataloguing the peculiarities of a society that is, in so many areas *verkrustet*—stuck in its ways, paralyzed by rules, laws and tradition. After the Wall fell, East Germans, pounded by change, looked at their Western neighbors and asked the same question, sometimes longingly, sometimes with boiling frustration: How could a country with such a powerful economy and such a successful democracy, saddle itself with so much ritual, so much rigidity, so much obedience, so much hunger for authority? Marc Fisher, *After the Wall: Germany, the Germans, and the Burdens of History* (New York: Simon & Schuster, 1995), p. 41.

149. Cit. according to Ellen K. Coughlin, "Willige Vollstrecker," in *Ein Volk von Mördern? Die Dokumentation zur Goldhagen-Kontroverse um die Rolle der Deutschen im Holocaust*, ed. Julius H. Schoeps (Hamburg: Hoffmann und Campe, 1996), p. 43.

150. Lothar Gall, in "Worte der Woche," *Die Zeit*, Sept. 27, 1996, p. 2.

151. Cf. Heleno Saña, *Das Vierte Reich: Deutschlands später Sieg* (Hamburg: Rasch und Röhring, 1990), pp. 80-81.

152. Elie Wiesel, *Der fünfte Sohn*, cit. according to Gerhard Zwerenz, *Die Rückkehr des toten Juden nach Deutschland* (Ismaning bei München: Hueber, 1986), p. 70.

153. Cf. Christian Schneider, "Geschichtliches zu einem methodischen Modeartikel: Das Interview als sozialwissenschaftliches Forschungsmittel und der historische Ort des Interpreten," *Mittelweg 36: Zeitschrift des Hamburger Instituts für Sozialforschung*, 5 (December 1996/ January 1997), 22.

154. When I arrived in Germany in 1982, the Pershing debate was at its hight. At that time the German playwright, Rolf Hochhuth, wrote: "It would only strengthen our elected representative, Helmut Kohl's position in the White House, if those who elected him, would find ways and means to save Germany from becoming target No. 1 in the Third and last world war. This would enable Kohl to say convincingly no in Washington to the untenable expectation of letting himself be conditioned, against the will of his compatriots, to become Reagan's obedient helper in the deployment of Pershing missiles in Europe." Hochhuth, "Kohl, Amageddon oder Sedanlächeln und Seife: Das kriegstreibende Herrengefühl der Nordamerikaner," *Die Zeit*, Aug. 1983, in *War hier Europa? Reden, Gedichte, Essays* (Munich: Deutscher Taschenbuch Verlag, 1987), p. 96.

155. This is a line from Goethe's poem "Der Erlkönig," where the Lord of the dark powers tries to lure the boy with the enticing call: "Willst feiner Knabe, du mit mir gehen? / Gar feine Spiele spiel ich mit dir!" ("My dear child, do you want to come with me? / Fabulous games I will play with you!")

156. "Splendid that no one knows that my name is 'Rumpelstilsken,' " from Grimm's *Fairy Tales*.

157. Alex Haley, *Roots: The Saga of an American Family* (Garden City, NY: Doubleday, 1976), p. 670.

158. Dominick LaCapra, "Representing the Holocaust: Reflections on the Historians' Debate" in *Probing the Limits of Representation: Nazism and the "Final Solution,"* ed., Saul Friedländer (Cambridge, MA: Harvard University Press; 1992), p. 110.

159. Cited accord. to Michael Wolfsohn, *Ewige Schuld? 40 Jahre deutsch-jüdisch-israelische Beziehungen*, Serie Piper 985 (Munich: Piper, 1988), p. 209.

160. Browning, *Ganz normale Männer*, p. 209.

161. Andrei S. Markovits, "Über das Unbehagen der Deutschen: Eine Antwort auf die eifrigen Kritiker der Studie 'Hitler's Willing Executioners,' " *Frankfurter Rundschau*, June 15, 1996, p. 18.

162. Wehler, "Stachel im Fleisch," p. 203.

163. Cf. Gudrun Lukasz-Aden, *Die schrecklichen Eltern—Generationskonflikt lebenslänglich: Wie die Nachkriegsgeneration mit ihren Eltern zurechtkommt*, Heyne Report, No. 10/43 (Munich: Heyne, 1989); Dörte von Westernhagen, *Die Kinder der Täter: Das Dritte Reich und die Generation danach* (Munich: Kösel, 1987).

164. Friedrich Meinecke, *Die deutsche Katastrophe* (Wiesbaden: Brockhaus, 1946).

165. Konrad Kwiet, "Judenverfolgung und Judenvernichtung im Dritten Reich: Ein historiographischer Überblick," in *Ist der Nationalsozialismus Geschichte? Zu Historisierung und Historikerstreit*, ed., Dan Diner (Frankfurt am Main: Fischer Taschenbuch Verlag, 1987), pp. 237-264, 294-306.

166. Hilberg, *Erinnerung*, p. 52.

167. Friedirich Dürrenmatt, *Theater: Essays, Gedichte und Reden* (Zurich: Diogenes, 1980), 56.

168. Dinita Smith, "Ein Interview mit Daniel Goldhagen," in *Ein Volk von Mörtdern?* Ed. Julius H. Schoeps, p. 49.

169. Axel Azzola, "Von Tätern, Tatmotiven und Taten: Zu und über Daniel Goldhagen, Hitler's willige Vollstrecker, ganz gewöhnliche Deutsche und der Holocaust," *Die Brücke: Forum für antirassistische Politik und Kultur*, No. 102 (July/Aug. 1998), p. 69.

170. Michael Crichton, *Dino Park*, trans. Klaus Berr (Munich: Knaur, 1991), pp. 52-53.

171. Mommsen, "Die dünne Patina," p. 15.

172. Goldhagen, *Hitler's Willing Executioners*, p. 190.

173. In recent literature Klaus-Michael Mallmann arrives at the same conclusion concerning the Lübeck Police Battalion 307, which carried out the massacre of Brest-Litiowsk. Mallmann writes: "A whole series of common place assumptions do not apply: The assumption that the perpetrators were made into murderers against their will, is just not plausible, because the riflemen of the firing squads were volunteers. The same holds true for the thesis according to which the men became used to brutality by gradually becoming accustomed to violence, because here there can be observed an acceleration of violence from zero to one hundred—the acceleration from murder to mass murder. The thesis about the irresistible power of indoctrination also misses the point, for there just hadn't been any time to get the wheels of propaganda rolling against the Judeo-Bolshevik threat. [In the honeymoon of the Hitler-Stalin Pact the German invasion of Russia had come out of the blue.] Mallmann, "Der Einstieg in den Genozid. Das Lübecker Polizeibataillon 307 und das Massaker in Brest-Litowsk Anfang Juli 1941," *Archiv für Polizeigeschichte* (1999), p. 85.

174. Golo Mann, "Plädoyer für die historische Erzählung," p. 242.

175. Cf. Julius H. Schoeps, "Vom Rufmord zum Massenmord: Die Nazis mußten den Vernichtungsantisemitismus nicht erfinden," in *Ein Volk von Mördern*, ed. Julius H. Schoeps, p. 138.

176. Paul K. Feyerabend, "Über einen neuen Versuch, die Vernunft zu retten," *Wissenschaftssoziologie: Studien und Materialien*, ed. Nico Stehr and René König, *Kölner Zeitschrift für Soziologie und Sozialpsychologie*, Sonderheft 18 (1975), 479.

177. Cit. according to Lion Feuchtwanger, *Das Haus der Desdemona oder Größe und Grenzen historischer Dichtung* (Frankfurt am Main: Fischer Taschenbuch Verlag, 1986), p. 151.

178. Gunter Hoffmann, "Die Welt ist wie sie ist," *Die Zeit*, Sept. 27, 1996, p. 10.

179. Cit. according to Otto Köhler, "Unter Deutschen," *Konkret*, 10 (Oct. 1996), p. 15.

180. Cf. Wilhelm Mommsen, *"Legitime" und "illegitime" Geschichtsschreibung* (Munich: R. Oldenbourg, 1930).

181. Wilhelm Mommsen, *Politische Geschichte von Bismarck bis zur Gegenwart* (Frankfurt am Main: Diesterweg, 1935), pp. 62, 66.

182. Hans-Ulrich Wehler, "Nachruf auf Theodor Schieder, April 11, 1908—October 8, 1984," *Geschichte und Gesellschaft*, 11 (1985), p. 143-152.

183. Wehler, "Stachel im Fleisch," p. 205. [The "Generalplan Ost" was the masterplan, devised by Himmler's *Rasse- und Sielungshauptamt* for preparing captured territories in the East for German settlement by means of "ethnic cleansing," enslavement and extermination of indigenous populations.]

184. 1999. *Zeitschrift für Sozialgeschichte des 20. und 21. Jahrhunderts*, 1992, H. 1, pp. 62-95.

185. Christof Dipper, "Auschwitz erklären," *Aschkenas*, 5, H. 1 (1995), 199-204.

186. Jürgen Habermas, "Geschichte ist ein Teil von uns: Warum ein 'Demokratiepreis' für Daniel Goldhagen?" *Die Zeit*, March 14, 1997, p. 13.

187. Wolfgang Wippermann, *Wessen Schuld? Vom Historikerstreit zur Goldhagen-Kontroverse* (Berlin: Elefanten Press, 1997), p. 105.

188. There must exist an English rendering of this short Goethe poem; perhaps Barker Fairley has translated it.

189. Cf. Hannah Ahrend, "Das Bild der Hölle," (1946) in *Nach Auschwitz. Essays und Kommentare* (Berlin, 1986), I, 59.

190. Wippermann, *Wessen Schuld?* p. 98.

191. Cf. Jörg Bremer, "die Arroganz der Vorurteile," *Frankfurter Allgemeine Zeitung*, Dec. 10, 1996, p. 34.

192. Cf. Speitkamp, "Die Historikerkontroverse und der Holocaust," p. 220 and Natan Szaider, "Wahnsinn mit System: Ein Gespräch mit dem Holocaustforscher Raul Hilberg," *Frankfurter Rundschau*, 15 July 2002, p. 12. Sznaider notes that long established conventional Holocaust research oriented itself on the Nuremberg International Military Tribunal. In the records of this tribunal the victims played a relatively unimportant role and when they appeared, then only from the perspective of the perpetrators. Israeli Holocaust research tends to be victim oriented, paying great attention to handed down written records of those who perished and on testimony of survivors.

193. Hilberg, *Erinnerung*, p. 48.

194. Cornelia Rabitz, "Fakten, Fakten, Fakten," und Michael Wuliger, "Kollektivgejaul: Goldhagens Buch und die deutsche Reaktion," *Allgemeine jüdische Wochenzeitung*, Aug. 22, 1996, p. 3; Gunter Hofmann, "Die Welt ist wie sie ist," p. 10.

195. Moshe Zimmermann, "Die Fußnote als Alibi," in *Ein Volk von Mördern?* Ed. Julius H. Schoeps (Hamburg: Hoffmann und Campe, 1996), p. 147.

196. Bremer, "Vorurteile," p. 34.

197. Hayden White, *The Content of the Form: Narrative Discourse and Historical Representation* (Baltimore and London: The John Hopkins University Press, 1987). [The passage, I am referring to, is in chapter 1 on p. 25 of the German edition.]

198. Cf. Jörn Rüsen, *Zeit und Sinn: Strategien historischen Denkens*, Fischer Wissenschaft, 7435 (Frankfurt am Main: Fischer Taschenbuch Verlag, 1990), p. 48 and 99.

199. Michael Wolfsohn, "Wattierte Erinnerung—Zur Geschichtspolitik in Deutschland," in *Geschichte und Politik: Eine Vortragsreihe*, ed., Bernd Heidenreich (Wiesbaden: Hessische Landeszentrale für politische Bildung, 1995), 52.

200. Hayden White, *Auch Klio dichtet oder die Fiktion des Faktischen: Studien zur Tropologie des historischen Diskurses* (Stuttgart: Klett-Cotta, 1986), p. 51.

201. Cf. Jörn Rüsen, *Historische Orientierung: Über die Arbeit des Geschichtsbewußtseins, sich in der Zeit zurechtzufinden* (Cologne: Böhlau, 1994), p. 226.

# THE NIGHTMARES OF RUTH BETTINA BIRN

## How the Subconscious Impedes the Judgment

During the Goldhagen debate Germany's leading news magazine *Der Spiegel* found in Ruth Bettina Birn, Canada's top Nazi-hunting scholar, a prestigious ally more than willing to help tarnish Daniel Jonah Goldhagen's academic reputation. In an interview Ms. Birn denigrated his book, *Hitler's Willing Executioners*, as a propagandistic tract which "draws the Holocaust as a devotional picture for the rich posthumous patrons in America, encouraging them to replace their feelings of self-doubt with emotional indignation." In a self-righteous tone she chastises Goldhagen for writing "in such a denouncing manner that circumspect, recognized scholars find themselves suddenly portrayed as revisionists who repress the truth." Finally, she suggested that "implicit and explicit hostile pressure" has been exerted to hinder the publication of her review of Goldhagen's book.[1]

### The "Rich Posthumous Patrons"

By the "rich posthumous patrons" Ms. Birn means, of course, "the rich Jews" who want to sponsor a chair for Holocaust Studies at Harvard. Who can blame them for that? The unfortunate victims who were devoured by the Holocaust were their relatives. And as the Goldhagen debate has shown, the study of the mass murder of six million Jews is perhaps not in the best hands when it is left to the conventional professional historians who shy away from grappling with this horrendous crime on an emotional level. Moreover, if it had not been for "the rich Jews," who would have exerted pressure on the American and Canadian governments to finally search for Nazi criminals who went into hiding in North America?

The Canadian Government didn't start with these investigations until 1987.[2] It proceeded only reluctantly and without deep moral conviction. What brought motion into the investigations was the push from Jewish organizations, such as the B'nai B'rith anti-Defamation League. Canadians of German or Eastern European origin continue to oppose what they call a "witch hunt,"[3] and it seems as if the Canadian government continues to proceed rather reluctantly and inconsequentially, so as not to upset these strong ethnic groups in its multi-cultural society.

Whatever the case may be, the prosecution of Nazi criminals never stood on top of Ottawa's list of priorities. "In contrast to the United States, nothing can be accomplished in Canada, absolutely nothing," was Simon Wiesenthal's complaint in the mid-eighties.[4] Since then there have been some changes: a Crimes against Humanity and War Crimes Section, where Ms. Birn is employed, was set up within the Department of Justice and given the task of investigating suspected Nazi criminals residing in Canada. But now as before, the results of those investigations remains rather meager. Indeed, the efforts of the "War Crimes Section" produced only a single conviction.

A recent personnel shuffle in the wake of a scandal that shook the unit, and increasing criticism on the part of the Jewish-Canadian community seem to have driven Canadian Nazi hunters to step up their activity. Nonetheless, Sol Littman, the Director of the Simon Wiesenthal Center in Toronto, draws this bleak conclusion:

> All in all, we can safely say that Canada started late, took the most difficult course, and failed miserably to bring Nazi war criminals to justice.
>
> Deep divisions on policy, strong differences on the merits of evidence, and, most ironic of all, accusations of anti-Semitism on the part of senior staff members, were damaging the morale of the unit and contributed to its failure.
>
> While the recent spurt of activity is encouraging, it is too early to tell whether it will be any more successful than what went on before.[5]

In sharp contrast to this half-heartedness and inefficiency, the United States takes a more resolute stand: among other things, the government placed the name of Kurt Waldheim, the former UN Secretary-General and Austrian president, on the list of "unwanted persons" and exerted pressure on Swiss banks to return assets seized by the Nazis from their Jewish victims. When U.S. Congressmen warn the president of Lithuania that his country will incur the displeasure of the U.S. government if he should continue to protect Nazi collaborators who "actively participated in the massacre of tens of thousands of Jews during German occupation,"[6] this rebuke is not only meant as lip service to Jewish-Americans, but also as a declaration of intent. This determination we owe in no small degree to the "rich posthumous patrons" about whom Ms. Birn talks so scoffingly.

*The Subconscious of the Historian*
Does Ms. Birn feel no shame in scolding Daniel Goldhagen for expressing deep emotions when he writes about the Holocaust? Is she neither willing nor able to understand what motivates the author of *Hitler's Willing Executioners* when she insinuates that he is being coached by "an experienced lawyer or a clever PR-expert?"[7] That is how Ms. Birn speaks about the feelings of an author whose father escaped the firing-squads of the Police Battalions and *Einsatzgruppen*. This from the daughter of a German navy veteran who confided to her that while on shore leave in Baltic ports, crew members of his ship had witnessed mass killings of Jewish men, women, and children![8]

What a vivid and disturbing work of history her study of *Die höheren SS- und Polizeiführer* (*The Upper-Echelon SS and Police Leaders*) could have turned out to be if she would have allowed the memory of what her father had told her, to be her guide![9] As is, the book bears witness to how her fantasy was stifled and how she was deprived of personal insights while attending the seminars of her mentor, Eberhard Jäckel, at the University of Stuttgart. In her foreword Ms. Birn thanks her husband for giving her comfort and courage when "the shadows of the black-clad German masters of yonder days haunted [her] in [her] dreams."[10]

Hayden White introduces his fascinating book, *Metahistory*, with a quotation from Gaston Bachelard: "We can only analyze what we have dreamt before."[11] What would have happened if the doctoral candidate Ruth Bettina Birn would have let visions from her nightmares flow into her historical interpretation? Did she fear incurring the displeasure of her *Doktorvater*, a man of the Hitler Youth generation? Perhaps more subconsciously than consciously, she avoided this risk. Her precaution insured that her historical findings were squeezed into an uninspired, and uninspiring, standardized dissertation, the kind of study that is produced year in, year out, at German universities. It is an undoubtedly useful guide that helps the reader to find his way through the ramified structures of Himmler's SS and police, but it is not living history in the tradition of Tucydides, Michelet, and Huizinga. In the powerful language of the German playwright, Rolf Hochhuth, Ruth Bettina Birn's dissertation,

> ...shows that our [German] nation, which welcomes it when artists chat about their idle dreams, will still not tolerate it when they do open their mouths to cry out what they have seen in their political nightmares.[12]

*The Debate has not only to do with Factual Correctness*
Could it be that Ms. Birn's scathing review of Goldhagen's book was not accepted for publication in the reputable journal *Holocaust and Genocide Studies*, because it is factually wrong and not because of "Jewish politics" as she insinuates? She misrepresents the content of *Hitler's Willing Executioners* and makes out of Daniel Goldhagen, the author, a racist strawman, a Simple Simon, who offers nothing but monocausal arguments.

"Would someone receive a Ph.D. at Harvard who begins by posing the question whether blacks and women are human beings like 'us'?"[13] Ms. Birn asks in her highly acclaimed review of Goldhagen's book. "Blacks" and "women" are biological categories. They suggest in the given context that Goldhagen ascribed to the Germans a kind of biological hereditary anti-Semitism. Need it be said that the political scientist, Daniel Goldhagen, rejects (just as much as his critics do) the notion that anti-Semitism is a genetic defect peculiar to the Germans? It also goes without saying that he does not regard the Third Reich and the Holocaust as the logical outcome of an allegedly genetic anti-Semitism.

Ms. Birn is also selective with the truth when she maintains that Goldhagen blends out the suffering of other Nazi victims by "overemphasizing" the massacre of the Jews. She claims this in her interview in *Der Spiegel*, as well as in her review of Goldhagen's book. There she writes:

He also overlooks the fact that millions of Soviet POWs were starved to death before it dawned on the German authorities that they had a problem with labour shortage.[14]

This intentional or unintentional misrepresentation of what Goldhagen really says is dispelled by a reference to the original text. On page 290 of the English version of his book Goldhagen writes:

> Despite the ardent and until then decisive ideological opposition to the employment of Russian "subhumans" within Germany—a purely ideological stance that had led the Germans to kill, mainly by starvation, 2.8 million young, healthy Soviet POWs in less than eight months—the policy was reversed during this period. In 1942, owing to ever more pressing economic need, the Germans stopped the decimation of Soviet POWs through starvation and began to use them as laborers, leading by 1944 to the presence of over 2.7 million Soviet citizens (many were not POWs) working in the German economy.

I'll spare myself the effort of juxtaposing further misrepresentations on the part of Ms. Birn with what Goldhagen actually says, for that would be "carrying coals to Newcastle." Goldhagen has already done just that in a 46 page rebuttal, entitled "The Fictions of Ruth Bettina Birn."[15]

In the foreword to *Eine Nation auf dem Prüfstand: Die Goldhagen-These und die historische Wahrheit*, containing Ms. Birn's and Norman Finkelstein's negative reviews, this rebuttal is, of course, brushed aside in a majestic gesture. There Hans Mommsen calls it "a by and large idle rejoinder." His colleagues will nod their heads in approval, but others will see through this and perceive how "the king of the roost" is trying to peck out an unwanted contestant.

A power struggle is definitely taking place in the academic community where every foul seems to be permitted. The article, "Holocaust und Geschichtsschreibung,"[16] a positive evaluation of Goldhagen's book, written by the German sociologist Helmut Dahmer, was excluded from the compiled volume *Geschichtswissenschaft und Öffentlichkeit*,[17] which was sponsored by *Zentrum für Antisemitismusforschung* of the Technical University of Berlin. Just as Ms. Birn had originally been asked by the editors of *Holocaust and Genocide*

*Studies* to submit her piece for publication, Dahmer was asked by Johannes Heil, the compiler of the volume in question, to contribute a chapter. The topic delegated to him was formulated as follows: "Expert criticism and/or psychological repression? The criticism of the book and the critics of Goldhagen as seen by psychologists, or: the historian, repression and the psyche."[18]

Dahmer accepted the invitation and wrote a paper on "The Holocaust and Historiography." He noted that mainstream historiography has thus far avoided dealing with the real issues when it comes to describing and analyzing this century of mass murder: Millions of perpetrators who were mobilized against millions upon millions of victims were no longer able to recall their murderous task.

> Whenever possible, historians have abstained from dealing with the "protagonists," i.e., with the countless "uninteresting" victims and perpetrators of this black century. Instead, they declared the history of social and economic structures with dynamics of their own—in other words—a historiography in which one neither "moralizes" nor "judges," to be the one and only kind of historiography, deserving to be called "serious," "scholarly" and "scientific," its mark of quality being that it is based upon research, conducted *sine ira cum studio* (with diligence and without anger).[19]

In summary Dahmer argued that Goldhagen's book must be recognized as an indicator of what is missing in academic historiography. In Germany it has encountered so much hostility, because it reminds the country's Holocaust "experts" that they have forgotten what is most important, namely the perpetrators who staged the Holocaust and the human beings who were devoured by it.

That was too much! The German "experts" in Holocaust research at the *Zentrum für Antisemitismusforschung* had expected a word of criticism from Dahmer, but not a severe reprimand. The *Zentrum* pulled the emergency break. The editor of the planned volume informed Dahmer that the aim was to "deliberately refrain from preparing a volume along the line of a pro or contra scheme."[20] The last thing people at the *Zentrum für Antisemitismusforschung* seemed to want was a discussion volume with *diverging* opinions. As Johannes Heil put it, Dahmer's paper,

> ...would stick out like a sore thumb, raising in every reader's and reviewer's mind the question of what is the purpose of this dissenting voice. Would he therefore do himself and everybody else the favor of withdrawing his paper?[21]

The notion that professional historians are not infallible, and that they, like everyone else, tend to repress that which shames, frightens or irritates them in whatever way, seems to have been so absurd to Johannes Heil that he outrightly rejected it. He wished to avoid a discussion about how subconscious factors lead German historians astray when they write about the Holocaust. Instead he had anticipated a discussion of "why professional criticism is perceived as repression"[22] (while it is not). Dahmer should have given a lecture on this topic to the "unenlightened" reading public. To put it bluntly, Heil would have liked it most of all if the sociologist, Helmut Dahmer, would have provided his colleagues in the various history departments with a clean bill of health by whitewashing what they write. This would have spared the historical profession the task of self-reflection, allowing them to return to business as usual after the hullabaloo over the book *Hitler's Willing Executioners* had calmed down. Some of them had already glanced with a jealous eye on this historiographical bestseller and asked themselves "why hardly anyone reads the books written by German historians."[23] And now they are busy trying to convince themselves that this simply has to do with their "reluctance to provide simple answers,"[24] and not at all with the fact that they have lost the ability to narrate history because of their "inability to mourn."[25]

This is not what the doctor says, but, rather a self-diagnosis on the patient. What is taken for granted in this diagnosis seems to serve as the foundation of mutual recognition among historians. Those who question the soundness of this make-belief foundation are viewed with mistrust and suspicion.

Thus the polite request addressed to Helmut Dahmer to "close the door on the way out" shows that in the Goldhagen controversy much effort goes into drawing borders in order to exclude unwelcome contestants. Consequently, Norman Finkelstein is not so far off the mark when he claims that a battle is being waged between conventional academic history and the specialized field of Holocaust Studies.[26]

*A Personal Note*

As a doctoral candidate of "Modern German History," I attended seminars with students who intended to major in Holocaust Studies. They were, as I recall, for the most part Jewish-American scholars. For the other members of the seminars who considered themselves to be budding dispassionate professional historians, they seemed not quite in step. They preferred books that were no longer in vogue or books which had never received much attention in the historical professions, books like Raul Hilberg's *The Destruction of the European Jews* (1961) or Lucy Dawidowicz's *The War against the Jews* (1975). I didn't get around to reading either work until after my general examination, because they had not been on my assigned reading list. What I had read were books "promising young scholars" were supposed to have read—books like Richard Levy's *The Downfall of the Anti-Semitic Parties in Imperial Germany* (1975) and Karl Schleunes' *The Twisted Road to Auschwitz* (1970). They were at that time *le dernier crie*.

My arrogance towards these Jewish-American students of Holocaust Studies dissipated a long time ago. In retrospect, it strikes me that they already knew then what I later became aware of here in Germany, the place of my origin. In and of itself the past does not constitute history; it only becomes history if we allow it to tell us who we are. There is no doubt in my mind that Daniel Jonah Goldhagen had the strength to stand up to the "experts," enabling him to write a path-breaking historical study because he opened himself up to the past and allowed it to tell him who he is.

## NOTES

1. Ruth Bettina Birn, "'Holocaust als Andachtsbild': Interview mit NS-Expertin Ruth Bettina Birn über Daniel Goldhagens Attacke auf Kritiker," *Der Spiegel*, Nov. 10, 1997, pp 266-267.

2. Honerable Jules Deschênes, Commisssioner, *Commission on War Criminals, Report* (Ottawa: Canadian Government Publishing Centre, 1986), Part 1: Public; Harold Troper and Morton Weinfeld, *Old Wounds: Jews, Ukrainians and the Hunt for Nazi War Criminals in Canada* (Chapel Hill and London: University of North Carolina Press, 1989), especially Chapter 7 "The Report and its Aftermath," pp 294-338.

3. Cf. John B. Gregorovich, ed., *On the Record: The Debate over alleged War Criminals in Canada—Letters to the Editor of The Whig-Standard* (Toronto: The Justinian Press, 1987); David Matas with Susan Charendoff, *Justice Delayed: Nazi War Criminals in Canada* (Toronto: Summerhill Press; 1987), especially Chapter 10 "Ukrainian-Jewish Relations," pp 163-186.

4. Cit. in Ansgar Skriver, "Nordamerika als Nazi-Asyl: Gravierende Versäumnisse der Behörden in den USA und Kanada," *Tribüne: Zeitschrift zum Verständnis des Judentums*, 24, H. 95 (1985), p. 109.

5. Personal telephone interview with Sol Littman, Canadian Representative, Friends of Simon Wiesenthal Center for Holocaust Studies, Toronto, May 7, 1998.

6. Letter to President Algirdas Brasauskas, signed by the Holocaust survivor Tom Lantos and 30 U.S. Congressmen, cited in "Lithuania: Warnung aus den USA," *Der Spiegel*, Dec. 1, 1997, p. 149.

7. Birn, "Holocaust als Andachtsbild," p. 266.

8. Cf. Sean Fine, "Nazi-Hunting Scholar under Fire for Views: Links with Anti-Zionist Angers CJC," *The Globe and Mail*, Jan. 26, 1998.

9. In the book, *Die höheren SS- und Polzeifüher: Himmlers Vertreter im Reich und in den besetzten Gebieten* (Düsseldorf: Droste, 1986), p. 6, Ruth Bettina Birn contends that her scientific analysis of criminal institutions must by necessity blend out the suffering of the victims ["läßt notwendigerweise die Leiden der Opfer außer Acht" (p. 69)]. Is this a rationalization or a valid historiographical argument? The question is worth debating. Fernand Braudel, the father of modern structural history, made no such claim. Even his book, *The Mediterranean*, which concentrates on such material factors as economic structures, vegetation, and climate, does not blend our, but rather shed light on the human experience.

10. Birn, *SS- und Polizeiführer*, p. ix.

11. Cit. in Hayden White, *Metahistory: die historische Einbildungskraft im 19. Jahrhundert in Europa*, transl. Peter Kohlhaas (1973; Frankfurt am Main: Fischer, 1991), p. 5.

12. Rolf Hochhuth, "Verbrannte Bücher -verbrannte Menschen," [Rede zum 50. Jahrestag der Bücherverbrennung; Wien, Konzerthaus, 20.5.1983], in *War hier Europa? Reden, Gedichte, Essays* (Munich: Deutscher Taschenbuch Verlag, 1987), p. 149.

13. Ruth Bettina Birn, "Revising the Holocaust," rev. of *Hitler's Willing Executioners* by Daniel Jonah Goldhagen, *The Historical Journal*, 40, I (1997), p. 213.

14. Birn; "Revising the Holocaust," p. 204.

15. *German Politics and Society*, 15, No. 3 (Fall 1997), pp. 119-165.

16. Helmut Dahmer, "Holocaust und Geschichtsschreibung. Nachlese zur Goldhagen-Kontroverse," *Archiv für die Geschichte des Widerstands und der Arbeit*, No. 15 (Fernwald: Germinal Verlag, 1998), pp. 441-462.

17. Johannes Heil and Rainer Erb, ed., *Geschichswissenschaft und Öffentlichkeit: Der Streit um Daniel J. Goldhagen*, Die Zeit des Nationalsozialismus, 14065 (Frankfurt am Main: Fischer Taschenbuch Verlag, 1998).

18. "Nach Goldhagen. Geschichte, Wissenschaft und Öffentlichkeit in den Neunzigern," (Konzept: Johannes Heil, ZfA Berlin. Manuskripteingang bis Ende Juni 1997), Stand 3.6.97 [provisional list of topics].

19. Dahmer, "Holocaust und Geschichtsschreibung," p. 443.

20. Johannes Heil, letter to Helmut Dahmer, Oct. 16, 1997.

21. *Ibid.*

22. *Ibid.*

23. Christof Dipper, "Warum werden deutsche Historiker nicht gelesen? Anmerkungen zur Goldhagen-Debatte," in Heil and Erb, ed., *Geschichtswissenschaft und Öffentlichkeit*, pp. 93-109.

24. "Scheu vor einfachen Antworten: Warum deutsche Historiker nicht gelesen werden," *Darmstädter Echo*, April 24, 1997 [Report on a lecture by Prof. Christof Dipper at the Technical University Darmstadt].

25. Cf. Alexander and Margarete Mitscherlich, *Die Unfähigkeit zu trauern: Grundlagen kollektiven Verhaltens*, Serie Piper, 168 (Munich: Piper, 1977).

26. Norman G. Finkelstein, "Daniel Goldhagen's 'Crazy' Thesis: A Critique of 'Hitler's Willing Executioners,'" *New Left Review*, No. 224 (July/Aug. 1997), pp. 82-85.

# KATER AND MOUSE

*Du bist ein kleiner Mann, ein Pförtner*
*eine Graue pfeifende Maus, die das Seil zernagt.*
*Das Seil, an dem ein Fallbeil hängt.*

—Gerhard Zwerenz

The First, and Only, Review of This Book by a Professional Historian, Michael Kater, The Canadian Centre for German and European Studies, York University, Toronto, Ontario

This book, really just an oversized essay, may be briefly dispatched at two levels: first, it is a mean-spirited *ad hominem* attack against three leading historians of Germany, and second, it argues, badly, that Daniel Jonah Goldhagen's thesis in his notorious doctoral dissertation, *Hitler's Willing Executioners*, is one-hundred-percent correct, and therefore unassailable.

On the first count, Kautz subsumes historians Hans Mommsen, Hans-Ulrich Wehler, and Eberhard Jäckel under the rubric "Hitler Youth and Anti-Aircraft Gunners" in an effort to smear them as former young Nazis. These passages are sufficiently libelous to stand up in a German court of law. Kautz viciously paints the entire Mommsen family as anti-Semitic, when he cites an entry in one of Wilhelm Mommsen's books of 1935, dedicated to his four sons, including Hans, "in the new Reich of Adolf Hitler" (p. 43). While it is well known that the older Mommsen, grandson of Theodor, was implicated in the Third Reich and after 1945 lost his Marburg chair in modern history because of this, it is equally well known that the Nazi-tainted past of their father has been a trauma for both Wolfgang J. and his twin brother Hans Mommsen. He, Wehler and Jäckel certainly were old enough to be members of the Hitler Youth and indeed anti-aircraft gunners at the end of the war, but service in these organizations was not voluntary, and, if they were in them, it would not necessarily have made them Nazis. Indeed, what we know of their work as historians and what they have told us so far in selective memoirs, suggests quite the opposite.

Kautz renders further bad judgment about these and other historians in present-day Germany. Wehler, Hans Mommsen, and Eberhard Jäckel are important, but they are not the only spokespersons of the current generation of German historians. Hans Mommsen's twin Wolfgang J. is equally significant, and so is Wolfgang Schieder, a younger colleague, and, even younger Jürgen Kocka, who in this book is introduced as a mere "vassal" (p. 38). Historians more in the middle of the ideological spectrum are ignored by Kautz, and so are notorious right-wingers such as Michael Stürmer and, worse, Ernst Nolte. It must have escaped Kautz that German historians to the right of the three scholars he targets are even less willing to abide Goldhagen.

From what I can see, Kautz attacks these three historians, who are stupidly and mendaciously linked to figures from the *Nibelungen* saga, and thereby to the anti-Semitic Richard Wagner, for their scholarly arguments against Goldhagen's radical thesis that all Germans always hated the Jews badly enough to kill them. More specifically, Wehler is taken to task for having admonished readers of the influential weekly *Die Zeit* to allow for the passions of Goldhagen's anti-German arguments. When I read that article in 1996, I found it a cautious and responsible judgment by a senior historian, not the cheap condescending comment that Kautz makes it out to be. Kautz derides Karl Schleunes' classic *The Twisted Road to Auschwitz* because it details the complicated path by which the Nazis eventually arrived at the radical mass murder. Schleunes' early "functionalist" view has been a cornerstone for Mommsen's argument that the "Final Solution of the Jewish Question" was part of a radicalization of anti-Semitic policy in the Third Reich since 1933, the last and most terrible part. This does not fit the opposing "intentionalist" school (of which Jäckel is actually a follower), least of all the non-differentiating Goldhagen. This journeyman scholar, whom Kautz repeatedly describes as a "Harvard historian," as if he had a chair, when in reality he is a political scientist without tenure, can do no wrong for the author; the fact that Goldhagen largely built on and repeated the pioneering work of Christopher Browning matters nothing to him.

There is no need here to dig further into the Goldhagen debate, let alone Kautz's skewed view of it, since this has been done ad nauseam ever since the publication of *Hitler's Willing Executioners*. Perhaps one could understand this malicious pamphlet better if one knew exactly what ax its author has to grind. He mentions an American and Canadian connection, which could suggest that he once tried to get a job on this continent but was unsuccessful. As a scholar of the Holocaust or the Third Reich, he is not at all known in either country. Questionable as it is, *"Hürnen Sewfriedte"* is the first "major" publication in what seems to be a junior academic post in his native Germany. He has obviously done a great disservice to Wehler, Mommsen, and Jäckel, but they can well afford to ignore these scribblings. Kautz may have done greater harm to the cause of Third Reich historiography, especially so since incomprehensibly, he found the Berlin Argument-Verlag as a publisher. Most of all, however, Kautz has hurt himself. While the speciousness of his argumentation is bad enough, the insulting manner of its delivery should prevent him from ever embarking on a serious university career.

*Response: An Attempt to enter Dialogue with a Compatriot*
The sheer vehemence of Michael Kater's review of my book, Gold-Hagen und die "hürnen Sewfriedte" suggests that in common with many of today's German historians, he has something he is struggling to forget. What strikes one immediately upon being confronted by his review is that he has limited his critique to a desperate defense of his German colleagues who—according to Kater—have been dastardly assailed by an impertinent, unqualified outsider. Apparently, solidarity with these colleagues takes absolute priority over dealing with a serious problem raised in my book.

This problem, as suggested in the book's subtitle, *Die Holocaust-Forschung im Sperrfeuer der Flakhelfer*, deals with the historical bias that infects a whole generation of German historians. Suffering from its Third Reich and World War II experience, this generation made passionless "objectivity" an overriding virtue in historical writing,[1] thereby allowing them to reconstruct in obsessive detail institutions and events, without ever having to grapple with those who used the institutions to commit atrocious crimes or concern themselves with the victims of these horrendous acts. It is this kind of depersonalized, dispassionate historiography, which has been extolled by the Mommsens and Wehlers for decades as the only kind of history, deserving sanctification as "scholarly history."

Anyone with even the faintest notion of the games academics play, can tell that Kater himself senses that his visceral defense of his German colleagues failed to do the job, so he plays the prestige game and launches into a vitriolic personal attack on a non-colleague. The world—and history—may be in need of those who march to a different drummer, but we can say goodbye to genuine *Wissenschaft*, if tenured professors persist in circling the wagons as if under attack by "bloodthirsty Apaches" whenever a stranger approaches their academic campgrounds. Kater has taken leave from scholarly discourse in this review. His message to me is: "I don't want to get to know this intruder. I don't want to hear anything he may have to say."

However, if Kater is a true scholar, he should be willing to engage in a scholarly debate in which we seek the truth rather than launching an unjustifiable *ad hominem* attack. For the purpose of that debate, it is irrelevant whether or not Daniel Goldhagen is a mere "political scientist without tenure" or whether I am known in Canada or the United States as a scholar of the Holocaust and the Third Reich. It doesn't matter if *"Hürnen Sewfriedte"* is my first or my third major publication; what matters is whether what I have to say regarding the debate over *Hitler's Willing Executioners* is true or false.

Isn't it true that in the discourse on the Holocaust, both scholarly and popular attention tends to focus on the "assembly-line" killing in the SS operated death camps so that we lose track of the massive slaughter that took place outside the camps? Isn't it true that it took a vast number of "willing executioners" to perform the grizzly task of disposing of thousands upon thousands of Jews in town after town and village after village? There needed to be "willing executioners" who had little or no scruples about shooting helpless women and children at point blank range.

Goldhagen confronted this undeniable historical fact by examining the German police battalions that operated behind the line in German-occupied territory. He subjected these units to a sociological analysis, which revealed that the enlisted men—and to a significant degree, the officers as well—constituted a representative sample of the German population. In civilian life they had been barbers, lumber retail merchants, and dock workers. Many of them were married and had fathered children. Nor were they, as some might suspect, handpicked ideological warriors, brainwashed in *Napolas* or in one of the *Ordensburgen*. Most of them had never been members of the Nazi party, let alone the SS. Is it any wonder that Goldhagen is preoccupied by the question: Why were typical German citizens not only willing, but eager to kill Jews?

In an attempt to find out, he studied a vast number of post-45 trial records pertaining to these killer cops. Kater is disdainful of this effort. From the height of his tenured position, he characterizes this tedious, time-consuming research as mere repetition of Christopher R. Browning's pioneer work *Ordinary Men: Reserve Police-Battalion 101*. To rectify this slight, one should point out that Goldhagen bases his conclusion on his study of at least twenty-five other police units. Granted, he pays greater attention to the unit studied by Browning than any of the others (it earns 65 reference entries), but this does *not* mean that he is merely covering the same ground as Browning.

To explain, it's worth reviewing what Browning says in the introduction to his book. There he comments on how the recorded statements of the perpetrators are frequently marred by distortions of memory, and outright lies. Other historians, he says, working with the same source material, might tell the story in a different way.[2] And Goldhagen does tell it differently. What Kater fails to realize is that Browning's *Ordinary Men* and Goldhagen's *Hitler's Willing Executioners* are based on very different explanatory models. Browning resorts to a behaviorist theory; namely the men are trained to kill after they arrive in Poland, repetition makes it easier.[3] Goldhagen approaches the topic as a cultural anthropologist who recognizes that human beings act out the values and customs inherent in their culture; in other words, they were pre-conditioned to kill by the culture in which they have been raised. This difference was made clear in my book where I pointed out the advantage of the latter mode of explanation. Hence, there is no need to elaborate further on the fundamental difference between these two approaches. Instead, I refer Professor Kater to pages 28-29 and 40-41, pages he seems to have overlooked.

Whatever Kater may think of the "notorious doctoral dissertation" of a "journeyman scholar," Goldhagen's book presents historians of the Holocaust and the Third Reich with numerous pertinent issues. The issue now becomes: Why did leading, professional, German historians refuse to take up the gauntlet thrown down by Goldhagen? In an attempt to answer this question, I subjected the public utterances on Goldhagen's book by three prominent German historians—Hans Mommsen, Hans-Ulrich Wehler, and Eberhard Jäckel—to a very close reading. To underscore certain points, I refer to other historians as well, but by and large I stick with the three named scholars.

In my scrutiny of what these three have to say about Goldhagen and in other comments they make on other subjects related to the Holocaust, I discern an identifiable psychological "state of mind" that pervades the German historical profession—a state of mind that throws considerable light on their reaction to the Goldhagen controversy.

Kater presumptuously lectures me on my choice of German historians to analyze. He insists that the three I have chosen are not an adequate sample. Hans Mommsen's twin brother Wolfgang J., he says, is equally significant, as are Wolfgang Schieder and Jürgen Kocka. He accuses me of ignoring historians more in the middle of the ideological spectrum and paying no attention to Michael Stürmer and Ernst Nolte, both notorious right-wingers. Here Kater is throwing in a red herring to make me appear ignorant. He is using one of the oldest (and cheapest) ploys, namely searching the bibliography for books the author hasn't cited and claiming this constitutes a fatal flaw.

I have lived in Germany long enough and I have closely followed the historians' debate of the eighties. I know where these people stand. Nolte, for example, would hear nothing of "ordinary Germans" ever having been, not only willing, but also eager executioners of Jews. "Wasn't the Bolshevik 'annihilation of a class' the logical precedent of the Nazi genocide?"[4] he asked. Nolte's rhetorical question sticks in my mind, as it does in Kater's. If one is to take it seriously, the policemen who slaughtered Jews were merely acting in self-defense. After all, Nolte reminds us, the President of the Jewish World Congress announced in 1939 that Jews would fight on the side of the allies in the war against Hitler.[5]

In writing my book, I didn't think it worthwhile to rehash the debates of the eighties or to speculate on what reactionaries like Nolte, Stürmer, Zitelmann and other right-wingers might say about Goldhagen. (Although I can't recall that they ever commented openly on the topic.) Nevertheless, if Kater is looking for a critical book on the Goldhagen controversy, which contains a tedious academic discussion of the historians' debate, let me recommend Wolfgang Wippermann's book, *Wessen Schuld? Vom Historikerstreit zur Goldhagen-Kontroverse*, Antifa Edition (Berlin: Elefanten Press, 1997).

Be this as it may, the point to be made here is that right-wing historians like Nolte, Stürmer, and Zitelmann didn't publish what they thought about *Hitler's Willing Executioners*. Instead, the charge against Goldhagen and his book was spearheaded by three leading *liberal* historians, namely by Hans Mommsen, Hans-Ulrich Wehler, and Eberhard Jäckel. They raved against Goldhagen, not only in professional journals read primarily by academics, but on various TV talk shows and in *Die Zeit*, one of Germany's leading weekly newspapers.

What does it say when three renowned historians, considered to be the *crème de la crème* of today's liberal German historiography lose control when confronted with a book on the Holocaust, which talks of the perpetrators as mass murderers responsible for their deeds and not pale, impersonal figures in history? What does it say when they prefer to see the perpetrators themselves as *victims*, victims of an inexorable history in which they played no role and had no will?[6] What does it say when three upstanding liberal German historians totally reject a book which provides graphic descriptions of the perpetrators deeds: smashed skulls, rivers of blood, frightened women begging for mercy, only to be laughed at?

This failure to respond appropriately has everything to do with unresolved problems in the personal backgrounds of the three historians concerned. It is important to recognize—as Kater concedes—that they belong to the *Hitler-Jugend* generation, which was drafted near the end of the war to serve as auxiliary anti-aircraft gunners to ward of the Flying Fortresses and Halifax bombers.[7] Jäckel was born in 1929, Hans Mommsen in 1930, and Wehler in 1931. Kater argues that their "service in [the *Hitler-Jugend* and in flak batteries] was not voluntary and...would not necessarily have made them Nazis." But this is a pedestrian argument and really misses the point.

As a historian of Nazi Germany, Kater knows as well as I do, that adolescents enjoyed being in the Hitler Youth. Wehler, for example, "war mit Hingabe dabei"[8] ("was a Hitler Youth in body and soul"). When war broke out and the *Hitler-Jugend* was integrated into the war effort, a new wave of enthusiasm seemed to go through the ranks of these youngsters.[9] At the same time, war confronted these boys with experiences that are extremely difficult for adolescents to cope with. Wehler lost his father at the age of eight. When the firestorm bombardments on Cologne started, he was drafted into a Hitler Youth fire brigade and had to help salvage casualties. "We had to enter burning buildings and had to drag out human beings who had been transformed into pieces of 'coal,' scarcely one meter long,"[10] he recounted in a recent interview.

Such experiences leave lasting scares on youthful psyches. I am grateful to Kater for having opened the subject so that I could address it further. Kater mentions that both Wolfgang J. Mommsen and his twin brother Hans, suffered the trauma of having a father with a Nazi-tainted past. *Trauma* is the right word for it. When discussing Hans Mommsen, Hans-Ulrich Wehler, and Eberhard Jäckel, we are talking about a traumatized generation with common early experiences. The former German Chancellor—and incidentally a trained historian—Helmut Kohl, was also a Hitler Youth. In April 1945 he was sworn in by *Reichsjugendführer* Arthur Axmann. War made him, like it made Wehler into a semi-adult who as member of a Hitler Youth fire brigade dug up dead bodies after the bombing raids on Ludwigsburg. In the rubble of the Third Reich this adolescent had to make it on his own from Berchtesgaden back to his native city further North.[11] The 19-year-old soldier Hans-Jochen Vogel was shot in the belly during the last days of the war while retreating with his *Wehrmacht* unit across the Alps. The way in which members of this generation turned their back on these formative experiences, and dutifully subjected themselves to the imposed re-educative process in democracy, liberalism, and also value-free science, determined how they would relate to their own Nazi past.

As distasteful as it may be to Kater to explore how the Hitler Youth generation relates to its Nazi past, one is, nevertheless, obliged to plumb the psyche of this workaholic reconstruction generation. In doing so, one reaches into murky, troubled waters where surprises await, surprises, which prove to be not so surprising after all. The two brothers, Hans-Jochen Vogel (born 1926) and Bernhard Vogel (born 1932), both sons of a Nazi father, made spectacular careers in post-war West Germany. Hans-Jochen was awarded a doctorate in law (*"summa cum laude"*) in 1950. While still a student, he joined the SPD and rapidly climbed the ladder of success in his party. In 1960 he became burgomaster of Munich; in 1972 he moved to Bonn to take up a ministerial post under Willy Brandt; and in 1983 he succeeded Herbert Wehner as Federal Chairman of the SPD.[12] Bernhard outdid his brother within the ranks of the CDU by becoming in succession first Prime Minister of Rheinland-Palatine and than Prime Minister of Thuringia.[13] In 1994, when the Americans turned over the accumulated holdings of the Berlin Document Center—the world's largest collection of Nazi Party documents—to the Bundesarchiv, Hans-Jochen and his brother vehemently objected to making their father's dossier accessible to the public.[14] Sadly, even today, the left-liberal Hans-Jochen Vogel and his conservative brother consider it their filial duty to protect their late father from prying eyes. Ironically, the same Hans-Jochen Vogel, who would like to keep his father's Nazi dossier off limits to researchers, is chairman of the *Verein "Gegen Vergessen—für Demokratie,"* an organization, dedicated to continuing research into the Nazi past.[15]

Michael Kater's conventional political yard stick, according to which the good guys are on the left and the bad ones on the right, doesn't seem to be of much use, if one wants to understand this ambivalent stance of the Vogel brothers, especially of Hans-Jochen, in regard to his family's Nazi past. No less important than the categories "left" and "right" is how close the topic under discussion gets to the skin. If Kater were to conduct interviews with German historians roughly his age or somewhat older, I believe he would encounter great resistance to a free discussion of the Third Reich or the Holocaust. In fact, the three German historians for whom Kater vouches so ardently would likely have great difficulty when it comes to talking about their own biological and academic fathers.

Hans Mommsen is not likely to agree that his father was a Nazi and a vile anti-Semite. Fact is that in the fall of 1933, just after Nazi Germany had withdrawn from the League of Nations and the first phase of Jewish exclusion from public life was well underway (legalization of the expulsion of Jews from the civil service and judiciary, from universities, and medicine), Mommsen *père* signed the "Declaration of Loyalty of University Professors and Teachers of other Institutions of Higher Learning to Adolf Hitler and the National Socialist State."[16] In the summer of 1940, after the fall of France, he officially joined the Nazi Party.[17] His book *Politische Geschichte von Bismarck bis zur Gegenwart* (Frankfurt am Main: Diesterweg, 1935) contains, among others, the following Nazi flavored passage:

> Step by step Jews gained control of literary and art criticism in the press and in journals. Richard Wagner was one of the first to address this trend and to point out the inherent danger. He was also one of the first to recognize that the Jewish question was a racial question that had nothing to do with religion. (p. 62)

In the same book by Father Wilhelm, Marx appears as "a typical representative of Jewish intellectualism, void of any roots in the *Volk* and the *Heimat*" (p. 66). Rosa Luxemburg is described as the "Jewess Rosa Luxemburg" and Kurt Eisner, the Prime Minister of the Bavarian revolutionary government, is called "a Jewish literate from Galicia" (p. 194). The Nazi storm trooper Horst Wessel who wrote the SA marching hymn and who was killed in a brawl is eulogized by Wilhelm Mommsen as a "shining symbol of all the good traits in National Socialism." For Mommsen *père*, Wessel not only "sacrificed" his life for the movement but is also the incarnation of the Nazi synthesis of social contradictions: "He was a worker and student. Hence, he embodies in his person the transcendence of intellectual and manual labor" (p. 244).[18] And when the world was watching the newly appointed German Chancellor with apprehension, because storm troopers like Wessel had trampled down all opposition, Mommsen Sr. attributed the "unwarranted" apprehension to the "hate campaign, waged by Jewish emigrants...which was wholeheartedly supported by Jewry abroad." (p. 259)

Should Kater be so tactless, as to point out these passages to his German colleague, the latter would probably mutter something about his father not really having been the author of these passages, that a long since forgotten *Oberstudienrat* Huhnhäuser had written the passages dealing with the Nazi seizure of power, and that, without his father's knowledge, an editor of Diesterweg Publishers had inserted modifiers into the book's manuscript, so that Marx became "der Jude Marx" and so on.[19]

If Kater wants to accept this explanation, okay. But would he please explain to me why Wilhelm Mommsen instigated in 1944 the republication of this book, from which he distanced himself after 1945? And above all, if he no longer identified with the book after helpers, advisors, and editors had dabbled with the manuscript, why did he dedicate it to his sons. The passage in question reads:

> I dedicate this book to my four boys who represent a fourth generation, which has not consciously experienced the war. This generation is thriving in unbroken strength, because it takes the experience of growing up in the Reich of Adolf Hitler for granted. Some of the members have already contributed in a decisive way to the Führer's vision. (p. 10)

Does Kater believe that here too "the hand that signed the paper"[20] was the hand of dear old *Oberstudienrat* Huhnhäuser? How do Hans and Wolfgang Mommsen feel about this dedication? Isn't that the question? What have our German fathers left to us? How do we feel about it? When are we going to stop making excuses for them?

The same goes for our intellectual fathers: Wehler's *Doktor-Vater* Theodor Schieder, one of the founding fathers of West German liberal historiography wrote in 1939 as a "promising young scholar" a memorandum, in which he urged various government agencies in Berlin to implement "a population shift of the greatest dimensions" in the newly annexed part of Western Poland, as well as the "*Entjudung* [getting rid of all Jews] in the rest of Poland."[21] The existence of the Schieder Memorandum was well known among professional historians in Germany by 1991. But Wehler had nothing to say about the eager participation of his mentor in the worst aspects of the Nazi racial policy until 1999, and then only, because he was pressured by younger non-mainstream historians, such as Götz Aly and Peter Schöttler at the German Historical Congress in Frankfurt/Main.[22] After this congress, Wehler conceded, "there is no way of getting around it, the political options, Schieder took prior to 1945, must be criticized."[23] Claiming to be surprised by the Schieder revelation, Wehler maintains that because of the "most recent discoveries" in the archives, which had been inaccessible prior to 1989, "the contours of a pro-Nazi activism" of Schieder and other German historians are now emerging "out of a hitherto impenetrable past."[24]

Wehler writes in the same apologetic article:

Schieder kept a strict silence on one thing: we could not get one word out of him about the thirties and forties, especially about the period from 1934 to 1944 when he was at the University of Königsberg [a think tank for *Volkstumsforschung*, where one contemplated the purity of race and blood]. This gave rise to vague suspicions...[but] clarification didn't seem very urgent to us.[25]

A strange, impersonal student-teacher relationship, but one that is significant nevertheless! Schieder's reserve and Wehler's lack of curiosity in what his professor was likely engaged in, is symptomatic of something German, or at least of a character trait that has become second nature to Germans after 1945.

Michael Kater should be familiar with this syndrome, for there is a little bit of Schieder in most older Germans, just as there is a little bit of Wehler in most younger ones. This is true even if they live in Canada and hold chairs at Canadian universities. German-Canadians—and I am one also—as compared to Canadians of Italian or Greek origin, tend to keep a low profile. Helmut Rauca, who was charged by the West German government with the responsibility for the death of 10,500 Jews in the city of Kaunas, was described by his Canadian neighbors as "a hard man to talk to."[26] When the Canadian government closed in on the Heidehof Home for the Aged in St. Catharines, Ontario, and accused 89-year-old Mr. Fast of having been a Nazi collaborator who had ties to a special police unit that exterminated Jews during the Second

World War, neighbors said they couldn't believe the charges. One of them is quoted as saying: "It's not possible. He's such a quiet man."[27] Sol Littman covered the Rauca 1982 extradition proceedings for the Canadian Brodcasting Corporation. He recalls the reaction of the young German immigrant who served as his TV crew's soundman: "He chose his words carefully, translating the words from his mother tongue. 'What's the point of raking up these coals?...Why can't we let bygones be bygones.' "[28] Not that all German-Canadians are as unsociable as Helmut Rauca, nor are they disinterested in the past, but when the Third Reich and the Holocaust are brought up, they tend to symbolically slam the door or they talk about the topic, as if it had nothing to do with them, the way Kater does.

In short, perhaps more than any other ethnic group in the multi-cultural mosaic of Canada, German-Canadians have complied with the wishes of the nation, as articulated by J. L. Granatstein, Professor Emeritus at York University (where Kater also teaches) and Director of the Canadian War Museum, when he writes: "Does it [the nation] tell immigrants that they must leave their Old World political baggage at the water's edge? I believe it should."[29] German-Canadians have followed Granatstein's dictum. They seek the approval of fellow Canadians by dumping much of their cultural and historical baggage at their ports of entry. They seek to impress by being quiet and orderly. But rub them the wrong way—the way my book seems to have rubbed Michael Kater—and it becomes all too apparent, how much they are still burdened by their Old World baggage.

But let us return to the German historians, not only to the three Kater feels I have so terribly wronged, but many of that generation. For when we come right down to it, the issue at stake is the student-teacher relationship of an entire generation of German historians who studied with Theodor Schieder, Werner Conze, Otto Brunner, and other founding fathers of post-45 German historiography, whose formative academic years fell within the period of the Third Reich. Also at issue is the student-teacher relationship of senior historians, like Eberhard Jäckel who studied with Gerhard Ritter, a *Doktor-Vater* who went into "inner emigration" during the Nazi period. Ritter managed to keep his rebellious thoughts so securely to himself that even the Gestapo was unaware of them and felt it safe to use him as a foreign propagandist.[30] Sadly, the pessimism expressed by the American historians Charles Maier concerning the academic sons of these tenured intellectual fathers seems fully justified. Their track record makes it all too clear that they lack the intestinal fortitude for intellectual and emotional patricide.[31]

Wehler's assertion that his mentor's dark secret had to remain a secret until now, because the archives were closed, just isn't true. Dissertations, books, articles, memorandums, and project descriptions written during the Nazi period were accessible at all times for those interested in them. Moreover, they were whispered about in archive cubicles, on campus lawns, and in student cafeterias, but it was not considered good form to incorporate them in scholarly discourse. On page 36 of my book, I quote extensively from a mean-spirited anti-Semitic article, written by a certain Heinrich Steitz.[32] The custodian of the archives in a small town had tipped me off about the article; I followed his lead and had no difficulty, finding it. Unearthing the article caused considerable embarrassment, because Steitz was a Doctor of Divinity who remained on the faculty list of the Department of Protestant Theology at the University of Mainz. After the war, he had written the officially sanctioned history of the Evangelical Church in Hesse and Nassau. To top it off, he was an honorary member of the "Hessische kirchengeschichtliche Vereinigung," an association, devoted to research on the history of the Protestant Church in Hesse.

It was quite clear to me that I would do myself no favor, if I'd show the article "Juden in Petterweil" by Heinrich Steitz to my faculty advisor at Darmstadt University. (He was, incidentally, a re-educated Wehrmacht lieutenant.) But it was impossible to keep my discovery entirely to myself; hence, I shared my find with a junior member of the department, with whom I enjoyed pleasant chats from time to time. He didn't welcome the revelation. He wondered whether I had gotten it right, since it had not been entered in the bibliography of Steitz's writings, contained in a *Festschrift*, published on the occasion of his 80th birthday.[33] I gained the impression that my patronizing "friend" considered the article a triviality, a banal anti-Semitic piece published in an obscure provincial journal. "Johnny Canuck" was insufficiently versed in the German way of life and in my naivete I had done something that bordered on the indecent. I left his office with the impression that this "friend" felt kind of sorry for me.

I suppose, Wehler felt kind of sorry for Goldhagen, when he "admonished readers of the influential weekly *Die Zeit* to allow for the passions of Goldhagen's...arguments." In a Sunday paper he is quoted as having said: "Goldhagen tut mir ein wenig leid"[34] ("I feel a bit sorry for Goldhagen"). If Kater interprets these written comments as genuine expressions of sympathy, there must be something wrong with his psychological antennae. If Mommsen, Wehler and Jäckel are Goldhagen's friends, the young historian has no need of enemies.

For Michael Kater all of the above will confirm his set opinion that "*Hürnen Sewfriedte*" "argues badly that Daniel Goldhagen's thesis...is one-hundred-percent correct, and therefore unassailable." If my German-Canadian compatriot only knew! I won't deny that it came to a certain meeting of minds between the son of a Jewish survivor who wants to know and a German refugee child who is driven by a comparable need. To say that Daniel Goldhagen's response to the opening section of my book manuscript was positive would be an understatement. "I read it with great interest and found it to be extremely interesting, insightful, and powerful," he wrote, "I look forward to receive [the entire manuscript] from you whenever you would like to share it with me."[35] His response to the manuscript in its entirety was: "I do have questions!" When we finally met at a conference in May 1999, both of us were too inhibited to address them. He didn't get around to tell me what bothered him about my work and I was too shy to ask him. Making small talk, we assured each other again and again that we really had to talk, but the conference ended without either one of us having mustered the courage for the kind of question-and-answer session that would have enabled us to really become friends.

However, I do sense where the problem lies. Daniel Goldhagen makes himself believe—must perhaps make himself believe, in order to feel halfway at ease in Germany—that the foreign imported process of re-education has made a new people out of the Germans and that they live in a model democracy. I nurture no such illusion. When I returned to Germany in 1982, I still saw the old elites in power wherever I looked. When Kater reminds me that I forgot to mention Hans Mommsen's twin brother Wofgang J., as well as Wofgang Schieder, the son of Theodor Schieder, he is inadvertently agreeing with me that these old elites have not faded away yet. They, as well as the Germans in general, are, of course, no longer Nazis. The victorious Allies had ordered them to be good Germans and they had obeyed. This political reorientation had by no means been a painful, soul-searching learning experience. On the contrary, as the distinguished psychoanalyst and social critic Horst-Eberhard Richter notes:

> It was...a longed-for adaptation, more of a mechanical process, to be sure; an escape from one kind of bondage into another. But for the sake of self-respect one had to make oneself believe that what was in reality an exchanged dependence, was one's own conviction. The conscience, which seemed to work all of a sudden, was a conscience imposed by external forces. And this conscience spoke English.[36]

Years ago, when I introduced a newly arrived young doctoral student from the University of Buffalo to a Darmstadt Professor of Political Science who had obtained his Ph.D. at the University of Florida, the latter tried to impress the young woman with his exaggerated casual deportment and with American slang he had picked up in Florida. Later when he had left, the young perceptive woman from Buffalo said to me: "That man is as fake as a three dollar bill!"

There are other points of friction between Goldhagen and I, but I leave it to Kater to read my book again, in order to find them. I have already put more effort into responding to his review than he has put into reviewing my book. In closing I'd like to set his mind to rest concerning my career prospects. It really wasn't necessary for him to black-list me, in order to prevent me "from ever embarking on a serious university career." Others have taken care of that already.

Fred Kautz<br>Darmstadt

## NOTES

1. Cf. "Objektivität als Heilmittel?" in Winfried Schulze, *Deutsche Geschichtswissenschaft nach 1945* (Münich: R. Oldenbourg, 1989), pp. 201-206.

2. Christopher R. Browning, *Ganz normale Männer: Das Reserve-Polizeibataillon 101 und die "Endlösung" in Polen*, trans. into German by Jürgen Peter Krause (Reinbek bei Hamburg: Rowohlt, 1993), p. 15.

3. Browning's book is in many ways the product of American education, as Kurt Vonnegut Jr. describes it in his Dresden novel, when he writes: "I think about my education sometimes. I went to the University of Chicago for a while after the Second World War. I was a student in the Department of Anthropology. At that time, they were teaching that there was absolutely no difference between anybody. They may be teaching that still." *Slaughterhouse-Five or the Children's Crusade: A Duty-dance with Death* (St. Albans: Panther Books, 1972), p. 13. In any event, the underlying concept of human nature in *Ordinary Men* fails to elucidate adequately why the policemen needed no or hardly any conditioning at all to kill Jews. A recent article on the massacre at Brest-Litovsk provides a graphic description on how ready the men of Police Battalion 307 were from the start to perform their grizzly task. Cf. Klaus-Michael Mallmann, "Der Einstieg in den Genozid: Das Lübecker Polizeibataillon 307 und das Massaker in Brest-Litowsk Anfang Juli 1941," *Archiv für Polizeigeschichte* (1999), p.p. 82-88.

4. Ernst Nolte, "Vergangenheit, die nicht vergehen will—Eine Rede, die geschrieben, aber nicht gehalten werden konnte," *Frankfurter Allgemeine Zeitung*, 6 June 1986, in *Vergangenheit, die nicht vergeht: Die "Historiker-Debatte", Dokumentation, Darstellung und Kritik*, ed. Reinhard Kühnl (Cologne: Pahl-Rugenstein, 1987), p. 36.

5. Cf. Heinrich Senfft, *Kein Abschied von Hitler: Ein Blick hinter die Fassaden des "Historikerstreits,"* Kleine historische Bibliothek, 2 (Hamburg: Hamburger Stiftung für Sozialforschung des 20. Jahrhunderts, 1990), p. 65.

6. On December 7, 2000 a panel discussion was held in Frankfurt/Main under the auspices of the Fritz Bauer Institut. The topic was "NS-Täter—Stand und Perspectiven der Forschung" ("Nazi Perpetrators: The Current State of Research and Prospects"). The consensus of the panelists Gerhard Paul, Klaus-Michael Mallmann, Gerd R. Ueberschär, and Ahlrich Meyer was that structuralist and functionalsit history à la Mommsen and Wehler is hampering research to this day. The category of "perpetrator" virtually doesn't exist in this conception of history; it only knows *Tatgehilfen*, i.e., aiders and abettors who acted under external pressures.

7. In the typescript of the American interogation officer Samson B. Knoll, who questioned Wilhelm Mommsen in April 1945, one reads: "The oldest son was last drafted into a FLAK unit and his whereabouts are at present unknown." Dennazification file of Wilhelm Mommsen, HstA Wiesbaden, Abt. 520 Fu 1835, II, cit. in Anne Chr[istine] Nagel, "'Der Prototyp der Leute, die man entfernen soll, ist Mommsen': Entnazi-

fizierung in der Provinz oder die Ambiguität moralischer Gewißheit," *Jahrbuch für Liberalismusforschung*, Vol. 10 (1998), p. 62, note 25.

8. Interview with Hans-Ulrich Wehler in *Versäumte Fragen: Deutsche Historiker im Schatten des Nationalsozialismus*, ed. Rüdiger Hohls and Konrad H. Jarausch (Stuttgart and Munich: Deutsche Verlags-Anstalt, 2000), p. 240.

9. Cf. Heinz Bude, *Deutsche Karrieren: Lebenskonstruktionen sozialer Aufsteiger aus der Flakhelfer-Generation*, edition suhrkamp NF 448 (Frankfurt am Main: Suhrkamp, 1987), p. 22.

10. Interview with Hans-Ulrich Wehler in *Versäumte Fragen*, p. 241.

11. Cf. Jürgen Leinemann, Paul Lersch, and Hartmut Palmer, "Der Bimbes-Kanzler," *Der Spiegel*, 21 Feb. 2000, pp. 44-55.

12. Cf. "Hans-Jochen Vogel—deutscher Politiker; SPD; Dr. jur.," *Munzinger-Archiv/Internat. Biograph. Archiv* 43/94.

13. Cf. "Bernhard Vogel—deutscher Politiker; Ministerpräsident von Rheinland-Pfalz (1976-1988) und Thüringen; CDU; Dr. Phil.," *Munzinger-Archiv/Internat. Biograph. Archiv* 50/99.

14. Anita Kugler, "Die Rückgabe der Vergangenheit," *die tageszeitung*, 20 June 1994, p. 3.

15. Dietmar Rothwange, "Interview mit Hans-Jochen Vogel, 'Kein Spaziergang,'" *ötv-magazin* 1/2 (1998), pp. 21-22.

16. Nationalsozialistischer Lehrerbund Deutschland / Sachsen, ed., *Bekenntnis der Professoren an den deutschen Universitäten und Hochschulen zu Adolf Hitler und dem nationalsozialistischen Staat*, 11. [?] Nov. 1933, p. 131. In his article "Die nationalsozialistische Machtergreifung an den deutschen Hochschulen. Zum politischen Verhalten akademischer Lehrer bis 1939," in *Die Freiheit des Anderen: Festschrift für Martin Hirsch*, ed. By hans-Jochen Vogel et al. (Baden-Baden: Nomos 1981),pp. 49-75, Michael Kater subjects 675 professors who signed this declaration to a statistical analysis. However, quantitative history brings him not much closer to the answer he really is looking for, namely: what kind of human being was that upright individual, whom Joachim Fest calls "Professor NSDAP?" I suppose that a painful question-and-answer session with Hans Mommsen about his father Wilhelm, in which the former could also ask Kater about his German father—"Die Deutschen sollten sich ihre Biographien erzählen" (Richard von Weitzsäcker)—would yield a more satisfactory answer than do mere calculations with percentages and formulas.

17. Cf. Helmut Heiber, *Walter Frank und sein Reichsinstitut für Geschichte des neuen Deutschlands* (Stuttgart: Deutsche Verlags-Anstalt, 1966), p. 767.

18. There are various versions about the violent death of the Brownshirt bard, Horst Wessel. According to the collectors album *Die Nachkriegszeit: Historische Bilddokumente, 1918-1934* ([Dresden, 1935]), published by the Eckstein-Halpaus and Waldorf-Astoria cigarette manufacturer, Wessel was ambushed and shot in his lodging room by Com-

munists on January 14, 1930. According to another version, the gunman fired at him from among a squad of Red Front street-fighters. Cf. Hans Peter Bleuel *Das saubere Reich* (Bern and Munich: Scherz, 1972), p. 3. Whatever the case may be, the violent death of Horst Wessel, whom Goebbels later stylized into a "blood witness," seems to have had just as much to do with rivalry over a prostitute, as over a clash of *Weltanschauung* between Nazis and Communists. Ali Höhler, the gunman, is said to have been the ex-pimp of Wessel's sweetheart. Hence, what Mommsen Sr. writes about Wessel is vile kitsch.

19. See interview with Hans Mommsen, in *Versäumte Fragen*, p. 164.

20. *The Hand that Signed the Paper* is the title of an allegedly autobiographical family saga, written by a Helen Demidenko. In 1995 the book was selected as Australia's best novel of the year and received the Miles Franklin Prize. The author gave in her book the impression that she had found the answer to a dark family secret, the answer to the question, as to why her Ukrainian father had participated in the massacre of Jews at Babi Yar and why her relatives had served as guards in Treblinka. Allegedly they had done so, in order to take revenge for what the Jews had done to the Ukrainians. The malaise, caused by this assertion , became one of Australia's greatest literary scandals, . when it was revealed that the book had actually been written by Helen Darville, the daughter of British emigrants. For an analysis of this Australian literary scandal, see: Robert Manne, The Culture of Forgetting: Helen Demidenko and the Holocaust (Melbourne: the Text publishing company, 1996).

21. Cit. in Angelika Ebbinghaus and Karl Heinz Roth, "Deutsche Historiker und der Holocaust," *1999: Zeitschrift für Sozialgeschichte des 20. und 21. Jahrhunderts*, No. 3 (1991), p. 8.

22. "Deutsche Historiker im Nationalsozialismus," moderation Otto Gerhard Oexle (Göttingen) and Winfried Schulze (Munich) in *42. Deutscher Historikertag, Frankfurt am Main 1998, Zeitgeschichte, Skriptenheft* III, p. 45-46; "Geschichte muß alle 20 Jahre neu geschrieben werden," [interview with Johannes Fried, President of the German Historical Association] in *Welt im Gespräch*, Sonderdruck zum 42. Deutschen Historikertag Frankfurt/Main; Volker Ullrich, "Hitlers willige Zunft – Ein Geleitwort zum Frankfurter Historikertag," *Die Zeit*, 3 Sept. 1998, p. 40; Franziska Augstein, "Schlangen in der Grube – Im Disput vereint: Der 42. Deutsche Historikertag," *Frankfurter Allgemeine Zeitung*, 14 Sept. 1998, p. 49; Ralph Bollmann, "Die Vordenker der Vernichtung – Das Beschweigen und Beschwichtigen ist vorbei: Auf dem 42. Deutschen Historikertag in Frankfurt am Main wurde aufgearbeitet, daß namhafte Geschichtsforscher der dreißiger Jahre die nationalsozialistische Umsiedlungs- und Volkstumspolitik legitimiert haben," *die tageszeitung*, 14 Sept. 1998, p. 16; Kurt Petzold, "Streit unter den Klio-Jüngern – Das Geschichtsbild von Karl E. Erdmann und die Probleme deutscher Historiker," *Neues Deutschland*, 9 Jan. 1998, p. 13; Winfried Schulze and Gerhard Oexle, ed., *Deutsche Historiker im Nationalsozialismus* (Frankfurt am Main: Fischer Taschenbuch Verlag; 1999).

23. Hans-Ulrich Wehler, "In den Fußstapfen der kämpfenden Wissenschaft – Braune Erde an den Schuhen: Haben Historiker wie Schieder sich nach dem Krieg von ihrer Vergangenheit ganz verabschiedet?" *Frankfurter Allgemeine Zeitung*, 4 Jan. 1999, p. 48.

24. Wehler, "Fußstapfen," p. 48.

25. Wehler, "Fußstapfen," p. 48.

26. Sol Littman, *War Criminal on Trial: Rauca of Kaunas*, 2nd ed. (Toronto: Keys Porter Books, 1998), p. 128.

27. Andrew Mitrovica, "Nazi Allegations Shock, Upset man, his Lawyer says," *The Globe and Mail*, 11 Dec. 1999.

28. Littman, p. 13.

29. J. L. Granatstein, *Who killed Canadian History?* (Toronto: HarperCollins, 1999), p. 85.

30. See Hannah Arendt, "Das Bild der Hölle" in *Nach Auschwitz: Essays und Kommentare* (Berlin, 1989), I, 59.

31. See Peter Schöttler, p. 26, n. 36.

32. Heinrich Steitz, "Juden in Petterweil," *Friedberger Geschichtsblätter: Beiträge zur Geschichte und Landeskunde der Wetterau*, 15 (1940), 76-83.

33. Heiko Wulpert, "Professor D. Dr. Heinrich Steitz: Bibliographie 1935-1985," *Jahrbuch der Hessischen Kirchengeschichtlichen Vereinigung* (1986), pp. 147-152.

34. Hans Mommsen, " 'Goldhagen tut mir ein wenig leid.' Der Bochumer Holocaust-Experte über die Folgen des jüngsten Historiker-Streits," *Deutsches Allgemeines Sonntagsblatt*, 3 April 1998.

35. Daniel Jonah Goldhagen, letter, 9 June 1997.

36. Horst-Eberhard Richter, *Die Chance des Gewissens: Erinnerungen und Assoziationen* (Munich: Deutscher Taschenbuch Verlag, 1988), pp. 52-53.

# INSTEAD OF A POSTSCRIPT

### Letter to my Children
### on the Occasion of the 50th Anniversary of VE-Day

Dear Rania and dear Jacob, in connection with your school project, "The End of the War and Germany's Capitulation in 1945," you asked me to tell you what I can remember. In return, I asked whether there was anything in particular you wanted to know, but you said you wanted to know everything. Everything? If only that would be possible! You have to understand that I was born during the war. Hence, I was still a child at that time and could hardly understand the things that I experienced.

That will also be the case with other adults you know: your classroom teacher, the director of your school, as well as the neighbours in our apartment building. Going by their age, I would say that most of them have experienced the war in one way or another. And because just about all members of this group have experienced the war, so that—when they look around—they only see people who had experiences, similar to their own, the majority tries to convince itself that what they have gone through was nothing unusual, by no means something so horrendous that it scarred them for life. One cannot have experienced death and destruction all around, and one cannot have escaped death and live afterwards as if nothing had happened. Firestorm bombardments, having to flee from one's home, and the loss of close relatives, leaves traces. To this add the question of how all this could happen and who is to blame? These are questions which arouse feelings of guilt and shame, not only in the war generation, but also in the children and grandchildren of the war generation. There are only a very few who are prepared to listen to the disquieting voices of the past.

The war, for me, has been such a decisive formative experience that I would be less than honest, if I would say, 'What happened, happened—forget it! Just look straight ahead into the future!' To help you understand, I have to reach back and tell you about your German-Canadian grandparents, about my father and mother.

*The Bessarabian Prehistory*
Your grandparents were ethnic Germans from Bessarabia, where they had a small farm. Bessarabia, as you must know, is a strip of land between Russia and Rumania, extending down to the Black Sea. The Djnester River constituted the border with the USSR, the River Pruth, the border with Rumania. According to your grandparents, Bessarabia must have been very beautiful. I heard about its fertile soil, about clean and tidy villages with blossoming acacia trees lining the streets, dissipating a pleasant sweet smell, with wells of fresh water where the cattle would quench their thirst. However, if I see nowadays reports on the news about Moldavia (Bessarabia has in the meantime become the Moldavian Republic), I start to think that in retrospect my parents must only have been able to see their native land through rose-coloured glasses, for to me the region looks pretty desolate. But it seems to be human nature to love one's native land, regardless of how it looks or whether it has a flourishing economy or not. Be this as it may, from time immemorial the strip of land between the Djnester and Pruth seems to have attracted its neighbors. In the past Russians and Rumanians quarreled about this piece of land and the way things are going they may quarrel over it again within the near future.

At the beginning of this story, Stalin, with the connivance of Hitler, seized control of Bessarabia. On June 27, 1940 the Soviet dictator gave the Rumanians four days to get out of Bessarabia. But the Red Army didn't even wait for the expiration of those four days; it crossed the Djnester River on June 28, 1940. Fascist Rumania, betrayed by its supposed ally, Adolf Hitler, was too weak to withstand the Soviet onslaught.

*The Russians are Coming, The Rumanians flee Head over Heels, Your Grandfather just wants to stay with Grandma*
The exchange of ownership of Bessarabia must have been pretty chaotic. The Rumanian army tried to take along everything that wasn't nailed down, but had then to discard most of its loot along the wayside, because of the hasty re-

treat. And although they didn't have a fighting chance against the Soviet invasion forces, the Rumanians, in a desperate effort, mobilized all able-bodied men. Your grandfather, who had already served as a conscript in a Rumanian artillery regiment, was called back, but like many Bessarabia-Germans who had been called back to active duty, he deserted.

Together with two other deserters, a Jew and an ethnic Hungarian from Transylvania, he hid himself in a cornfield, in order to return to his family once the Rumanian army had moved out of sight. He didn't want to retreat with the Rumanians to Rumania proper and abandon your grandmother in Soviet administered Bessarabia. If he had done so, he might never have seen her again.

*"Home to the Fatherland" Departure from Bessarabia*
According to a secret clause of the Hitler-Stalin Pact, under which Bessarabia was severed from Rumania and annexed to the Soviet Union, the Bessarabia-Germans were to be transferred to Nazi Germany. They were urged by the Germans to "come home to the fatherland." In compliance with this call (was it an invitation or coercion?) your grandparents, together with their children, left their house and home in Bessarabia on October 13, 1940. On a trek organized by a German-Soviet commission they were routed in the direction of Nazi Germany.

You cannot imagine what that must have been like, nor can I.

Hundreds and thousands of people left their house and home in order to start a new life in Germany. Whole villages got underway, moving with horse-drawn wagons. One statistical tabulation mentions 11,630 wagons and 22,922 horses. But these figures refer only to the transportation of 20,301 persons. Another count mentions an additional 15,273. There must have been even more horses and wagons. Then 30,461 people were supposed to have been transported by trucks and 22,337 by rail.

The first destinations were the Danube ports Kilia and Reni, and the Black Sea port Galatz. There the German Relocation Commission loaded the horses and wagons on ships, in order to move them to Germany.

Able-bodied men, your grandfather among them, were sent ahead. From Galatz, Rumania, to the transit camp Prachowa, also in Rumania, they were transported on Danube steamships. From there they were moved by rail. Women, children and elderly people were moved by rail from Jargara, Rumania, to the Danube port of Reni, then by Danube steamships to a transit camp in Prachowa. Your grandmother, Leni (my older sister and your aunt who lives now in Canada), my older brother Willie, as well as Ida (a cousin of mine) were on this transport.

*Death of my older Brother*
The transit camp in Prachowa consisted of provisional barracks and tents. Since it was already getting colder, Willie contracted pneumonia while bedded in the tent on the bare ground. The medical support staff took him from my mother, urged her to join the next transport, assuring her that there was no need to worry because her son would be sent after her in a special transport for those too sick to be moved by regular means. However, something went wrong. Later in the transit camp in Austria, your grandparents received an official letter from Silesia containing Willie's death certificate. What actually happened to Willie is a mystery to this day. Other Bessarabia-German resettlers who had relatives on hospital trains and ships also received death notices from Silesia. Till she died, your grandmother could not quite believe that Willie was dead. She thought that he might have lost his name tag, so that he was confused with someone else and that he might still be living today, without knowing, where his parents are. My worst suspicion is that the Rasse- und Siedlungshauptamt of the SS, which organized the gigantic transferal operation, classified critically ill patients as "lebensunwert" ("not worth bothering with"), and just let them starve to death.

*The Transit Camp St. Anna*
In any case, after the medical support staff had taken her son from her, your grandmother, together with Leni and Ida, got on the next transport to Austria. Your grandparents met each other again in the castle of the small Austrian town of Fischelham, which served as another transit camp. The next morning they were routed to Ried im Innkreis and quartered in the nunnery

St. Anna, which had been requisitioned from the nuns to make room for the arriving Bessarabia-Germans.

There they stayed for a whole year. Your grandfather worked for a local coal retail merchant and later in a brewery, while your grandmother got a job as a seamstress in a military tailorshop. She had the fondest memories of the camaraderie that existed between the seamstresses, cutters, pressers, and pattern makers. At lunchtime one of them would go over to the tavern next door and bring back grub and a big mug of beer, which would be passed around and all would drink out of it.

What I have to tell you here too, is that in this SS-operated camp the resettlers were also subjected to extensive Nazi brainwashing. They were given lectures, in which the *Volk* was extolled and "the Jew" vilified. In the Kindergarten little Ida learned Nazi songs like "Adolf Hitler soll uns führen in die neue Zeit..." ("Let Adolf Hitler lead us into the new age..."). My sister Leni was indoctrinated with the Nazi gospel in the school. Soldiers with the Iron Cross and Close Combat Badge on their tunic visited the school and described the war, in which Germany (at this time still seemed invincible), as a grand adventure. The kids must have eaten this up. For famous tank commanders and flying aces must have been idols to them, the way DJs and basketball players are the idols of kids nowadays.

And before I forget, the Nazis bestowed on your grandmother the "honor" of making her *"Blockwartin"* (Block Warden) or something like that. In this official position she was, according to her, *only* required to collect contributions for the *Winterhilfswerk* (Winter Relief). I have the suspicion that this is an understatement on the part of my mother. For if you ask German people who were adults during the Nazi period, what they had done during those critical years, most of them will say that they *"only"* did this or that, which didn't hurt anybody. That just can't be true. For if all Germans had done *only* those relatively harmless things, which they recalled afterwards, the support the Nazis received from amongst the people wouldn't have added up to anything and they never could have done the horrendous things they did.

It is reasonable to assume that your grandmother did more than just go from door to door to canvas for the Winter Relief. Studies on the Third Reich tell us that it was part of the Block Warden's duty to observe the neighbourhood and to report irregularities to higher authorities. I find it hard to believe that your grandmother maliciously spied on neighbours and deliberately denounced those who had stepped out of line, for she was a good-natured woman who was not interested very much in politics. However, she had always been a law-abiding German with undue respect for authority. It might be quite possible that she readily divulged information about the neighbourhood when Nazi officials came and asked her.

Moreover, the ethnic German resettlers were also screened for "racial purity." Those who had only ancestors of "German blood" were considered to be the best. The Nazis intended to resettle them in the newly conquered Polish territories. The others, in whose family tree one detected intermarriages with Russians, Bulgarians or Rumanians, were classified as "inferior" human stock. They were to be resettled in Germany proper to be deployed as wage earners in the economy, mainly in the armaments industry and the mining sector.

That almost happened to uncle Theodor, the husband of your grandfather's sister Elsa. The Nazis claimed to have found Japanese ancestors in his family tree. I still recall uncle Theodor; his face did indeed look somewhat Asiatic. Nonetheless, a benevolent official must have closed both eyes in his case, for he and his family were resettled along with other Bessarabia-Germans in West Prussia.

In our family tree the Nazis found neither on your grandfather's side, nor on your grandmother's side anything that could have aroused their suspicion.

*Here my Story begins: Birth and Baptism*

But I am going too fast. Before narrating the continuation of the odyssey to West Prussia, I must stop and tell you that my story begins in the resettlement camp St. Anna in Ried, Upper Austria. I was born there on August 30, 1941. It was a sensation of sorts, because I was the first child of Bessarabia-German resettlers to be born in the camp. The Lagerführer—there is a picture of him in his black SS uniform in the family album in Canada—congratulated my mother and presented to her a bouquet of flowers. When it came to choosing a name for me, little Ida was supposed to have said: "Why don't you just call him

Adolf Hitler?" Fortunately I was spared being stigmatized with the "Führer's" whole name. However, in the spirit of the times my parents burdened me with the middle name "Adolf." As embarrassing as it is, on my baptismal certificate there is this shameful middle name, giving testimony as to what political state of mind my parents were in at the time.

*Tuschinwald, where I escaped an Early Death just by the Skin of my Teeth*
Soon after my birth and after little Ida had been returned to her mother, we were routed to the next transit camp, namely to Tuschinwald in the vicinity of Lodz (which had been renamed Litzmannstadt by the Nazis). In Tuschinwald we had to wait for another year before we were settled on a farm. The conditions in the camp were intolerable. Our family, now consisting of four persons, had to share a two-room dwelling with another family of six—a quarrelsome grandfather and an infirm grandmother among them. The air is said to have been suffocating. No matter how penetrating the stench, the grandfather from the other family would not tolerate that the cramped quarters be aired by opening the window. And the stench must have been nauseating indeed, because the grandmother of the other family was so infirm that she tipped over the chamber pot when she tried to sit on it. On top of this, the rooms were ice cold and infested with bed bugs.

I was two months old at the time, and my mother told me that I cried at the top of my lungs in reaction to the bed bugs and the stench. She also told me that eventually I got very sick and almost died. To save my life, I was transferred to the pediatric ward in a hospital in Lodz. For the duration of my stay there my mother was quartered in an adjacent camp for resettlers, so she could easily come to the hospital and breast-feed me. After I had recuperated somewhat, my mother took me back to Tuschinwald, where I got as sick again.

To save my life once more, the Red Cross nurse in the camp made arrangements for my admission to the camp clinic. There I was kept until my parents were settled on a farm. Eventually my sister Leni, who was eleven at the time, also got so sick that she spent more time in the hospital than in the transit camp.

In April 1942, it was finally our turn for settlement on a farm. In anticipation your grandparents and your Aunt Leni were sent on to the next resettlement camp in Neumark County in West Prussia. In accordance with the urgent advice from the doctors, I was left in the clinic in Tuschinwald. My parents were to leave me there until they got settled on "their" new farm.

However, more time passed before they got a farm. The one that had originally been set aside for them had, in the meantime, been given to other resettlers. They had to wait another month in the camp in Neumark, before a farm was found for them.

*Erinnere mich, lass uns miteinander rechten! (Jes. 43,26)*
By May 1942 they got a farm. It was only 6 km from Neumark in the village of Neuhof. To settle my parents on this farm, the people of the Rasse- und Siedlungshauptamt of the SS had simply dispossessed a Polish farmer whom they had assured earlier that he would not be affected by the resettlement program. This farmer, by the name of Arendt, was given notice in the morning and my parents came to the farm the same afternoon. This means that my parents became the benefactors of stolen property.

Concerning your question about my recollections, they begin on this farm near the village of Neuhof. I still remember a fabulous rocking horse. The Polish farmer Arendt, who was put in quarters nearby, had made it for me. Your grandparents kept in contact with him. At his request, they employed his nephew, a student by the name of Alphons Kuklinski, as a farm hand.

I remember him as my first real friend. Here my own recollections and what I have been told by my parents mingle together. Alphons liked me. He carried me on his shoulders. When he hitched up the horses, he let me ride shotgun with him. And when we passed people, he proudly said: "Fritz ist mein Freund!"

My friend Alphons died. Because the Nazis no longer had enough able-bodied men to draft for their genocidal war, they conferred German citizenship on Alphons and drafted him, against his will, into the Wehrmacht. He was killed in action during the Normandy Invasion.

*Fleeing from the Red Army*

On January 19, 1945 we had to flee head over heels from Neuhof, West Prussia, because the Red Army was closing in and could not be stopped. My younger brother Paul had been born just one week earlier. My father fetched my mother and my new brother Paul in all haste from the hospital. Then a hog was hastily butchered so that we would have provisions for the long uncertain journey. Everything that could possibly be taken along was heaved on two covered wagons, including a heavy sowing machine with cast iron legs, which also went on the trip with us when we immigrated from Germany to Canada.

The westward trek lasted nine weeks. At the end of March, or in the beginning of April, we arrived in Öftinghausen, Diepholz County, in Lower Saxony. I have faint, dark recollections of this fearful odyssey. We had two horse-drawn covered wagons. My father led the way in the first one, drawn by two mares named Liesa and Starucha. My sister, who was thirteen at the time, followed with the lighter wagon, pulled by a red mare, named Korsa. You have to remember the names Liesa, Starucha, and Korsa, for it were these horses that saved our lives. Without them we most surely would have succumbed.

I sat in the first wagon with my mother and my new brother who was, at the start of this frightful journey, only six days old. I believe that I still can remember his little white knitted jacket. It was bitter cold. Nonetheless, I didn't want to stay in the back of the wagon where there was shelter and squeezed myself on the driver's seat beside my father. I wanted to see. What there was to see was the trek of refugees, slowly creeping westward, and at intervals German military convoys moving in the opposite direction, hurled at the Red Army close on our heels.

In my ears I can still hear the horse's hoofs pounding the frozen ground. How these poor beasts must have suffered! They ceaselessly had to pull these heavy wagons. There was no time to stop, for we dreaded falling in the hands of the Russians. When my sister Leni's hands and face were frozen stiff and she could no longer hold the reigns, your grandfather would unhitch Korsa, let her trot beside the two lead horses, and hitch the second wagon onto the first one, so that Leni could join us for a while, in order to warm up.

Vaguely, I remember that we crossed a river during the middle of the night. How does one describe something that one has forgotten but by which one is haunted nevertheless? It must have been the Oder River. So that the wagons would not thunder uncontrollably down the bank of the river, my father stuck heavy logs between the spokes of the wheels.

In disconnected memory fragments, I recall that we drove over ice and that there was the risk of breaking through or sliding sideways into the water. But was it really like that? Can a river like the Oder freeze over? Perhaps it was a pontoon bridge we crossed, built by Wehrmacht engineers.

As much as I try, from here on my memory fails me and I cannot recall what else we experienced on this hazardous journey. Neither can I recall any kind of emotion that I must have experienced, as my smaller brother was slowly dying before my eyes. Was I aware that his life was hanging by a thread? How did I cope with this? I don't know.

*Death of my Younger Brother*

According to what my mother told me, we were left behind in Soltau near Lüneburg because Paul was in urgent need of medical attention. But the doctors and nurses came too late. He died in agony. It's a wonder he hung on to life for so long. His funeral in Soltau was interrupted by aerial bombardment.

A few years ago, while visiting acquaintances in Fallingbostel, I made a trip to the nearby town of Soltau. I wanted to see Paul's grave and if that didn't exist anymore, at least the entry in the burial records. No one answered the door at the parsonage when I knocked, and in the city hall I was received with polite indifference and told that no one could help me. A local historian, a young woman, to whom I was referred in a bookstore, promised me that she would do some research on my behalf, but I never heard from her again.

*Arrival in Öftinghausen, Lower Saxony*

On March 25 we arrived in Diepholz County, Lower Saxony—our final destination. I remember this fairly well. What I can't remember, I have heard from my parents and from Leni.

It was a beautiful spring day, sun was shining in a cloudless sky. The trek we had joined in Soltau halted in the village of Schmalförden. Our wagons stood at the intersection. We enjoyed the warm spring weather and waited to be quartered on various farms. Leni tells me that she had me on her lap and that she was picking lice from my head. Trekking for weeks on end cross country while war is going on is not very sanitary!

We were assigned to the farm of Heini Schwenecker in Öftinghausen. That was quite convenient at the start, for farmer Heini had been part of the German occupation force in Norway and became a POW of the British. My father managed his farm till he was released. That my father could do well, for he was a farmer.

On the farm there was also a grandmother—the mother of farmer Heini. We, as refugees, were an abomination in her eyes. Only grudgingly did she let us get water from the pump, which was in the farm house. Heinz, the oldest son of farmer Heini, was filthy and malicious. If he and his grandmother had their way, they would have quartered us in the stable and stored plows and other farm utensils in our living space. Of Aunt Minna, the farmer's wife, I have fond memories. She always tried to defuse tension and secretly she supplied us with food.

If my memory is correct, we initially lived in various rooms in the farm house, first in the living room, than in two rooms in the garret. Eventually we were quartered in the *"Backhaus,"* a small separate building, which contained the oven for baking bread. There we had a kitchen and another small enclosure which served as our bed- and living-room. In front of these two cells, was an anteroom containing a hearth with a big kettle used for bailing pig-slop.

*The End of the War*
Somehow I also remember May 8, 1945, the day of the German surrender. It must have been announced on the radio. The horses were hitched up, in order to join other villagers in looting the nearby barracks of the Reich Labor Service. People took everything they could lay hands on: food stuff, uniforms, Venetian blinds. What I can remember most is a Reich Labor Service wedge cap, which I got to wear, and a Nazi history book with many pictures of Wehrmacht soldiers, which fascinated me, as well as dinner plates with the Reich Labor Service emblem. The latter we took with us to Canada.

Then the British army came. I remember the first British soldiers. There was distant shots. A while later, figures emerged from the woods and across the meadow towards the farm. They were British soldiers, "Tommies," as we called them. They had shot a buck and wanted to skin it and carve up the carcass. These British soldiers were not hostile at all and tried to communicate with us. One pulled out of his wallet snapshots of his wife and children and showed them to us. I have fond memories of these Brits. Later I was to wear a similar uniform in the Canadian Army.

That was the actual end of the war. What we experienced in the subsequent weeks were accompanying symptoms of the total collapse of the "Thousand Year Reich." Since the farm of Heini Schwenecker was quite a distance from the village, it was an ideal hiding place for fugitive German soldiers who wanted to avoid being taken prisoner by the British. It is deplorable how the hard-hearted mother of farmer Heini sent them away. They were hungry, constantly watching to avoid British patrols, and they were exhausted. The barn would have had plenty of space to give them a chance to rest. With a small piece of bacon farmer Heini's mother sent them on their way. Afterwards she acted in front of my mother as if she had shared her last slice of bread with them.

Now the farm was also visited regularly by liberated Eastern Europeans (who had formerly been utilized as slave labor in the German economy), so-called DPs, and by Allied POWs. These appreciated the isolation of the farm, for here they could slaughter a hog or a cow without permit and make moonshine booze, without being disturbed. I remember two Serbs in their peculiar uniforms especially well. When they came, it was party time. They generously shared their loot with us and they always had gallons of Schnapps, which they drank like water.

*Travels in a Defeated and Divided Country*

Part of my post-war memories have to do with travel. The roads and the rail system had been badly damaged during the war. Because of a shortage of gasoline, traffic had virtually come to a standstill. The few trains in operation were overcrowded.

Once my mother traveled with me to Bassum or Bremen. At one station we waited for a connecting train. But this train was so full that one had to push and shove to get inside. With the help of other passengers who pushed and pulled, my mother managed to get inside. But I was left standing on the platform yelling "Mama!" as the train pulled out of the station.

The station master, a man with the red cap, took care of me. He telephoned the next station, leaving the message that he would put me on the next train. When I arrived at the next station, my mother was greatly relieved, as was I.

I also remember illegal border crossings into the Russian Zone of Germany. Here I have to explain to you that soon after the war discord broke out between the victorious Allies—between the Russians, on the one side, and the Americans, the British, and the French, on the other. As a result, the Russian zone of occupation was sealed off from the Western zones.

Most of your grandmother's relatives had ended up after the war in the Russian Zone. Your grandmother was constantly toying with the idea of moving there. Not only the reunion with her relatives who lived there made such a move attractive to her, but also the fact that the Russians expropriated the big German land owners, the Junkers, whom they rightly held responsible for the war, in order to distribute the land to the landless. Her brother Albert and her sister Paula had gotten small farms this way.

We wanted to visit this aunt. Her farm hand, a young fellow who had just recently returned from Russia where he had been a POW and who was preparing to join the garrisoned *Volkspolizei*, the People's Police, came to fetch us from the British Zone. I remember that he had on his book shelve heavy volumes which had the head of Lenin stamped in the cover. On the way back we encountered two enlisted men from the People's Police. It turned out that they, too, were Bessarabia-Germans. My parents, as well as they, were happy to have met each other. The two policemen wished us a safe return home.

We were caught by a Russian patrol when we tried to cross the border illegally. We had just come out of the woods, were crossing a clearing, and felt unobserved, when all of a sudden Russian soldiers, wearing fur caps and carrying Kalashnikows sub-machine guns appeared and yelled "Stoi!"

We were in great fear of them, but to them, catching us was great fun. Since my mother spoke Russian, she was able to communicate with them. They told her that they had observed us for some time and that they had been waiting for us in their hideout.

My father was escorted away separately. My mother, my sister, and me were handed over to the People's Police at the border checkpoint. When mother asked the Russians what was going to happen to her husband, the Russians laughed and told her, she should find herself another man.

The People's Police kept us for a day in a dismal cell. Whether we were reunited with your grandfather there, at the checkpoint, before we were released into the British Zone, or whether he followed us to the West days later, I can't remember. All I can recall is the feeling of uncertainty we had concerning his fate. Your grandmother feared that the Russians might send him to Siberia.

*Burned Child Plays with Matches*
Yes, and how did we children pass the time while events of world historical significance touched our lives? You asked me about the games we played. Strange, I recall most vividly the dangerous games we played. Helmut, the farmer's son, who was a year younger, and I, strayed through the nearby woods. A sand pit in the woods, into which people threw all kinds of junk, was, for us, a kind of adventure playground. There we found discarded ammunition, bayonets, steel helmets, and Nazi badges. Using pliers, Heinz, Helmut's older brother, and we, used to remove the projectile from rounds of ammunition, strew the sticks of cordite from the ammunition shell onto the ground, and set them aflame. The percussion caps of the bullets we put on a stone and hit with a hammer to get a bigger bang. We can consider ourselves fortunate that nothing happened to us. Other children who played with ammunition lost limbs, eyesight, even their lives.

But not all games we played were dangerous. Helmut preferred to play farmer. Pine cones were his cows, acorns his sheep. The animals on the farm also offered opportunity for play. There was a big dog by the name of Prinz who had been taught to pull a small cart with rubber wheels, which was used to transport milk containers. And then there was a small dog, a bitch, by the name of Minka. These were our companions. Riding the farm horses was also great fun, bare-back, of course.

Our mare Liesa first changed ownership to farmer Heini, who subsequently sold her to a grocery store owner in the nearby village of Schweringhausen. This grocer hitched her to his covered wagon, with which he traveled from village to village and from farm to farm in order to sell his goods. When he stopped at the Schweneker farm, Helmut and I would compete to offer hands full of grass to "our" Liesa. Frequently, we got into heated arguments over whether the mare belonged to Helmut or to me.

*Elementary School in Schmalförden*
Somehow a kind of "normality" returned. Schools opened up again and I started grade one in the small red brick schoolhouse in the village of Schmalförden. My classroom teacher, Haffner was his name, was—like many other teachers at that time—an old Nazi who had learned nothing. During the war he had been an artillery captain. He limped somewhat, because he had been wounded in one leg during combat in Russia. He was very proud of his wounded leg. To really impress us, and to make us feel like wimps who lacked the stamina once cultivated in the Hitler Youths, he would demonstrate in Völkerball (a game, in which one disqualifies the players inside a ring by shooting them down with a ball) how he could dodge the ball, even though he had a stiff leg.

Aside from that, he was a class tyrant. For the smallest infraction one got from him a slap in the face, for more serious offenses one had to bend over to be beaten on the buttock with a stick. He loved music, was the organist in the village church, and whoever had a good singing voice, got good grades not only in music, but also in mathematics, social studies and other subjects—except for the two boys of the village communist. They really had beautiful voices, but that didn't help them a bit; they were Haffner's whipping boys. While sadistically humiliating the two sons of the village communist, Haffner was ingratiating when it came to the children of the well-to-do farmers. Them, he treated with kid gloves, because the parents provided him with sausages and sides of ham.

It can't have escaped your attention that I didn't like my teacher, nevertheless, there are some fond memories of the school in Schmalförden. We made class excursions to excavation sights where they were digging up pre-historic graves that contained urns, stone axes, and bronze fibulas. We had to write compositions on the stone axes and arrowheads found in the fields. At best, I got the note "Satisfactory" in them, but there was a children's encyclopedia, which I won in an art contest sponsored by the local savings bank. I remember stories and poems from my German reader and I am overjoyed when I find them again in your readers. And I remember *Heimatkunde* and geography, which catered to my need for "roots," as well as to my longing for faraway places.

*Goodbye Germany!*
But Lower Saxony offered no real basis for the start of a new life. One refugee family after the other drifted away. Many immigrated to the United States; in 1955 we immigrated to Canada. But that is another story, which I will tell some other time.

*The Search for Meaning*
As I told you in the beginning, the war and its aftermath have deeply affected the life of your father. On the one hand, it relieves me a great deal that you asked me about my war experiences, on the other, I am struggling with a great deal of inner resistance against writing down my memories as a war child because these contain experiences from which children should be spared. And yet it is a childhood I love, because it is my very own childhood. This childhood is connected to the darkest chapter in German history, so that it would have been impossible to tell you about my early years without mentioning this dark side. To tell you about this dark side was not easy for me, because I didn't want to burden your minds.

However, our German past would be an even greater burden to you if I would spread a blanket of silence over it. I have tried, therefore, to transform for you the "deceptiveness" of words into a treasure of knowledge for the present. In doing so, I have tried to make you aware that the call to come "heim ins

Reich" ("home to the fatherland")—a call which lured your grandparents to the "Reichsgau Danzig-Westpreußen"—was by no means a humanitarian gesture on the part of those of kin. The call was part of the devious "Generalplan Ost," which had been devised to subjugate indigenous people in Eastern Europe to the German "master race."

In my narrative, I go the way of Jules Michelet, the French historian who is in many ways unsurpassed. I go back to the sources. I become once more the child of yonder days in order to perceive the meaning contained in the texture of the events, not the meaning construed by a modern verbacious historiography. You will be overwhelmed soon enough by "the hard-brained chatter of irresponsible frivolity" (Disraeli) of the adherents of a supposedly stringent modern historiography, adherents who flatter themselves at having learned the lesson of statistics and of having replaced the evasive language of history with the universal language of mathematics.

Strictly in accordance with Michelet, I also give a voice to my brother Paul who died before he was able to speak, and to Alphons Kuklinsky who had to hold his tongue at the time. And if it was impossible to make such protagonists speak, I make them at least visible, as for example my younger brother Paul who only remains in my memory as a baby wearing a white knitted jacket. In dealing with the horrendous past, I was not content with greeting these protagonists with a casual "hello!" I wanted to accompany them back to their graves, to separate them from the living so that their shadows could calm each other, allowing me to put the lid on the urns. For although it behooves us to lament their untimely death, we have nevertheless the right to lead an unburdened life of our own.

*Your Father*
*Started on May 9, 1995*

HANS MOMMSEN
Born 1930, son of Wilhelm Mommsen and twin of Wolfgang J. Mommsen; from 1941 attended the Städtische Realgymnasium in Marburg; in 1951 studied History, German Literature, and Philosophy at Marburg; at University of Heidelberg Teaching Assistant of Werner Conze; dissertation at the University of Tübingen under the supervision of Hans Rothfels; Doctorate in Philosophy 1959; Habil. 1967; 1960-61 researcher at the Munich Institut für Zeitgeschichte; 1968-1996 Professor of Modern History at the Ruhr University in Bochum. He is perhaps Germany's most prominent historian and Goldhagen's most ardent opponent.

HANS-ULRICH WEHLER
Born 1931 in Freudenberg near Siegen; father killed in action when he, Wehler, was eight; admitted in recent interview his enthusiastic participation in the Hitler Youth; studied History, Sociology, and Economics at Athens, Ohio, and Bonn, and Cologne; Doctorate of Philosophy 1962 and Habil. 1968, both under the supervision of Theodor Schieder; in 1971 appointed Chair in Modern History at the new University of Bielefeld, where he became one of the founders of the so-called "Bielefeld School" (the "Historische Sozialwissenschaft"), a structuralist approach to history; one of the founders and co-editors of the journal *Geschichte und Gesellschaft*; noteworthy spokesman in recent debate over the plight of the German refugees; retired in 1996.

EBERHARD JÄCKEL
Born in 1929 in Wesermünde; attended Gymnasium in Dortmund, Fulda, and Arnsberg; commenced university studies after World War II at Göttingen and continued at Tübingen, Freiburg i. Br.; Gainsville, Florida, and Paris; 1955 Doctorate in Philosophy, Doktor-Vater, Gerhard Ritter; 1961 Habil. at Kiel; 1967-97 Chair for Modern History at the University of Stuttgart; a Hitler specialist but his source book *Hitler: Sämtliche Aufzeichnungen 1905-1924* (1980) contains forgeries by Konrad Kujau who was exposed in 1983 as the forger of the so-called *Hitler Diaries*. Jäckel is considered to be one of Germany's leading left liberal historians.

RUTH BETTINA BIRN
Born in 1952 in Stuttgart; university studies in History, Oriental Studies and Ethnology in Munich, Tübingen and Stuttgart; dissertation "Die höheren SS- und Polizeiführer: Himmlers Vertreter im Reich und in den besetzten Gebieten" written under the supervision of Eberhard Jäckel; 1985-86 postdoctoral fellow at MIT; since 1986 conducted investigations on suspected Nazi war criminals for Australian, Canadian and U.S. governments; since 1991 Chief Historian of the Crimes against Humanities and War Crimes Section of the Canadian Department of Justice. *Der Spiegel* introduced her in its anti-Goldhagen campaign to German readers as the "most knowledgeable expert on questions concerning the Holocaust."

# BIBLIOGRAPHY

## The Goldhagen Controversy

*Contributions by Daniel Jonah Goldhagen*

Goldhagen, Daniel Jonah. *Hitler's Willing Executioners: Ordinary Germans and the Holocaust*. London, Little, Brown and Company, 1996.

——*Hitlers willige Vollstrecker: Ganz gewöhnliche Deutsche und der Holocaust*, trans. Klaus Kochmann. Berlin: Siedler, 1996.

——"Das Versagen der Kritiker," *Die Zeit*, 2 Aug. 1996, pp. 9-14.

——"The Fictions of Ruth Bettina Birn." *German Politics and Society*, 15, No. 3 (Fall 1997), 119-165.

——"Ein neuer Vermeidungsdiskurs: Antwort auf die im Spiegel veröfentlichten Anwürfe." *Frankfurter Rundschau*, 18 Aug. 1997.

——Rebuttal of Finkelstein's Essay "Daniel Goldhagen's 'Crazy Thesis'." Submitted to *Der Spiegel*, but not published.

——"Außer Acht gelassen wissenschaftliche Redlichkeit." Rebuttal of M. Jeissmann's article "Der Schutz des allmächtigen Autoren." *Frankfurter Allgemeine Zeitung*, 12 Nov. 1997, p. 15.

——Letter to the editor [open letter to Prof. Claus Arndt]. *Die Zeit*, 5 Feb. 1998, p. 58.

——Letter to the editor [Response to Volker Ulrich's review. Eine Nation auf dem Prüfstand, by Ruth Bettina Birn and Norman Finkelstein. *Die Zeit*, 23 April 1998, p. 62.

——"Willing Executioners: The Paradigm Challenged-Victims Testimony, Critical Evidence, and New Perspectives in the Study of the Holocaust." *Tikkun*, 13, Nr. 3 (1999), S. 40-47. [Ins Deutsche übersetzt von Fred Kautz, erschienen unter dem Titel "Die Notwendigkeit eines neuen Paradigmas," in: Ellsässer, Jürgen und Andei S. Markovits, Hrsg., *"Die Fratze der eigenen Geschichte,"* S. 80-102.

——" 'Deutsche Lösung' für den Balkan: Um das Völkermorden zu beenden, muß die Nato Serbien besiegen, besetzen und umerziehen." *Süddeutsche Zeitung*, 30. (April/May 1999), S. 17.

## Reaction to Goldhagen

Arndt, Claus. "Moralische Leere: Ein Brief nach Amerika, der nie beantwortet wurde." [Open letter to Daniel Jonah Goldhagen]. Die Zeit, 13 Jan 1998, p. 13.

Ash, Mitchell G. "Die Debatte über Goldhagen im Internet." die tageszeitung, 16 July 1996, p. 12.

Augstein, Rudolf. "Was dachten die Mörder?" [Spiegel Interview with Daniel Jonah Goldhagen]. Der Spiegel, 12 Aug 1996, pp. 50-55.

Azzola, Axel. "Von Tätern, Tatmotiven und Taten: Zu und über Daniel Jonah Goldhagen, 'Hitlers willige Vollstrecker, ganz gewöhnliche Deutsche und der Holocaust'." Die Brücke: Forum für antirassistische Politik und Kultur, H. 102 (July/Aug. 1998). p. 69.

Baring, Arnulf. "Dianas Tod oder Die neue Zurückhaltung: Und Anmerkungen zum Medienspektakel Goldhagen." Frankfurtrer Allgemeine Zeitung, 8 April 1998, p. 11.

Becker, Ulrich, et al Goldhagen und die deutsche Linke oder die Gegenwart des Holocaust. Antifa Edition. Berlin: Elefanten Press, 1997.

Birn, Ruth Bettina (in collabortation with Volker Riess). "Revising the Holocaust." The Historical Journal, 40, No. 1 (March 1997), 195-215.

——" 'Holocaust als Andachtsbild': Interview mit NS-Expertin Ruth Bettina Birn über Daniel Goldhagens Attacke auf Kritiker." Der Spiegel, 10 Nov. 1997, p. 266-267.

——and Voler Riess. "Das Goldhagen-Phänomen oder: Fünfzig Jahre danach." Geschichte in Wissenschaft und Unterricht, 49, H. 2 (Feb. 1998), 80-95.

Bodemann, Y. Michael. "Das Böse und die ganz normalen Guten." die tageszeitung, 7 Aug. 1996, p. 18.

Bremer Jörg. "Die Arroganz der Vorurteile." Frankfurter Allgemeine Zeitung, 10 Dec. 1996, p. 34.

——"Der Verführer, der nicht überzeugt—Lesung vor leeren Stühlen: Israel bleibt skeptisch gegen Goldhagens einfache Antworten." Frankfurter Allgemeine Zeitung, 29 Nov. 1997, p. 35.

Broder, Henryk M. " 'Ich bin stolz'...über Goldhagen Vater und Sohn." Der Spiegel, 20 May 1996, p. 58.

Buchholz, Martin. "Goldhagen ist an allem schuld." Neues Deutschland, 24 Sept. 1996, p. 16.

Cowell, Alan. "Holocaust Wrangling: U.S. Scholar takes Case to Berlin." International Harald Tribune, 9 Sept. 1996, p. 8.

Dahmer, Helmut. "Holocaust und Geschichtsschreibung: Nachlese zur Goldhagen-Kontroverse." [This paper was commissioned as a contribution for the compilation Geschichtwissenschaft und Öffentlichkeit (Frankfurt am Main: Fischer Taschenbuch Verlag, 1998), but was subsequently rejected by the editors Johannes Heil and Rainer Erb.]

——"Geschichte ohne Akteure: Goldhagens Buch ist eine Defizitanzeige." Die Zukunft, 11 (1997), 23-26. [Abridged version of "Holocaust und Geschichtsschreibung: Nachlese zur Goldhagen-Kontroverse."

——"Holocaust en geschichschrijving: De Goldhagen-controverse opnieuw bezien." In *Wiens Schuld?: De impact van Daniel Jonah Goldhagen op het holocaustdebat*. Ed. Rolf Binner, Otto van de Haar and Jan-Willem Bos (Antwerpen: Standaart Uitgeverij, 1998), p. 231-244. [Dutch version "Holocaust und Geschichtschreibung: Nachlese zur Goldhagen-Kontroverse."]

——"Das Elend der Goldhagen-Kritik: Geschichte ohne akteure." *Die Brücke: Forum für antirassistische Politik und Kultur*, H. 99 (Jan/Feb 1998), 53-57. [Abridged version of "Holocaust und Geschichtsschreibung: Nachlese zur Goldhagen-Kontroverse."]

Davis, Katia. "Es wispert die Journaille: Wir wollen die Kanaille! Woher die Aufregung über Goldhagens Buch 'Hitlers willige Vollstrecker' rührt/Eine Betrachtung." *Neues Deutschland*, 24 Mai 1996, p. 11.

——" 'Da hat nicht Hitler einfach den Schalter angeknipst': Mit Daniel Jonah Goldhagen sprach Katia Davis für ND über sein Buch Hitlers willige Vollstrecker." *Neues Deutschland*, 26 Aug. 1996, p. 11.

Dönhoff, Marion Gräfin. "Mit fragwürdiger Methode: Warum das Buch in die Irre führt." *Die Zeit*, 6 Sept. 1996, p. 7.

Elsässer, Jürgen. "Ist Deutschland unheilbar? Revanche gegen Goldhagen: Ganz gewöhnliche Deutsche und ihr Unterbewußtes." *literatur konkret*, 23 (1998/99), 14-15.

Elsässer, Jürgen und Andrei S. Markovits. *"Die Fratze der eigenen Geschichte": Von der Goldhagen-Debatte zum Jugoslawien-Krieg*. Antifa Edition. Berlin: Elefanten Press, 1999.

Enderlein, Michael. Rez. zu *Gold-Hagen und die "hürnen Sewfriedte": Die Holocaust-Forschung im Sperrfeuer der Flakhelfer*, von Fred Kautz. *zoon politikon: Darmstädter Studierenden-Zeitschrift*, Nr. 3, Okt. 1998, S. 18.

Fine, Sean. "Nazi-hunting Scholar under fire for Views: Link with with anti-Zionist enrages CJC." *The Globe and Mail*, 26 Jan. 1998.

Finkelstein, Norman G. "Daniel Jonah Goldhagen's 'Crazy Thesis': A Critique of Hitler's Willing Executioners." *New Left Review*, No. 224 (July/Aug. 1997), p. 39-87.

——"Alls und nichts erklärt." Auszüge aus seinem Aufsatz "Daniel Goldhagen's 'Crazy Thesis'." *Der Spiegel*, 18 Aug. 1997, p. 56-62.

——" 'Ein fadenscheiniger Schwindel': Antwort auf Daniel Jonah Goldhagens Beitra 'Ein neuer Vermeidungsdiskurs'." *Frankfurter Rundschau*, 22 Aug. 1997, p. 7.

——und Ruth Bettina Birn. *Eine Nation auf dem Prüfstand: Die Goldhagen-These und die historische Wahrheit*. Mit einer Einleitung von Hans Mommsen. Transl. Bernd Leineweber. Hildesheim: Claassen, 1998.

——"Meine Seite, deine Seite." [Comments on Volker Ulrich, "Goldhagen auf dem Prüfstand"]. *Die Zeit*, 28 Mai 1998, p. 62.

Franz, Markus "Preis für den Beobachter der willigen Vollstrecker." *die tageszeitung*, 11 March 1997, p. 4.

Fürstenberg, Doris. "Mein Onkel: Versuch über einen 'ganz normalen Täter'—Zum Holocaust Gedenktag." *Die Zeit*, 15 Jan 1998, pp. 11-13.

Gall, Lothar. Comments on Goldhagen's book in "Worte der Woche." *Die Zeit*, 27 Sept. 1996, p. 2.

Geulen, Christian, [Harald Atmanspacher and Thomas Kluck]. "Historisieren um Identität zu stiften? Ein Jahr Goldhagen auf deutsch: Die Transformation des Holocaust in ein nationalgeschichtliches Ereignis." *Frankfurter Rundschau*, 5 Aug. 1997.

"Goldhagen und die Deutschen." *Psyche: Zeitschrift für Psychoanalyse und ihre Anwendung*, 51, H. 6 (June 1997).

"Goldhagen ein Quellentrickser?" *Der Spiegel*, 11 Aug. 1997, *Der Spiegel*, 11 Aug. 1997, pp. 156-158.

"Die Goldhagen-Debatte: Deutsche Holocaust-Forscher und entdecken und bewältigen eine Tabubruch." *Gegenstandpunkt*, 4 (1996), pp. 29-42.

Goldmann, Robert B. "People, Not Polemics on a Book Tour in Germany." *International Harald Tribune*, 20 Dec. 1996, p. 9.

Habermas, Jürgen. "Geschichte ist ein Teil von uns: Warum ein 'Emokartiepreis' für Daniel J. Goldhagen? Eine Laudatio." *Die Zeit*, 14, 14 March 1997, pp. 13-14.

Heil, Johannes. Letter to Helmut Dahmer. 16 Oct. 1997.

Herbert, Ulrich. "Aus der Mitte der Gesellschaft: Der Zusammenhang zwischen Antisemitismus in Deutschland und dem millionenfachen Mord an den Juden darf nicht wegdiskutiert werden." *Die Zeit*, 14 June 1996, pp. 5-6.

——Letter to the editor. *Der Spiegel*, 25 Aug. 1997, p. 12.

"Holocaust book makes big debut in Germany." *Stars and Stripes*, 8 Aug. 1996.

Jansen, Christian. "Der ganz normale Ablaßhandel—Zwei Jahre nach dem Goldhagen-Schock: Das Buch 'Hitlers willige Vollstrecker' einfach ein Medienstrohfeuer—In der Geschichtsforschung spielt es keine Rolle." *Die Woche*, 30 April 1998, p. 30.

Jeismann. "Der Schutz des allmächtigen Autors—Rechsanwälte lesen lassen: Wie Daniel Goldhagen mit seinen Kritikern verfährt." *Frankfurter Allgemeine Zeitung*, 17 Dec. 1997, p. 41.

——"Rechtsschutz: Nachtrag zu Goldhagen." Frankfurter Allgemeine Zeitung, 17 Dec. 1997, p. N5.

Kahlenberg, Friedrich. "Die Bilder sind echt: Das Bundesarchiv in Koblenz widerspricht Zweiflern." *Die Zeit*, 29 Sept. 1996, p. 10.

Kater, Michael H. Rez. zu *Gold-Hagen und die "hürnen Sewfriedte": Die Holocaust-Forschung im Sperrfeuer der Flakhelfer*, von Fred Kautz. *Australian Journal of Jewish Studies*, 15 (2001), 129-131.

Kautz, Fred. "Die Historiker sind beleidigt: Ihre feinfühligen Einwände gegen das Buch von Daniel Jonah Goldhagen." *Die Brücke: Forum für antirassistische Politik und Kultur*, No. 97 (Sept./Oct. 1997), pp. 45-46.

——"Von Aug- bis Finkel-Stein: die Goldhagen-Debatte zusammengefaßt und auf den neuesten Stand gebracht." *Die Brücke: Forum für antirassistische Politik und Kultur*, No. 98 (Nov./Dec. 1997), pp. 62-63.

——"Warum taten sie, was sie taten?" Fred Kautz und Andreas Klärner im Gespräch mit Daniel Jonah Goldhagen. *Die Brücke: Forum für antirassistische Politik und Kultur*, No. 99 (Jan./Feb. 1998), pp. 51-53.

——"Zu Chief Historian Birns Scheltrede und Klagelied: Eine unerbetene Einmischung." *Die Brücke: Forum für antirassistische Politik und Kultur*, No. 100 (March/April 1998), pp. 62-63.

——"Die Alpträume von Frau Birn: Wie das Unbewußte deutschen Historikern bei der Befassung mit dem Holocaust ins Handwerk pfuscht." *Jungle World*, 20 May 1998, p. 17.

——"Unterschiedliche Perspektiven gemeinsamer Historie." Leserbrief zum Bericht vom 24. Sept. 1998, "Die 'hürnen Sewfriedte': Der Darmstädter Kautz schreibt ein Buch über deutsche Historiker." im Lokalteil. *Darmstädter Echo*, 26. Okt. 1998, S. 19.

——" 'An Attempt to enter Dialogue with a Compatriot.' Response from the author to Michael Kater's Review of *Goldhagen und die "hürnen Sewfriedte"* by Fred Kautz. *Australian Journal of Jewish* Studies, 15 (2001), 131-148.

Kershaw, Ian. "Trauma der Deutschen." *Spiegel spezial*, Nr. 1 (2001), S. 6-13.

Köhler, Jörg. "Goldhagen Debatte: Wie antisemitisch sind die Deutschen? Gespräch mit Professor Israel Gutman, Jerusalem." *Neues Deutschland*, 10 Sept. 1996, p. 3.

Köhler, Otto. "Der gewöhnliche Deutsche." *Konkret*, 6 (June 1996), pp. 14-16.

——"Unter Deutschen." *Konkret*, 10 (Okt. 1996), pp. 14-17.

Kunath, Robert C. "Reflections on the Goldhagen Controversy." *The Psychohistory Review: Studies of Motivation in History and Culture*, 27, No. 3 (Spring 1999), 83-99.

Küntzel, Mathias. "Finkelsteins Freunde: auf die antizionistische Kritik an Goldhagen hat man in Deutschland nur gewartet." *Jungle World*, 20 May 1998, p.16..

Leicht, Robert. "Ein Urteil, kein Gutachten: Warum der Streit sich lohnt:" *Die Zeit*, 6 Sept. 1996, p. 7.

Littman, Solomon Israel. "Schuld, die das Gewissen eines jeden Deutschen zerfrißt." Leserbrief zum Bericht vom 24. Sept. 1998, "Die 'hürnen Sewfiedte': Der

Darmstädter Kautz schreibt ein Buch über deutsche Historiker." im Lokalteil. *Darmstädter Echo*, 29. Okt. 1998, S. 27.

——"Die Verweigerung: Goldhagen und die Flakhelfer." Rez. zu *Goldhagen und die 'hürnen Sewfriedte': Die Holocaust-Forschung im Sperrfeuer der Flakhelfer* von Fred Kautz. *Neues Deutschland*, 2. Feb. 2002.

——"Der zermürbende Kampf von Frederic Kautz gegen den akademischen Betrieb." Rez. zu *Goldhagen und die "hürnen Sewfriedte": Die Holocaust-Forschung im Sperrfeuer der Flakhelfer* von Fred Kautz. *graswurzel revolution*, Mai 2002, S. 14.

Loewy, Hanno: "Wider die allzu schnelle Erledigung: Anmerkungen zu Daniel Goldhagens Erklärung von Motiven für den Holocaust." *Frankfurter Rundschau*, 15 June 1996, p. 18.

Mallmann, Klaus-Michael. "Der Einstieg in den Genozid: Das Lübecker Polizeibataillon 307 und das Massaker in Brest-Litowsk Anfang Juli 1941." *Archiv für Polizeigeschichte* (1999), 82-88.

Markovits, Andrei S. "Über das Unbehagen der Deutschen: Eine Antwort auf die eifrigen Kritiker der Studie 'Hitler's Willing Executioners'." *Frankfurter Rundschau*, 15 June 1996, p. 18.

Mayntz, Gregor. "Die Deutschen—ein Volk von Mördern?" *Rheinische Post*, 11 Sept. 1996.

*Mittelweg 36: Zeitschrift des Hamburger Instituts für Sozialforschung*, 5 (Dec. 1996/Jan. 1997).

Mommsen, Hans. "Die dünne Patina der Zivilisation," *Die Zeit*, 30 Aug. 1996, pp. 14-15.

"Nach Goldhagen, Geschichte, Wissenschaft und Öffentlichkeit in den Neunzigern." (Konzept: Johannes Heil, ZfA Berlin, Manuskripteingang bis Ende Juni 1997), Stand 3.6.97. [Provisional list of themes for the Fischer Taschenbuchverlag volume *Geschichtswissenschaft und Öffentlichkeit in den neuziger Jahren* (1998), Ed. Johannes Heil and Rainer Erb, essentially a compilation of anti-Goldhagen contributions.]

——"'Goldhagen tut mir ein wenig leid.' Der Bochumer Holocaust-Experte über die Folgen des jüngsten Historiker-Streits." *Deutsches Allgemeines Sonntagsblatt*, 3. April 1998.

Naumann, Michael. Letter to the editor [Comments on behalf of Henry Holt & Co. Publishers concerning Volker Ulrich's rev. of *Eine Nation auf dem Prüfstand* by Ruth Bettina Birn and Norman G. Finkelstein]. *Die Zeit*, 23 April 1998, p. 62.

"Neuer Streit um Kollektivschuld: die Deutschen, Hitlers willige Mordgesellen?" *Der Spiegel*, 20 May 1996, pp. 48-77.

Niroumand, Mariam. "Little Historians: Das Buch des amerikanischen Politologen Daniel Johna Goldhagen wird keinen Historikerstreit auslösen." *die tageszeitung*, 13 April 1996, p. 10.

Pan, Peter. "Die Diskussion der Goldhagen-Kontroverse in Deutschland: Medienereignis oder Vermeidungsdiskurs?" *zoon politikon: Darmstädter Studierenden-Zeitschrift*, Nr. 7, Okt. 1999, S. 1-2.

Pätzold, Kurt. "Auf der breiten Spur der deutschen Täter: Anmerkungen zu Goldhagens Buch über Hitler, die Deutschen und den Judenmord." *Neues Deutschland*, 17/18 Aug. 1996, p. 12.

——"In memoriam Daniel J. Goldhagen? Jahresüberblick auf einen brisanten Historikerstreit." *Junge Welt*, 8 Jan. 1998, pp. 10-11.

——"Auf dem Seziertisch: Warum jetzt noch ein Buch zum Streit über das Buch von Daniel J. Goldhagen, hrsg. Von Johannes Heil und Rainer Erb." *Junge Welt*, 2/3 Mai 1998, p. 12.

Pohl, Dieter. "Die Holocaust-Forschung und Goldhagens Thesen." *Vierteljahreshefte für Zeitgeschichte*, 45, H. 1 (Jan. 1997), pp. 1-48.

Rabitz, Cornelia. "Fakten, Fakten, Fakten." *Allgemeine jüdische Wochenzeitung*, 22 Aug. 1996, p. 3.

Raulff, Ulrich. " 'Herz der Finsternis'—Daniel Jonah Goldhagens Ästhetik des Grauens." *Frankfurter Allgemeine Zeitung*, 16 Aug. 1996, p. 27.

——"Letzte Quellen: Der Holocaust im Licht des Fin de siècle." *Frankfurter Allgemeine Zeitung*, 16 Aug. 1996, p. 27.

Redner, Harry. "Goldhagen's German Supporters: A Review Essay on the Work of Fred Kautz and Helmut Dahmer." *The Australia/Israel Review*, 24, Nr. 2, 29. )Jan/Feb. 1999), S. 23-25.

Reid, Kalvin. "Writer opens Pandora's box of German history: Ex-St. Catharines man object of scorn for his views on German involvement in Holocaust." *The Standard*, 18. September 1999, S. 1-2.

Riemer, Jeremia M. "Der Menschlichkeit gerecht werden: Daniel Goldhagens Buch 'Hitlers willige Vollstrecker' wird häufig missverstanden—eine Zwischenbilanz der Kritik." *die tageszeitung*, 29 Aug. 1996, p. 10.

Riess, Volker. Letter to the editor. *Die Zeit*, 23 April 1998, p. 62.

[Rothwange, Dietmar]. "Ohne Emotion: Kollege kritisiert etablierte Historiker." *das ötv magazin*. Nr. 10/11 (Oktober/November, 1999), S. 36.

Rüsen, Jörn. "Den Holocaust erklären—aber wie? Überlegungen zu Daniel J. Goldhagens Buch *Hitler's Willing Executioners*." *Frankfurter Rundschau*, 25. June 1996, p. 11.

"Scheu vor einfachen Antworten: Warum deutsche Historiker nicht gelesen werden." *Darmstädter Echo*, 24 April 1997. [Article on a lecture held by Prof. Christof Dipper at the Technicla University Darmstadt].

Schirrmacher, Frank. "Wunderheiler Goldhagen." *Frankfurter Allgemeine Zeitung*, 13 Sept. 1996, p. 1.

―――"Verdreht: Ein Streit um Goldhagen." *Frankfurter Allgemeine Zeitung*, 19 Aug. 1997, p. 29.

―――Schneider, Peter. "Face it. There is No 'German Gene'." *International Herald Tribune*, 6. Dec. 1996, p. 11.

Schoeps, Juliu H., ed. *Ein Volk von Mördern? Die Dokumentation zur Goldhagen-Kontroverse um die Rolle der Deutschen im Holocaust*. campe paperback Hamburg: Hoffmann und Campe, 1996.

―――" 'Warum Deutsche Juden mordeten': Hitlers willige Vollstrecker stellt Fragen die viele nicht hören wollen." *Neues Deutschland*, 13 Aug. 1996, p. 11.

Schulte, Bettina. "Die Forschung fängt erst an—Korrekturen an Goldhagen: Vorträge über den Holocaust an der Universität Freiburg." *Frankfurter Rundschau*, 13 Feb. 1997, p. 7.

Siedler Verlag, ed. *Briefe an Goldhagen*. [Letters to Goldhagen, introduced and answered by him]. Berlin: Siedler, 1997.

Sternburg, Wilhelm von. *Warum wir? Die Deutschen und der Holocaust*. Berlin Aufbau Taschenbuch Verlag, 1996.

Teppich, Fritz. "Wovon leider nicht geredet wird: Fritz Teppich, ein Jude in Deutschland, zur Diskussion über Goldhagens Buch *Hitlers willige Vollstrecker*." *Neues Deutschland*, 9 Aug. 1996, p. 10.

Trilse-Finkelstein, Jochanan. "Goldhagens Reise durch Deutschland: *Hitlers willige Vollstrecker* und ein Medienspektakel." *Neues Deutschland*, 22 Sept. 1996, p. 13.

Ullrich, Volker. "Goldhagen und die Deutschen." *Die Zeit*, 13 Sept. 1996, p. 2.

―――"Goldhagen ohne Ende: Die neue Kritik entwertet die Holocaust-Studie nicht." *Die Zeit*, 22 Aug. 1997, p. 7.

―――"Goldhagen auf dem Prüfstand: Ruth Bettina Birn und Norman G. Finkelstein attackieren den internationalen Bestseller *Hitlers willige Vollstrecker*." *Die Zeit*, 2 April 1998, p. 52.

Wippermann, Wolfgang. *Wessen Schuld? Vom Historikerstreit zur Goldhagen-Kontroverse*. Antifa Edition. Berlin: Elefanten Press, 1997.

―――"Goldhagen an die Tafel! Wie deutsche Historiker den Wissenschaftler Daniel Goldhagen demontieren." *Jungle World*, 27 Nov. 1997, p. 23.

―――" 'Holoporn': Die Goldhagen-Kritik wird obzön—Der Fall Finkelstein." *Jungle World*, 20 May 1998, p. 15.

Wolfram, Winfried. "Ein Buch gegen nationale Bocksgesänge: Daniel J. Goldhagen—Diskussion in Berlin über die Deutschen und den Holocaust." *Neues Deutschland*, 9 Sept. 1996, p. 11.

Wuliger, Michael. "Kollektivgejaul: Goldhagens Buch und die deutsche Reaktion." *Allgemeine jüdische Wochenzeitung*, 22 Aug. 1996, p. 3.

Zuckermann, "Perspektiven der Holocaust-Rezeption in Israel und Deutschland." *Aus Politik und Zeitgeschichte. Beiträge zur Wochenzeitung "Das Parlament."* B 14/98, 27 March 1998, p. 19-29.

"Zu Protokoll." Excerpts from the "Talk-im-Turm" talkshow on Sat 1 TV Station. 28 April 1996. *Konkret*, 6 (June 1996), p. 17-19.

Zwerenz, Gerhard. "Samisdat im dritten Jahrtausend." *Ossietzky: Zweiwochenschrift für Politik, Kultur, Wirtschaft*, 13. Jan. 2001, S. 22-24.

### Anti-Semitism, National Socialism, Holocaust

Arendt, Hannah. *Nach Auschwitz: Essays und Kommentare*. Berlin: 1989.

Bleuel, Hans-Peter. *Das saubere Reich*. Bern und München: Scherz, 1972

Birn, Ruth Bettina. *Die höheren SS- und Polizeiführer: Himmlers Vertreter im Reich und in den besetzten Gebieten*. Düsseldorf: Droste, 1986.

Broszat, Martin. "'Holocaust' und die Geschichtswissenschaft." *Vierteljahreshefte für Zeitgeschichte*, 27 (1979), 285-298.

——"Plädoyer für eine Historisierung des Nationalsozialismus." *Merkur: Deutsche Zeitschrift für europäisches Denken*, 39, H. 5 (May 1985), 373-385.

——and Saul Frieländer [an exchange of letters]: "A Controversy about the Historicization of National Socialism." *Yad Vashem Studies*, 19 (1988), 1-47.

Browning, Christopher. *Ganz normale Männer: Das Reserve-Polizeibataillon 101 und die "Endlösung" in Polen*. Transl. into German by Peter Krause. Reinbek bei Hamburg: Rowohlt, 1992.

Buchbvender, Ortwin and Reinhod Sterz, ed. *Das andere Gesicht des Krieges: Deutsche Feldpostbriefe 1939-1945*. Munich: Beck, 1982.

Dawidowicz, Lucy S. *The War against the Jews, 1933-45*. Tenth Aniversary Edition. 1975, New York: Viking Penguin, 1987:

Demant, Ebbo. " 'Machen Sie fertig den Galgen für 12 Mann': Interviews mit den früheren KZ-Bewachern Kaduk, Erber und Klehr." *Der Spiegel*, 29 Jan. 1979, p. 29-34.

Dipper, Christof. "Auschwitz erklären." *Aschkenas*, 5, H. 1 (1995), 199-204.

Friedländer, Saul. *Kitsch und Tod: Der Widerschein des Nazismus*. Transl. from French into German by Michael Grendacher. Paris: Edition du Seul, 1982; Munich: Deutscher Taschenbuch Verlag, 1986.

——"Die Dimension des Völermords an den Juden." *Merkur: Deutsche Zeitschrift für europäisches Denken*, 45, H. 7 (July 1991), 557-568.

——ed. *Probing the Limits of Representation: Nazism and the "Final Solution"*. Cambridge, MA: Harvard University Press, 1992.

Fuhr, Eckhard. "Deutsches Aufarbeiten." *Frankfurter Allgemeine Zeitung*, 8 April 1997, p. 1.

Hamburger Institut für Sozialforschung, ed. *Vernichtungskrieg: Verbrechen der Wehrmacht 1941bis 1944—Ausstellungskatalog.* Hamburg: Hamburger Edition; 1996.

Hilberg, Raul. *Die Vernichtung der europäischen Juden.* Reexamined and augmented edition. Transl. from the English into German by Christian Seeger, Harry Maor, Walle Bengs and Wilfried Szepan. 3 vol. Frankfurt am Main: Fischer Taschenbuch Verlag, 1990.

——*Sonderzüge nach Auschwitz.* Transl. from English into German by Giesela Schleicher. Slightly revised version of the German 1st edition: Frankfurt am Main: Ullstein, 1987.

Hillgruber, Andreas. *Der 2. Weltkrieg 1939-45: Kriegsziele und Strategien der großen Mächte.* Stuttgart: Kohlhammer, 1982.

Hohmann, Joachim S. "Gegen das Gift des Revisionismus: eine internationale Wissenschaftler-Tagung an der Pariser Sorbonne." *Tribüne: Zeitschrift zum Verständnis des Judentums,* 27, H. 105 1988), pp. 43-48.

Jatho, Jörg-Peter. *Das Gießener "Frietagskränzchen": Dokumentation zum Mißlingen einer Geschichtslegende—zugleich ein Beispiel für Entsorgung des Nationalsozialismus.* Fulda: Ulenspiegel-Verlag, 1995.

Kater, Michael H. *Das "Ahnenerbe" der SS 1935-1945: Ein Beitrag zur Kulturpolitik des Dritten Reiches.* Studien zur Zeitgeschichte. Hrsg. vom Institut für Zeitgeschichte. Stuttgart: Deutsche Verlags-Anstalt, 1974.

Kaufmann, Alfred. "Bethlehem die Weihnachtsstadt." *Orient-Rundschau,* 13, No. 12 1 Dec. 1931, 133-135.

Klee, Ernst. *Deutsche Medizin im Dritten Reich: Karrieren vor und nach 1945.* Frankfurt am Main: S. Fischer, 2001.

Klemperer, Victor. *LTI: Notizbuch eines Philologen.* 14th ed. Leipzig: Reclam, 1996.

Kogon, Eugen. *Der SS-Staat: Das System Das System der deutschen Konzentrationslager.* 22nd ed. Heyne Sachbuch, No. 19/9. Munich, 1946; Munch: Heyne, 1974.

Kuball, Michael. *Familienkino: Geschichte des Amateurfilms in Deutschland.* Reinbek bei Hamburg: Rowohlt Taschenbuch Verlag, 1980. Vol. II.

Lenz, Hans-Friedrich. *"Sagen Sie Herr Pfarrer, wie kommen Sie zur SS?" Bericht eines Pfarrers der Bekennenden Kirche über seine Erlebnisse im Kirchenkampf und als SS-Oberscharführer im Konzentrationslager Hersbrück.* Gießen: Brunnen Verlag, 1982.

Levy, Richard S. *The Downfall of the Anti-Semitic Political Parties in Imperial Germany.* New Haven, CT: Yale University Press, 1975.

Littman, Solomon Israel. *War Criminal on Trial: Rauca of Kaunas.* 2. erweiterte Aufl. Toronto: Key Porter Books, 1998.

Lozowick, Yaacov. *Hitlers Bürokraten: Eichmann, seine willigen Vollstrecker und die Banalität des Bösen.* Aus dem Englischen in Deutsche übers. von Christoph Münz. Zürich: Pendo, 2000.

Meinecke, Friedrich. *Die deutsche Katastrophe.* Wiesbaden: Brockhaus, 1946.

Mommsen, Hans. "Die Realisierung des Utopischen: Die Endlösung der Judenfrage" im '*Dritten Reich*': *Geschichte und Gesellschaft*, 9 (1983), 381-420.

Nationalsozialistischer Lehrerbund Deutschland/Sachsen, Hrsg. *Bekenntnis der Professoren an den deutschen Universitäten und Hochschulen zu Adolf Hitler und dem nationalsozialistischen Staat.* 11. 11. Nov. 1933.

Neumann, Franz. *Behemoth: Strukturen und Praxis des Nationalsozialismus 1933-1944.* Frankfurt am Main: Fischer Taschenbuch Verlag, 1984.

Niroumand, Mariam. "Mit Kastner war die Diaspora angeklagt—Gespräche mit dem israelischen Journalisten Tom Segev, der die Rolle der zionistischen Staatsgründer neu debattieren will." *die tageszeitung*, 21 Nov. 1994, p. 15.

Pulzer, Peter G. J. *The Rise of Political anti-Semitism in Germany and Austria.*: New York: Wiley, 1964.

Reemstma, Jan Philippe. "Terrorratio: Überlegungen zum Zusammenhang von Terror, Rationalität und Vernichtungspolitik." In *"Vernichtungspolitik": Eine Debatte über den Zusammenhang von Sozialpolitik und Genozid im nationalsozialistischen Deutschland.* Ed. Wolfgang Schneider. Schriftenreihe des Hamburger Instituts für Sozialforschung. Hamburg: Junius, 1991.

Reifurth, Dieter and Viktoria Schmidit-Linsenhoff. "Die Kamera der Henker: Fotographische Selbstzeugnisse des Naziterrors in Osteuropa." *Fotogeschichte: Beiträge zur Geschichte und Ästhetik der Fotografie*

Rüter Ehlermann, Adelheid, H. H. Fuchs and C. F. Rüter. *Justiz und NS-Verbrechen: Sammlung Deutscher Strafurteile wegen nationalsozialistischer Tötungsverbrechen 1945-1966.* Amsterdam: University Press Amsterdam, 1974.

Speitkamp, Winfried. "Die Historikerkontroverse und der Holocaust." *Geschichtsdidaktik: Probleme, Projekte, Perspektiven*, 12, H. 3 (1987), 217-228.

Steitz, Heinrich. "Juden in Petterweil." *Friedberger Geschichtsblätter: Beiträge zur Geschichte und Landeskunde der Wetterau*, 15 (1940), 76-83.

## The Present of the Past

Aretin, Karl Otmar von. "Die Bedeutung des 8. Mai 1945 in der deutschen Geschichte." In *Deutschland 1945-1949: Ringvorlesung im Sommersemester 1985.* Ed. Hans-Gerd Schumann. THD-Schriftenreihe Wissenschaft und Technik. Vol. 49. Darmstadt: Technische Hochschule Darmstadt, 1989.

Baier, Lothar. *Volk ohne Zeit: Essay über das eilige Vaterland.* Wagenbach Taschenbbuch, 182 Berlin: Wagenbach; 1990.

# BIBLIOGRAPHY / 175

Bar-On, Dan. *Legacy of Silence: Encounter with Children of the Third Reich*. Cambridge, MA: Harvard University Press, 1989.

Bude, Heinz. *Deutsche Karrieren: Lebenskonstuktionen sozialer aufsteiger aud der Flakhelfer-Generation*. edition suhrkamp. NF 448. Frankfurt: Suhrkamp, 1987.

———*Bilanz der Nachfolge: Die Bundesrepublik und der Nationalsozialismus*. Suhrkamp taschnbuch wissenschaft 1020. Frankfurt am Main: Suhrkamp, 1992.

Commission of Inquiry on War Criminals. *Report*. Part I: Public. By the Honourable Jules Deschênes. [Bekannt unter dem geläufigeren Namen Deschênes-Report]. Ottawa, Canada, 30 December 1986.

Cowell, Alan. "Germany Wants to be 'Normal', but History Keeps Getting in the Way." *International Harald Tribune*, 25 Nov. 1997, p. 1 and 4.

Davies Alan. "A Tale of two Trials: Antisemitism in Canada." *Jews and Christians during and after the Holocaust*. Theme I of *Remembering for the Future*. Papers to be presented at an International Scholar's conference to be held in Oxford, 10-13 July, 1988. Oxford, New York, Frankfurt am Main: Pergamon Press, 1988, pp. 306-314.

Feuck, Jörg. " 'Wir wollen unsere Arbeit im stillen machen': Der Kampfräumdienst kümmert sich um das explosive Kriegserbe." *Frankfurter Rundschau*, 29 July 1994.

Fischer, Marc. *After the Wall: Germany, the Germans and the Burdens of History*. New York: Simon & Schuster, 1995.

Greiner, Ulrich. " 'Mein Name sei Schwerte'—Ein deutsches Leben: der frühere Rektor der Technischen Hochschule Aachen, bekannt als Hans Schwerte, war Hauptsturmführer der SS und hieß Hans Ernst Schneider." *Die Zeit*, 12 May 1995.

Habermas, Jürgen. *Eine Art Schadenabwicklung*. edition suhrkamp, 1453. Frankfurt am Main: Suhrkamp, 1987.

Gregorovich, John B. *On the Record: The Debate over alleged War Criminals in Canada , Letters to the Editor of the Whig-Standard*. Toronto: The Justinian Press, 1987.

Janssen-Jurreit, ed. *Lieben Sie Deutschland? Gefühle zur Lage der Nation*. Serie Piper, vol. 368. Munich: Piper, 1985.

"Kanada: Ferne Greuel—Jahrzehntelang blieben alte und neue Nazis unbehelligt. Jetzt wird die Justiz aktiv." *Der Spiegel*, 18 Jan. 1988, p. 124.

Kohl, Helmut. "Katholisch, liberal, patriotisch." In *Mein Elternhaus: ein deutsches Familienalbum*. Ed. By Rudolf Pörtner. Munich: Deutscher Taschenbuch Verlag, 1984, pp. 358-364.

Lukasz-Aden, Gudrun. *Die schrecklichen Eltern—Generationskonflikt lebenslängglich: Wie die nachkriegsgeneration mit ihren eltern zurechtkommt*. Heyne Report, No. 10/43. Munich: Heyne, 1989.

Leinemann, Jürgen, Paul Lersch und Hartmut Palmer. "Der Bimbes-Kanzler." *Der Spiegel*, 21. Feb. 2000, S. 44-55.

Manne, Robert. *The Culture of Forgetting: Helen Demidenko and the Holocaust.* Melbourne: The Text Publishing Company, 1996.

Matas, David und Susan Charendoff. *Justice Delayed: Nazi War Criminals in Canada.* Toronto: Summerhill Press, 1987.

Mayr, Walter. " 'Ich bin doch immun': Spiegel-Reporter Walter Mayr über das zweite Leben des SS-Mannes Hans Schneider." *Der Spiegel,* 8 May 1995, pp. 94-97.

Mitscherlich, Alexander and Margarete. *Die Unfähigkeit zu trauern: Grundlagen kollektiven Verhaltens.* Serie Piper, 168. 1967; Munich: Pipewr 1977.

Mitrovica, Andrew. "Nazi Allegations Shock, Upset man, his lawyer says." *The Globe and Mail,* 11. Dec. 1999.

Moser, Tilman. *Vorsicht Berührung: Über Sexualisierung, Spaltung, NS-Erbe und Stasi Angst.* suhrkamp taschnbuch, 2144. Frankfurt am Main: Suhrkamp, 1992.

Posener, Gerald. *Belastet: Meine Eltern im Dritten Reich.* Transl. by manfred Schmitz. Berlin: Das neue Berlin; 1994.

Richter, Horst-Eberhard. *Die Chance des Gewisses: Erinnerungen und Assoziationen.* Hamburg: Hoffmann und Campe, 1987.

Rothwange, Dietmar. "'Kein Spaziergang' Interview mit Hans-Jochen Vogel." *das ötv magazin.* Nr. 1/2 (Januar/ Februar, 1998), S. 21-22.

Saña, Heleno. *Die verklemmte Nation: Zur Seelenlage der Deutschen.* Munich: Knesebeck & Schuler; Munich: Knaur, 1992.

——*Das Vierte Reich: Deutschlands später Sieg.* Hamburg: Rasch und Röhring, 190.

Schneider, Peter. *Deutsche Ängste: Sechs Essays.* Sammlung Luchterhand, 782. Darmstadt: Luchterhand, 1988.

Skriver, Ansgar. "Nordamerika als Nazi-Asyl: Gravierende Versäumnisse der Behörden in den USA und Kanada." *Tribüne: Zeitschrift zum Verständnis des Judentums,* 24, H. 95 (1985), S. 19-29.

Troper Harold und Morton Weinfeld. *Old Wounds: Jews, Ukrainians and the Hunt for War Criminals in Canada.* Chapel Hill und London: University of North Carolina Press, 1989.

Westernhagen, Dörte von. *Die Kinder der Täter: Das Dritte Reich und die Generation danach.* Munich: Köyxel, 1987.

Wolfsohn, Michael. *Ewige Schuld? 40 jahre deutsch-jüdisch-israelische Beziehungen.* Serie Piper, 985. Munich: Piper, 1988.

——"Wattierte Erinnerung—Zur Geschichtspolitik in Deutschland." In *Geschichte und Politik: eine Vortragsreihe.* Ed. by Bernd Heidenreich. Wiesbaden: Hessische Landeszentrale für politische Bildung, 1995, pp. 41-52.

Zuckermann, Moshe. "Perspektiven der Holocaust Rezeption in Israel und Deutschland." *Aus Politik und Zeitgeschichte.* Beilage zur Wochenzeitung "Das Parlament". B 14/98. 27 March, 1998, pp. 19-29.

## Historians and Historiography

Aly, Götz. *Macht, Geist, Wahn: Kontinuitäten deutschen Denkens*. Berlin: Argon, 1997.

Ariès,Philippe. *Ein Sonntagshistoriker: Philippe Ariès über sich*. Transl. from French into German by Eva Groepler. Frankfurt am Main: Haine; 1990.

Augstein, Franziska. "Schlangen in der Grube: Im Disput vereint Der 42. Historikertag." *Frankfurter Allgemeine Zeitung*, 14. Sept. 1998, S. 49.

Böhm, Hiltraud. "Zur Person: Helmut Böhme." *Frankfurter Allgemeine Zeitung*, 7 Dec. 1989.

Böhme, Gernot: "Sinn und Gegensinn—Über die Dekonstruktion von Geschichten." *Psyche: Zeitschrtift für Psychoanalyse und ihre Anwendung*, 44, H. 7 (July 1990), 577-592.

Bollmann, Ralph. "Die Vordenker der Vernichtung." *die tageszeitung*, 14. Sept. 1998, S. 16.

Bracher, Karl Dietrich. *Zeitgeschichtliche Kontroversen—um Faschismus, Totoalitarismus, Demokratie*: Munich: Piper, 1976.

Broder, Henryk M. "Eine ABM-Maßnahme?" In *Erbarmen mit den Deutschen*. Hamburg: Hoffmann und Campe, 1993, pp. 74-79.

Bude, Heinz. *Bilanz der Nachfolge: Die Bundesrepublik und der Nationalsozialismus*. suhrkamp taschenbuch wissenschaft 1020. Frankfurt am Main: Suhrkamp, 1992.

Ebbinghaus, Angelika und Karl Heinz Roth. "Vorläufer des 'Generalplans Ost'. Eine Dokumentation über Theodor Schieders Polendenkschrift vom 7. Oktober 1939." 1999. *Zeitschrift für Sozialgeschichte des 20. und 21. Jahrhunderts*, Nr. 1 (1992), S. 62-95.

Ebbinghaus, Angelika und Karl Heinz Roth. "Deutsche Historiker und der Holocaust." 1999. *Zeitschrift für Sozialgeschichte des 20. und 21. Jahrhunderts*, Nr. 3 (1992), S. 7-10.

Emmrich, Michael. "Die Fehler eines Studenten: Der Sozialhistoriker Michael Kater habe sich zum 'Diener' der SS gemacht meint Ernst Klee—Vorwurf und Antwort." *Frankfurter Rundschau*, 30. Okt. 2001, S. 20.

Feuchwanger, Lion. *Das Haus der Desdemona oder Größe und Grenzen historischer Dichtung*. Frankfurt am Main, Fischer Taschenbuch Verlag, 1986.

Fried, Johannes. "Geschichte muß alle 20 Jahre neu geschrieben werden." [Interview mit Johannes Fried, Präsident des Deutschen Historikerverbands] in *Welt im Gespräch*. Sonderdruck zum 42. Historikertag, Frankfurt am Main, 1998.

Geertz, Clifford. *Dichte Beschreibung: Beiträge zum Verstehen kultureller Systeme*. Transl. from Englisch to German by Brigitte Luchesi and Rolf Bindemann. suhrkamp taschenbuch wissenschaft, 696. Frankfurt am Main: Suhrkamp, 1983.

Ginzburg, Carlo. "Spurensicherung: Der Jäger entziffert die Fährte, Sherlock Holmes nimmt die Lupe, Freud liest Morelli—die Wissenschaft auf der Suche nach sich selbst." In *Spurensicherung: Über verborgene Geschichte, Kunst und soziales*

*Gedächtnis.* Berlin: Wagenbach 1983; rpt. Munich: Deutscher Taschenbuch Verlag, 1988, pp. 78-125.

——Beweis und Möglichkeiten. Postscript to *Die wahre Geschichte von der Wiederkehr des Martin Guerre* by Natalie Zemone Davis. Frankfurt am Main: Fischer Taschenbuch Verlag, 1989, pp. 185-213.

Granatstein, J. L. *Who killed Canadian History?* Toronto: HarperCollins, 1998.

Gross, Raphael. "Die verspätete Holocaustforschung." *Buchzeichen.* Beilage zum *Tages-Anzeiger*, 8. Oktober 2001, S. 11.

Habermas, Rebekka and Niels Minkmar, ed. *Das Schwein des Häuptlings: Sechs Aufsätze zur historischen Anthropologie.* Wagenbach Taschenbuch, 212. Berlin: Wagenbach, 1992.

Heiber, Helmut. *Walter Frank und sein Reichsinstitut für Geschichte des Neuen Deutschlands.* Stuttgart: Deutsche Verlags-Anstalt, 1966.

Heym, Stephan. *Der König David Bericht.* 1972; Frankfurt am Main, Fischer Taschenbuch Verlag, 1974.

Hilberg, Raul. *Unerbetene Erinnerung: Der Weg eines holocaust-forschers.* Transl. From English to German by Hans Günther Holl. Frankfurt am Main: Fischer, 1994.

Himelfarb, Gertrud. "Helden, Schurken, Kammerdiener: Über Perspektiven der Geschichtsschreibung." *Merkur: Zeitschrift für europäisches Denken*, 45, H. 7 (July 1991), 1025-1038.

Hofmann, Gunter. "Die Welt ist wie sie ist: die Geschichtswissenschaft wirkt in ihrer Mehrheit konservativ und zufrieden. Doch worauf gründet dieses Selbstbewusstsein?" *Die Zeit* 27 Sept. 1996, p. 10.

Hohls, Rüdiger und Konrad H. Jarausch, Hrsg. *Versäumte Fragen: Deutsche Historiker im Schatten des Nationalsozialismus.* Stuttgart und München: Deutsche Verlags-Anstalt, 2000.

Höhne, Heinz. "Schwarzer Freitag für die Historiker—'Holocaust': Fiktion und Wirklichkeit." *Der Spiegel*, 29 Jan. 1979, pp. 22-23.

Iggers, Georg G. *Deutsche Geschichtswissenschaft: eine Kritik der traditionellen Geschichtsauffassung von Herder bis zur Gegenwart.* Transl. from English to German Christian M. Barth. Munich: Deutscher Taschenbuch Verlag, 1971.

Jeismann, Michael. "Gegenverkehr—Anthropologische Wende: Der 41. Historikertag in München." *Frankfurter Allgemeine Zeitung*, 23 Sept. 1996.

Kühnl, Reinhard, Hrsg. *Vergangenheit die nicht vergeht: Die "Historiker-Debatte, Dokumente, Darstellung und Kritik.* Köln: Pahl-Rugenstein, 1987.

La Capra, Dominick. *Geschichte und Kritik: Fischer Wissenschaft, 7395.* Frankfurt am Main: Fischer Taschenbuch Verlag, 1987.

Leinemann, Jürgen. "Der doppelte Außenseiter." [about Ernst Nolte] *Der Spiegel*, 30 May 1994, p. 30.

Loewenberg, Peter. *Decoding the Past: The Psychohistorical Approach.* Berkeley and Los Angeles: University of California press, 1984.

Mann, Golo. *Erinnerungen und Gedanken : Eine Jugend in Deutschland.* Frankfurt am Main: Fischer, 1986.

——"Plädoyer für die historische Erzählung" (1979). In *Wissen und Trauer: Historische Portraits und Skizzen.* Leipzig: Reclam, 1991, pp. 232-243.

Mommsen, Wilhelm: *Politische Geschichte von Bismarck bis zur Gegenwart*: Frankfurt am Main: Diesterweg, 1935.

Nagel, Anne Chr[istine]. "'Der Prototyp der Leute, die man entfernen soll, ist Mommsen'. Entnazifizierung in der Provinz oder die Ambiguität moralischer Gewißheit." *Jahrbuch zur Liberalismus-Forschung,* 10 (1998), 55- 91.

Nichols, Alden. *Germany after Bismarck: The Caprivi Era, 1890-1894.* Cambridge, MA: Harvard University Press, 1958.

Nietsche, Friedrich. "Nutzen und Nachteil der Historie für das Leben." In *Werke in drei Bänden.* Ed. Karl Schlechta. Munich: Hanser, 1954, pp. 209-285.

Oexle, Gerhard Otto (Göttingen) und Winfried Schulze (München), Moderatoren. "Deutsche Historiker im Nationalsozialismus." Zeitgeschichte, Skriptheft III. 42. Deutscher Historikertag, Frankfurt am Main, 1998.

Petzold, Kurt. "Streit unter den Klio-Jüngern: Das Geschichtsbild von Karl E. Erdmann und die Probleme deutscher Historiker." *Neues Deutschland,* 9. Jan. 1998, S. 13.

Rancière, Jaques. *Die Namen der Geschichte: Versuch einer Poetik des Wissens.* Transl. Eva Modenhauer. Frankfurt am Main: Fischer, 1994.

Ritter, Gerhard. *Luther: Gestalt und Tat.* 7th ed. Stuttgart: Deutsche Verlags Anstalt, 1983.

Rüsen, Jörn. *Zeit und Sinn: Strategien historischen Denkens.* Fischer Wissenschaft, 7435. Frankfurt am Main: Fischer Taschenbuch Verlag, 1990.

——"Was ist Geschichtskultur? Überlegungen zu einer neuen Art über Geschichte nachzudenken." In *Historische Orientierung über die Arbeit des Geschichtsbewusstseins, sich in der Zeit zurechtzufinden.* Köln: Böhlau, 1994, pp. 211-234.

Schötter, Peter. "Aus Muse Klios Lebenswelt: Der 40. Historikertag in Leipzig bestätigt die Vorurteile über die Natur der Zunft." *Die Zeit,* 7 Oct. 1994, p. 53.

——*Geschichte als Legitimationswissenschaft, 1918-1945.* suhrkamp taschenbuch wissenschaft, 1333. Frankfurt am Main: Suhrkamp, 1997.

Schulin, Ernst, ed. *Deutsche Geschichtswissenschaft nach dem Zweiten Weltkrieg (1945-1965).* Schriften des historischen Kollegs, 14. Munich: Oldenbourg, 1989.

Schulze, Winfried, und Otto Gerhard Oexle, Hrsg. *Deutsche Historiker im Nationalsozialismus.* Die Zeit des Nationalsozialismus. Frankfurt am Main: Fischer Taschenbuch Verlag, 1999.

Senfft, Heinrich. *Kein Abschied von Hitler: ein Blick hinter die Fassaden des "Historikerstreits."* Kleine Historische Bibliothek. Hamburg: Hamburger Stiftung für Sozialforschung des 20. Jahrhunderts, 1990.

Smith, Gary and Hinderk M. Emrich, ed. *Vom Nutzen des Vergessens.* Einstein Bücher. Berlin: Akademie Verlag, 1996.

Sontheimer, Kurt. "Wider die Leisetreterei der Historiker." *Die Zeit* 4 Nov. 1994, p.15.

Stern, Fritz, ed. *Geschichte und Geschichtsschreibung: Möglichkeiten, Aufgaben, Methoden—Texte von Voltaire bis zur Gegenwart.* Munich: Piper, 1966.

——*The Failure of Illiberalism: Essays on the Political Culture of Modern Germany.* Chicago: The University of Chicago Press, 1971.

Struck, Hanna. "Kostbares Vermächtnis hinterlassen: Zum Tode von Eugen Kogon, Harry Buckwitz and Werner Nachmann." *Tribüne: Zeitschrift zum Verständnis des Judentums,* 27. H. 105 (1988), pp. 66-71.

Suchsland, Rüdiger. "Erkenntnis ohne Interesse? Der 41. Historikertag in München." *Frankfurter Rundschau,* 23 Sept. 1996.

Treml, Manfred. " 'Schreckbilder'—Überlegungen zur Historischen Bildkunde: Die Präsentation von Bildern an Gedächtnisorten des Terrors." *Geschichte in Wissenschaft und Unterricht,* 48, H. 576 (May/June 1997), 279-294.

Thukydides. *Geschichte des Peloponnesischen Krieges.* Transl. and with introd. by Peter Landmann. Bibliothek der Antike. Zurich and Munich: Artemis, 1976.

Ullrich, Volker. "Die Kränkung des Widespenstigen." [About Hans Mommsen] *Die Zeit,* 22 Nov. 1996.

——"Hitlers willige Zunft: Ein Geleitwort zum Frankfurter Historikertag." *Die Zeit,* 3. Sept. 1998, S. 40.

Weber, Wolfgang. *Priester der Klio: Historische-sozialwissenschaftliche Studie zur Herkunft und Karriere deutscher Historiker und zur Geschichte der Geschichtswissenschaft 1800-1970.* 2nd ed. Europäische Hochschulschriften, Reihe III, Geschichte und ihre Hilfswissenschaften, Vol. 216. Frankfurt am Main: Lang, 1987.

Wehler, Hans-Ulrich. "Nachruf auf Theodor Schieder (11 April 1908 - 8 Oct. 1984)," *Geschichte und Gesellschaft,* 11, H. 1 (1985) 143-153.

——"Geschichte—von unten gesehen. Wie bei der Suche nach dem Authentischen Engagement mit Methode verwechselt wird." *Die Zeit,* 3 May 1985, p. 64.

White, Hayden. *Auch Klio dichtet oder die Fiktion des Faktischen: Studien zur Tropologie des historischen Diskurses*: Stuttgart: Klett-Kotta, 1986.

——*Die Bedeutung der Form: Erzählstrukturen in der Geschichtsschreibung.* Transl. from English to German by Margit Smuda Fischer Wissenschaft, 7417. Frankfurt am Main: Fischer Taschenbuch Verlag, 1990.

——*Metahistory: Die historische Einbildungskraft im 19. Jahrhundert in Europa.* Transl. from English to German by Peter Kohlhaas. 1973; Frankfurt: Fischer, 1991.

——"In den Fußstapfen der kämpfenden Wissenschaft: Braune Erde an den Schuhen Haben Historiker wie Schieder sich nach dem Krieg von ihrer Vergangenheit ganz verabschiedet?" *Frankfurter Allgemeine Zeitung*, 4. Jan. 1999, S. 48.

Will, Michael, "Zapfenstreich am Alten Friedhof: Wie sich die Stadt Darmstadt wissenschaftliche Leistungen aus dem Billiglohn-Sektor besorgt-und denjenigen, der sie erbracht hat, anschließend kalt lächelnd ins Nichts fallen lässt," *DA: Direkte Aktion: Anarchosyndikalistische Zeitung*, 26, H. 20316, Nr. 152 (July/Aug 2002), S. 5.

## Sociology of Knowledge

Elias, Norbert. *Engagement und Distanzierung. Arbeiten zur Wissenssoziologie I.* Ed. and transl. by Michael Schröter. Frankfurt am Main: Suhrkamp 1987.

Feyerabend, Paul K. "Über einen neueren Versuch die Vernunft zu retten." *Wissenschaftssoziologie: Studien und Materialien*. Ed. by Nico Stehr and René König. Kölner Zeitschrift für Soziologie und Sozialpsychologie, Sonderheft 18 (1975), 479-514.

Huber, Ludwig. "Das Problem der Sozialisation von Wissenschaftlern Ein Beitrag der Hochschuldidaktik zur Wissenschaftsforschung." In *Wissenschaftsforschung: eine Vorlesungsreihe*. Ed. by Peter Weingart. Campus Paperbacks. Frankfurt am Main/New York: Campus, 1975, p. 58-90.

Oelkers, Jürgen. " 'Scientific Community' eingeschlossene oder aufgeschlossene Gesellschaft?" *Neue Politische Literatur*, 20, H. 141-159.

Freud Sigmund. "Die Verneinung." In *Gesammelte Werke*. 4th ed. Vol XIX. 1948; Frankfurt am Main: Fischer, 1968.

Habermas, Jürgen. *Zur Logik der Sozialwissenschaften*. suhrkamp taschenbuch wissenschaft, 517, Frankfurt am Main: Suhrkamp Taschenbuch Verlag, 1982.

Weber, Max. *Gesammelte Aufsätze zur Wissenschaftslehre*. Ed. by Johannes Winkelmann. 7th ed. Tübingen: Mohr, 1988.

Gombrich, Ernst H. *Das forschende Auge: Kunstbetrachtung und Naturwahrnehmung*. Special volume of the Edition Pandora. Frankfurt /New York: Campus, 1994.

## Miscellaneous

Böll, Heinrich. "Brief an einen jungen Nichtkatholiken" (1966). In *Aufsätze, Kritiken, Reden*. Köln: Kiepenheuer & Witsch, 1967, S. 230-241.

Crichton, Michael. *Dino Park*. Transl. from Klaus Berr. München: Knaur, 1991 [Engl. *Jurassic Park*. New York: Alfred A. Knopf].

Delius, Friedrich Christian. *Der Spaziergang von Rostock nach Syrakus*. Reinbek bei Hamburg: Rowohlt, 1995.

Dürrenmatt, Friedrich. *Theater: Essays, Gedichte und Reden*. Zurich: Diogenes, 1980.

Elias, Norbert. *Engagement und Distanzierung. Arbeiten zur Wissenssoziologie I*. Hrsg. und Transl. from Michael Schröter. Frankfurt am Main: Suhrkamp, 1987.

Essinger, Helmut and Klaus Liebe-Harcourt "Offener Brief: Wissenschaftler der Gutachterkommission melden sich zu Wort." *THD-Intern*, 15 Oct. 1992. p. 6.

Feyerabend, Paul K. "Über einen neueren Versuch, die Vernunft zu retten." *Wissenschaftssoziologie: Studien und Materialien*. Hrsg. von Nico Stehr and René König. Kölner Zeitschrift für Soziologie und Sozialpsychologie, Sonderheft 18 (1975), 479-514.

Huber, Ludwig. "Das Problem der Sozialisation von Wissenschaftlern—Ein Beitrag der Hochschuldidaktik zur Wissenschaftsforschung." In *Wissenschaftsforschung: Eine Vorlesungsreihe*. Hrsg. Peter Weingart. Campus Paperbacks. Frankfurt am Main/New York: Campus, 1975, S. 58-90.

Freud, Sigmund. "Die Verneinung." In *Gesammelte Werke 4*. Aufl. Bd. XIX. 1948; Frankfurt am Main: Fischer, 1968.

Gombrich, Ernst H. *Das forschende Auge: Kunstbetrachtung und Naturwahrnehmung*. Sonderband der Edition Pandora. Frankfurt am Main/New York: Campus, 1994.

Habermas, Jürgen. *Zur Logik der Sozialwissenschaft. Suhrkamp taschenbuch wissenschaft*, 517. Frankfurt am Main: Suhrkamp Taschenbuch Verlag. 1982.

Haley, Alex. *Roots: The Saga of an American Family*. Garden City, NY: Doubleday, 1976.

Hebel, F. "Senat lehnt Ehrenpromotion von Azis Nesin ab." *THD-Intern*, 15 Oct. 1992, p. 6.

Hochhut, Rolf. *War hier Europa? Reden, Gedichte, Essays*. Munich: Deutscher Taschenbuch Verlag, 1987.

"Kanal Brutal: Der Widerstand gegen den täglichen Horrortrip auf dem Bildschirm wächst weiter—vier von fünf Deutschen haben die TV-Gewalt satt." *Focus*, 27 June 1994, pp. 143-148.

Mann, Golo. "Plädoyer für die historische Erzählung" (1979). In *Wissen und Trauer: Historische Portais und Skizzen*. Leipzig: Reclam, 1991, S. 232-243.

Mommsen, Wilhelm. *Politische Geschichte von Bismarck bis zur Gegenwart*. Frankfurt Am Main: Diesterweg, 1935.

Mauerer, Doris. "Keine Pfauenfeder im Krähenpelz: Zum 200. Geburtstag der Dichterin Anette Freiin von Droste-Hülshoff—ein Leben zwischen Anpassung und Trotz, Resignation und Wut." *Die Zeit*, 10 Jan. 1997, p. 56.

Nichols, Alden. *German after Bismarck: The Caprivi Era, 1890-1894*. Cambridge, MA: Harvard University Press, 1958.

Nietzsche, Friedrich. "Nutzen und Nachteil der Historie für das Leben." In *Werke in drei Bänden*. Hrsg. von Karl Schlechta. München: Hanser, 1954, S. 209-285.

Oelkers, Jürgen. "Scientific Community' eingeschlossene oder aufgeschlossene Gemeinschaft?" *Neue Politische Literatur*, 20, H. 2(1975), 141-159.

Olschanski, Reinahard. "Lebensnahe Philosophie." *Darmstädter Echo*, 25. Mai 2001, S. 22.

Rancière, Jaques. *Die Namen der Geschichte: Versuch einer Poetik des Wissens*. Übers. von Eva Moldenhauer. Frankfurt am Main: Fischer, 1994

Ritter, Gerhard. *Luther: Gestalt und Tat*. 7. Aufl. Stuttgart: Deutsche Verlags-Anstalt, 1983.

Rüsen, Jörg. *Zeit und Sinn: Strategien historischen Denkens*. Fischer Wissenschaft. 7435. Frankfurt am Main: Fischer Taschenbuch Verlag, 1990.

——"Was ist Geschichtskultur? Überlegungen zu einer neuen Gesichte nachzudenken" In *Historische Orientierung: über die Arbeit des Geschichtsbewusstseins, sich in der Zeit zurechtzufinden*. Köln: Böhlau, 1994, S. 211-234.

Schiller, Friedrich. "Der Verbrecher aus verlorener ehre—Eine wahre Geschichte." In *Schillers Werke*. Nationalausgabe. Weimar: Hermann Böhlau, 1954. Vol. XVI.

Schrötter, Peter. "Aus Muse Klios Lebenswelt: Der 40. Historikertag in Leipzig bestätigt die Vorurteile über die Natur der Zunft." *Die Zeit*, 7 Oktober 1994, S. 53

Schulin, Ernst. Hrsg. "Deutsche Geschichtswissenschaft nach dem zweiten Weltkrieg (1945-1965)." *Schriften des historischen Kollegs*, 14. München: Oldenbourg, 1989.

Schulze, Winfried. "Deutsche Geschichtswissenschaft nach 1945." *Historische Zeitschrift*, Beiheft NF, Bd. 10. München: Oldenbourg, 1989.

Smith, Gary and Hinderk M. Emrich, Hrsg. *Vom Nutzen des Vergessens*. Einstein Bücher. Berlin: Akademie Verlag, 1996.

Sontheimer, Kurt. "Wider die Leisetreterei der Historiker." *Die Zeit*, 4 November 1994, S. 15.

Stern, Fritz, Hrsg. *Geschichte und Geschichtsschreibung: Möglichkeiten, Aufgaben, Methoden—Texte von Voltaire bis zur Gegenwart*. München: Piper, 1966.

——*The Failure of Liberalism on the Political Culture of Modern Germany*. Chicago: University of Chicago Press, 1971.

Struck, Hanna. "Kostbares Vermächtnis hinterlassen: Zum Tode von Eugen Kogon. Harry Buckwitz und Werner Nachmann." *Tribüne: Zeitschrift zum Verständnis des Judentums*, 27, H. 105 (1988). S. 66-71.

Suchsland, Rüdiger. "Erkenntnis ohne Interesse? Der 41. Historikertag in München." *Frankfurter Rundschau*, 23 September 1996.

Toilstoi, Leo N. *Krieg und Frieden*. Transl. by Werner Bergengruen, with a postscript by Heinrich Böll. 2 vols. Munich: Deutscher Taschenbuch Verlag, 1990.

Tournier, Michel. *Der Erlkönig*. Transl. by Hellmut Waller. Frankfurt am Main: Fischer Taschebuch Verlag, 1984.

Treml, Manfred. "Schreckensbilder—Überlegungen zur Historischen Bilderkunde: Die Präsentation von Bildern an Gedächtnisorten des Terrors." *Geschichte in Wissenschaft und Unterricht*, 48. H. 5/6 (May/June), 279-294.

Thukydides. *Geschichte des Peloponnesichen Krieges*. Übers. und mit Einführung und Erläuterungen versehen von Peter Landmann. Bibliothek der Antike. Zürich und München: Artemis: 1976.

Tucholsky, Kurt. *Panter, Tiger & Co.: Eine neue Auswahl aus seinen Schriften und Gedichten*. Hrsg. von Mary Gerold-Tucholsky. Reinbek bei Hamburg: Rowohlt, 1954.

Ullrich, Volker. "Die Kränkung des Widerspenstigen." [Transl. from Hans Mommsen] *Die Zeit*, 22 November 1996.

Vonnegut Jr., Kurt. *Slaughterhouse-Five or the Children's Crusade: A Duty-dance with Death*. St. Albans: Panther Books, 1972.

[Viefhaus, Marianne]. "Verunsicherung? Missverständnis? Demokratischer Vorgang?" *THD-Intern*, 15 Oct. 1992, p. 6.

Weber, Max. *Gesammelte Aufsätze zur Wissenschaftslehre*. Hrsg. from Johannes Winkelmann. 7. Aufl. Tübingen: Mohr, 1988.

Weber, Wolfgang. "Priester der Klio: Historisch-sozialwissenschaftliche Studie zur Herkunft und Karriere deutscher Historiker und zur Geschichte der Geschichtswissenschaft 1800-1970." 2. Aufl. Europäische Hochschulschriften, Reihe III, Geschichte und ihre Hilfswissenschaften, Bd. 216. Frankfurt am Main: Lang, 1987.

Wehler, Hans-Ulrich: "Nachruf auf Theodor Schieder (11 April 1908–8 Oktober 1984)." *Gesichte und Gesellschaft*, 11, H.1 (1985) 143-153.

——"Geschichte—von unten gesehen. Wie bei der Suche nach dem Authentischen Engagement mit Methode verwechselt wird." *Die Zeit*, 3 Mai 1985, S. 64.

White, Hayden. *Auch Klio dichtet oder die Fiktion des Faktischen: Studien zur Tropologie des historischen Diskurses*. Stuttgart: Klett-Cotta, 1986.

——*Die Bedeutung der Form: Erzählstrukturen in der Geschichtsschreibung*. Trans. from Margit Smuda. Fischer Wissenschaft, 7417. Frankfurt am Main: Fischer Taschenbuch Verlag, 1990.

——*Metahistory: Die historische Einbildungskraft im 19. Jahrhundert in Europa*. Transl. from Peter Kohlhaas. 1973; Frankfurt am Main; Fischer, 1991.

Zwerenz, Gerhard. *Der Widerspruch: Autobiographischer Bericht*. Texte zur Zeit. 1974; Berlin: Aufbau Taschenbuch Verlag, 1991.

# INDEX

## A

Aachen 43,109
Abicht, Ludo 108
Abraham, David 71
academic historians 2,13
academic law enforcement officers 1,33,90
academic screening 61-62,64
Adolf Hitler Boarding School xiv,xix
aesthetics 4,14,16-17
Aly, Götz 93,103,136
American higher education 61
Ankara 63
anthropology 22,25,28
anti-Semitism 16,19,24-25,29-33,35,49-50,52-56, 73,82,89,91,97,107-108,116,118
apologists 98
Aretin, Karl Otmar Freiherr von 64-65
Ariès, Philippe 39,45,107
Aryan 6,30,52,56-57
atavistic dimensions of history 2,46
Augstein, Rudolf 19-20,32,73,104,111,143
Auschwitz 14-17,19,23,46,48,50,52,74-75,78-79, 83,102-103,107,113-114,122,126
Axmann, Arthur 132

## B

Balkankämpfer und Orientfreunde 109
Banality of Evil 31
Bassermann dynasty 12
Bauer, Yehuda 60,108,141
BBC 56
*Behemoth* viii,38,106
Berlin Document Center xvi,133
Beromünster 56
Bessarabia xviii,47,101,146-148,150,158
Bethlehem 57-58
Bialystock 88
Biberstein, Ernst 29
Birn, Ruth Bettina 115-119,123-124
Black Forest (Bibrach) 45
Bloch, Marc 16,37
Bochum 1,33,51,66,88,144
Bodemann, Y. Michael 2,15,102
Bohemia 50
Böhme, Helmut 64,110
Böll, Heinrich 1,102
bombardment 42-43,132,145,154
Borodino 47
Bracher, Karl Dietrich 14,98,103
Brandt, Willy 133
Braudel, Fernand 37,39,123
Broszat, Martin 12-13,92,103

Browning, Christopher vii,xx,8,21-22, 34-36,78,104-105,112,127,129,141
Brunner, Otto 137
Bude, Heinz 105,142
Bund der Asienkämpfer 109
*Bürgertum in Deutschland* 12,103

**C**

Carnegie, Dale 74
CDU 133,142
Chicago Black Hawks 62
collaborator vii,51,77,117,137
collective guilt 23,27,29,31,42,75,98
Concentration Camps 78
Conze, Werner vii,xii,xxi,92,94,137
Crichton, Michael 86,112
Czernowitz 70,79

**D**

Dachau Concentration Camp 18
Darmstadt x,xiii,xv,xvii-xviii,6,29,42-43, 63-66,68,93,103,124,138,140-141
Darville, Helen (also Demidenko) 143
Dawidowicz, Lucy S. 122
Demant, Ebbo 103
*Der Erlkönig* 46,108,113
*Der Verbrecher aus verlorener Ehre* 103
Deschênes, Jules 123
Deutschland 12,26,102-103,107, 109,111,114,142-144
Dibelius, Otto 29
*Die Zeit* xviii,10,32-33,49,67,102-103, 105-107,109-111,113,124,126,131,139, 143
Dipper, Christof 93-94,124
discreditation 25,60

documentary model of historical understanding 18
documents xv,5-6,8,14-16,18,87,103,133
Droste-Hülshoff, Annette von 44,107

**E**

Emrich, Michael 110
Erber, SS Oberscharfüher 16,103
Erdmann, Karl Dietrich 144
Essinger, Helmut 110
euthanasia 56
Euthanasia Program 55

**F**

Faschismus 103
Fast, Jakob 137
*Faust* 8,62,110
Febevre, Lucien 16,37
Fest, Joachim 40,65,138,142
Filbinger, Hans Karl 6
Final Solution x,7,21,24,52,59, 78,112,126
Finkelstein, Norman G. 119,122,124
Fischer, Fritz xii,xxi,64,102,104-107, 112-114, 123-124,144
Fisher, Marc 104,111
Flakhelfer vii,xi,xx,35,37,42-43,47, 59,69,105,127,142
Fontane, Theodor 4
Franz, Günther 6
Frankfurt x,xiv,xxi,1-2,30,37,74,79, 102,104-107,110,112-114,123-124,134, 136,141-144
*Frankfurter Rundschau* xxi,1,79,102, 106,112,114
Freud, Sigmund 11,19,81,108

# INDEX

Friday Circle 56-57
Frisch, Max vii
Fuchs, H. H. 109
Führer xi,xv-xvi,21,26,30-31,37-38, 43,49,65,96,135,151
functionalist 7,49,59,98,107-108,126

## G

Gall, Lothar 2,12,74,103,111
Geertz, Clifford xv,xxi,25,105
Generalplan Ost 92-93,96,113,161
Gestapo 55-57,96,138
ghetto 11,23,28,70,79
Gießen 55-56,109
Ginzburg, Carlo xix,xxi,25,39
Goethe, Johann Wolfgang von 4,8,54,96,112,114
Goldhagen, Daniel Jonah x,1,7,11,45-46,68,74-75,79,89,91,97, 101-102,104-105,110-111,115,122, 124-125,144
Goldhagen, Erich 70-71,79,91,96
Graham, Billy 39
Green, Gerald 12
Gregorovich, John B. 123
Greiner, Ulrich 109

## H

Habermas, Jürgen 20,25,68,95, 104-105,113
Habilitationsschrift 62,109
Haley, Alex 82,112
Harvard xi,1,4,8,16,21-22,27,32-33, 51,60,80,88-90,109,112,115,118,126
Heidehof Home for the Aged 136
Heil, Johannes 120-121,124,141
Heine, Heinrich 32-33

Hersbrück Concentration Camp 31
Hess, Rudolph x,6,29,31,56,114, 138,144
Hessisches Staatsarchiv 6
Hilberg, Raul 5,11-12,23-24,40-41,45, 50-52,54,83,97-98,102-104,106-108, 112,114,122
Hilberg Wall 5
Himmler, Heinrich 16,33,49,113,118,123
historiography viii,xi,4,6-7,16,37-38, 46-47,58,80-85,95,99-100,110,120, 127,131,135, 137,161
*Historische Sozialwissenschaft* 6,88
history of events viii,48-49
Hitler, Adolf
vii,ix-xiii,xv-xvi,xix-xx,2,8-9,22, 24,26,30-31,33-35,37-40,42,44,46, 48-49,52,54-55,59-60,65,68-69,74, 83-84,89,91-92,95-96,98-99,102-106, 108-113,115,117-118,121,124-125, 127-129,131-135,141-143,146-147, 149,151,159
Hitler Youth vii,xix,22,24,35,37-40,42, 44, 46,60,69,106,117,125,132-133,159
*Hitler's Willing Executioners*
x-xi,2,9,26,31,34,59,68,74,83-84,89, 91-92,95,99,100,103-105,110-113,116, 18-119,122,125-126,128-130,132
Hochhuth, Rolf 6,111,118,124
Holocaust
vii-viii,x-xii,xx-xxi,1-5,7,11-15,17,19-22, 27,32-33,35-36,40,47-49,51,59-60,68,71, 73-74,76-82,84-85,87,89,97-99,102-104, 107-108,111-112,114-115,117-124, 127-128,130-131,133,137,143-144

## I

Iggers, Georg G. 38
Imgart, Dagmar 109

indifference 4,33,36,54-56,58-60,154
Institut für Zeitgeschichte xxi,12
Irving, David 3
Israel x,xx-xxi,40-41,60,76,78,83, 97-98,100,114

## J

Jäckel, Eberhard
 xii-xiii,xvi,1,11-12,20,22,24-27,29, 32-33,37,39-41,46,50,54,65-66,68-70, 80,88-89,92,94-98,104,106,108,110, 117,125-127,130-132,137, 139
Jansen, Christian 108
Jatho, Jörg-Peter 55,109
Jeismann, Michael 102
Jerusalem 57
Judenräte 50
Jünger, Ernst 4,144

## K

Kaduk, SS Master Sergeant 14-16,103
Kater, Michael H. xii-xiii,xx-xxii, 125,127-137,139-140,142
Kaufmann, Alfred 56-58
Klee, Ernst xxiii
Klemperer, Victor 7,102
Kocka, Jürgen 32,126,130
Kohl, Helmut 43,74,76,78, 107-108,111,123,132
Kuball, Michael 102

## L

LaCapra, Dominick 112
Lenz, Hans-Friedrich 105
Levy, Richard S. 50,52-54,108,122
Liebe-Harkort, Klaus 110
literature xiv,4,17,54,62,65,68,74, 87,90,113

Littman, Sol xiv,xviii,xxi,116,123, 137,144
Luther, Martin xv-xvi,29-30,56-58
Lutheran xvii,29-30,56-58

## M

Maier, Charles 138
Mann, Golo 6-7,50,52,88,90,94, 102-103,109,113,125,143
Manne, Robert 109,143
Maser, Werner 65
mass murder 2-4,17,28-29,32-33,54-55, 60,73,78,85,87,113,115,120,126,131
Mayr, Walter 109
*Mein Kampf* 8,49
Meinecke, Friedrich 112
Mekita, Stan 62
mercy killing 55-56
Michelet, Jules 40,83,101,106,118,161
Milgram experiment 21
Mitscherlich, Margarete and Alexander 19,104,124
Mommsen, Hans
 xiii,xvi,1-2,7-8,12,19-20,22,27,32,37, 46-47,51,53-55,66,73-75,80,87,91,96, 102-103,105,108,119,125-126,130-132, 134,140,142-144
Mommsen, Wilhelm 37-38,91-92, 96,113,125,134-135,142
Mommsen, Wolfgang 92,135
Moravia 50
Mörike, Eduard 4
Mussolini 35

## N

Napoleon 47,67,71,83
national character 26,51

# INDEX

National Socialism 12,14,22,25,31, 35-36,48-49,51,61,76,95,103,134
Nationalsozialismus 103,105-106, 109,112,124,142-144
Nesin, Aziz 63-64,110
Neuhof, Kr. Neumark 152-153
Neumann, Franz 5,38,106-107
new school of history 39
*Nibelungen* xi,105,126
Nichols, J. Alden 109
Niemöller, Martin 29-30
Nolte, Ernst xvi,39,96,98,126, 130-131,141
NSDAP 54,142

## O

Oberstudienrat Huhnhäuser 135
Olden, Rudolf 65,113,141
Owen, Claude xiv,108

## P

Palestine 57,82
perpetrators ix,xii,2,5,9,11,19,21-22, 24,27,32,36,41,50,59-60,71,75,79,85, 88,91, 98, 108,113-114,120,129,131
Police Battalion 101 8,11,17,21,32,34,78
Pope 12
pornography of horror 2
privacy laws 10-11
Protestant Germans 29-30,138
Pulzer, Peter G. J. 53,109

## Q

question of guilt 14,97-98

## R

Rauca, Jakob 136,144
Raulff, Ulrich 2,4-5,14-17,102-103

Redner, Harry xiv
re-education 37,40,60,140
Re-education Officers 38
refugees 41,153,155
Regional Court of Kassel 56
Reichs Sicherheits Hauptamt xi
Reichsbischoph Müller xv
Reid, Kalvin xvii,xxi
Reitlinger, Gerald vii,xx
repression 4,23,44,120-121
responsibility 20,31-32,36,68, 77-78,85,98,101,136
revisionists 66,115
Ritter, Gerhard 92,96,137-138
Robertson, Pat 39
*Roots* 82
Rosenberg, Hans 83
Rothwange, Dietmar xvii,xxi,142
Russia 31,43,71-72,80-81, 88,113,119,146,150,153,157-159

## S

Salin, Marshal 25
Schieder, Theodor 92-94,96, 113,135,137,140
Schieder, Wolfgang 126,130
Schmalförden, Kr. Diepholz 155,159-160
Schneider, Hans Ernst 109
Schneider, Peter 17-18,103
Schöttler, Peter 136,144
Schröder, Gerhard 76
Schröder, Hans-Christoph 65
Schwerte, Hans vii,62,109-110
Second World War 137,141

Siegfried Line 1,33
Soltau 154-155
Soviet Union 47,65,82,147
SPD 133,142
SS-Hauptsturmführer 110
State University of New York xviii
Steitz, Heinrich 29-30,105,138,144
Stierlin, Helm 65
Stone, David 86-87
Storm, Theodor 43,90
structuralists ix,97,99
Stürmer, Michael 96,126,130-131
Suchsland, Rüdiger 102
Syrian Orphanage in Jerusalem 57

T
*The Destruction of the European Jews* 5,23-24,40,51,122
*The Politics of Memory* 5,106
thick description 2,24,28,70
Third Reich vii-viii,xii,xv,12-13,20, 29-30,43,46,54,58,92,96,103,118, 125-128,130,132- 133,137,150
Tolstoy, Leo 47,71-72,107,110
trauma 43,45,81,125,132
Turkey 63

U
Ullrich, Volker 32,102,105,143
"Urworte, Orphisch" 96
United States Holocaust Museum 5

V
Vogel, Bernard 133,142
Vogel, Hans-Jochen 132-133,142

W
Wallenstein 12,103

Wanasee Protocol 7
*War and Peace* 47,71,107
Warthegau 47
Weber, Wolfgang 106
Wehler, Hans-Ulrich xi-xiii,xx,1,6, 11-12,19-20,22-27,29,32-33,37,39-41, 46,54,60-61,65-70,80,88-89,92,94-96, 98,104,106,108-110,112-113,125-127, 130-132, 135-136,138-139,141-142,144
Wehner, Herbert 133
Wehrmacht vii,ix,xv-xvi,10,43, 45,79,132,138,154
Weiss, Peter 12,14
West Prussia xvii-xviii,42,79,150,152-153
White, Hayden 59,99,111,114,117,123
Wiener, Reinhard, Petty Officer 9
Will, Elisabeth 57-58
Will, Heinrich 56-57
Will, Michael xi1
Wippermann, Wolfgang xviii,32, 96-97,114,131
*Wissenschaft* xvii,60,71-72,106, 110,113-114,124,128,144
Wol xii,xiv,xx,47,92,96-97,100,106, 109, 112,114,125-126,130-132,135
Wolhynia 47
World War I vii-viii,xvii,26,36,42,57,97,127
World War II vii-viii,xvii,xiv,26,42,97, 127,137,141

Z
Zandern, Liman von 57
Zitelmann, Rainer xiii,64-66,96,98,131
Zwerenz, Gerhard xviii,xxi,111,125

ALSO PUBLISHED by BLACK ROSE BOOKS

## HOW THE FIRST WORLD WAR BEGAN
*The Triple Entente And The Coming Of The Great War Of 1914-1918*
*Edward E. McCullough*

By reviewing the events of the pre-1914 period, the responsibility of Germany for the outbreak of the war is reconsidered. The book begins with a short account of the situation after the Franco-Prussian War, when France was isolated and Germany secure in the friendship of all the other Great Powers, and proceeds to describe how France created an anti-German coalition. The account of the estrangement of England from Germany attempts to correct the usual pro-British prejudice and to explain the real causes of this development.

> Historian Edward McCullough pulls no punches in this controversial book. He offers new insights into the Great War. —*St. Catharine Standard*

For 32 years, EDWARD E. MCCULLOUGH has taught as a university teacher in Montrèal and he is currently Professor Emeritus at Concordia University. His research work on European history has been published in numerous reviews.

368 pages, bibliography, index
Paperback ISBN: 1-55164-140-2    $28.99
Hardcover ISBN: 1-55164-141-0    $57.99

## CHILE AND THE NAZIS
*From Hitler to Pinochet*
*Graeme S. Mount*

Based on documentary evidence from the archives of the Chilean Foreign Office, and from U.S., British, German, and, intercepted, Japanese documents, Mount is one of the first authors to provide evidence of the events and circumstances surrounding Chile's reluctance to sever diplomatic ties with Nazi Germany allowing it to maximize its opportunities there, influencing Chilean politicians, military operations, and the popular media.

> Mount reveals the conflict, the espionage, and the difficulty with policy which resulted from widespread Nazi influence...all issues that continue to be of importance even now, after the return of democracy to Chile.
> —Professor Florentino Rodao, Asóciacion de Estudios del Pacífico

> A hitherto little-known, but fascinating aspect of twentieth-century history.
> —Stan Hordes, Latin American and Iberian Institute, University of New Mexico

GRAEME S. MOUNT teaches history at Laurentian University in Sudbury, Ontario. He is author of *The Caribbean Basin: An International History* and *Invisible and Inaudible in Washington: American Policies toward Canada during the Cold War.*

204 pages
Paperback ISBN: 1-55164-192-5    $19.99
Hardcover ISBN: 1-55164-193-3    $48.99

# ALSO PUBLISHED by BLACK ROSE BOOKS

**GERMANY EAST** *Dissent and Opposition*
Bruce Allen

This work on the scope of dissent in East Germany integrates the post World War II uprising and the birth of the opposition forces with the 1980s social change movements, as well as developments since the destruction of the Berlin Wall.

Thoroughly documented, but readable enough to allow general readers to see dissent for what it is: the inevitable uprising of a suffering people.—*Books in Canada*

BRUCE ALLEN, an autoworker and trade-union activist, is author of numerous articles on development in Central and Eastern Europe.

    191 pages, biography
    Paperback ISBN: 0-921689-96-9    $18.99
    Hardcover ISBN: 0-921689-97-7    $47.99

**EUROPE** *Central and East*
Marguerite Mendell, Klaus Nielsen, editors

This volume of essays examine changes in the former USSR and the eastern bloc thereby placing them in a larger historical and sociological perspective. Contributors include: Mihailo Crnobrnja, Jerzy Hausner, Bob Jessop, Tadeusz Kowalik, Domenico Mario Nuti, Birgit Muller, Hilary Wainwright, Claire Wallace.

The list of participants is impressive.—*Canadian Book Review Annual*

MARGUERITE MENDELL and KLAUS NIELSEN are both associated with the Karl Polanyi Institute in Canada, and internationally. This book is part of the series *Critical Perspectives on Historic Issues*.

    298 pages
    Paperback ISBN: 1-895431-90-5    $19.99
    Hardcover ISBN: 1-895431-91-3    $48.99

**LOOKING EAST LEFTWARDS** *Former "State Socialist" World, Volume 2*
David Mandel

This collection, covering Russia, the Ukraine, Belarus, Hungary, Poland, China, and Cuba combines a unique variety of genres, interviews, diaries, and essays, that provide both analytical insight and a concrete sense of the complex socio-political and cultural processes at work in these societies. Key, in this account of the "post-Communist" regime, is an essay by the editor, entitled "Travels Through Russia, Belarus and the Ukraine: Diaries, Summer—Fall 1996".

DAVID MANDEL is co-founder of the School for Worker Democracy in Moscow. He teaches political science at the University of Quebec, in Montreal, Canada.

    250 pages, index
    Paperback ISBN: 1-55164-098-8    $24.99
    Hardcover ISBN: 1-55164-099-6    $53.99

ALSO PUBLISHED by BLACK ROSE BOOKS

## PURE SOLDIERS or BLOODTHIRSTY MURDERERS
*The Ukranian 14th Waffen-SS Galicia Division*
Sol Littman

Between 1950 and 1955, thousands of veterans from the notorious German-led, Ukrainian 14th Waffen-SS Galicia Division emigrated to North America with the full consent of the respective governments despite immigration regulations in force at the time that forbade entry to all who served in any branch of the SS. The Jewish community fought a brief, but futile, battle to persuade those governments to deny them entry, denouncing them as a "sinister legion" of "bloodthirsty murderers"—war criminals who had engaged in the mass murder of thousands of innocent civilians.

On the other hand, a well-organized body of Division supporters insisted there was nothing "sinister" or "murderous" about the young men who had volunteered to serve in its ranks. They declared them exceptional soldiers who obeyed the international rules of war, praised them for being dedicated soldiers who harbored no hatred for Jews, guarded no concentration camps, and committed no crimes against humanity.

At issue then was the nature of the Division and its war record. Were they "pure soldiers" as many of their supporters contended, or, were they, to use Daniel Goldhagen's phrase, among Hitler's willing executioners?

*Pure Soldiers or Bloodthirsty Murderers* traces the 14th Waffen-SS Galicia Division's fortunes from its formation in April 1943, to its surrender to the British in May 1946, from immigrant farm workers in Britain, Canada and the USA, to Cold War CIA assassins. Along the way it attempts to shed some light on this acrimonious dispute that has continued to the present day.

SOL LITTMAN is former Canadian Director of the Simon Wiesenthal Center, author of *War Criminal on Trial*, founding editor of *The Canadian Jewish News* and the First Director of B'nai Brith Canada's "League for Human Rights." He also served with the Anti-Defamation League in the U.S. and has enjoyed a longstanding working relationship with both the Canadian Jewish Congress and the World Jewish Congress.

    256 pages, bibliography, index
    Paperback ISBN: 1-55164-218-2     $24.99
    Hardcover ISBN: 1-55164-219-0     $53.99

ALSO PUBLISHED by BLACK ROSE BOOKS

**MANUFACTURING CONSENT** Noam Chomsky and the Media
*Mark Achbar, editor*

Charts the life of America's most famous dissident, from his boyhood days running his uncle's newsstand in Manhattan to his current role as outspoken social critic. Included are exchanges between Chomsky and his critics, historical and biographical material, filmmakers' notes, a resource guide, more than 270 stills from the film, and, 18 "Philosopher All-Stars" Trading Cards!

Juicily subversive, bristling and buzzing with ideas.—*Washington Post*

You will see the whole sweep of the most challenging critic in modern political thought.—*Boston Globe*

One of our real geniuses...an excellent introduction.—*Village Voice*

An intellectually challenging crash course in the man's cooly contentious analysis in a package that is clever and accessible.—*Los Angeles Times*

...challenging, controversial.—*Globe and Mail*

...lucid and coherent statement of Chomsky's thesis.—*Times of London*

...invaluable as a record of a thinker's progress towards basic truth and basic decency.—*Guardian*

264 pages, 270 illustrations, bibliography, index
Paperback ISBN: 1-55164-002-3     $26.99
Hardcover ISBN: 1-55164-003-1     $55.99

---

send for a free catalogue of all our titles
BLACK ROSE BOOKS
C.P. 1258, Succ. Place du Parc
Montréal, Québec
H2X 4A7 Canada
or visit our web site at: http://www.web.net/blackrosebooks

To order books:
In Canada: (phone) 1-800-565-9523 (fax) 1-800-221-9985
email: utpbooks@utpress.utoronto.ca
In United States: (phone) 1-800-283-3572 (fax) 1-651-917-6406
In UK & Europe: (phone) London 44 (0)20 8986-4854 (fax) 44 (0)20 8533-5821
email: order@centralbooks.com

Printed by the workers of
MARC VEILLEUX IMPRIMEUR INC.
Boucherville, Québec
for Black Rose Books Ltd.